TRUE STORIES

Anthony French

Writing as Anna Lane

True Stories

Author's Note

Back in the days when I was teaching Astrology and Psychology I often found myself engaged in what I call incidental counseling. I was not a licensed counselor, nor had I studied that craft, but I'd always had a sympathetic ear. And perhaps the subjects I was teaching encouraged those I came in contact with, mostly women, to share their stories with me.

I won't attempt to explain the appeal of these stories of anguish and redemption, tragedy and triumph; but since I have been a writer for even longer than I've been a teacher, it came to pass that I adopted my Anna Lane persona and brought some of them to the light of paper.

Herein are fifteen of those stories, originally published in the late '80s, early '90s. All the names of persons and places have been changed, of course, but the essential facts are all there, and as far as I know, they are all true stories.

True Stories
Contents

PUTTING MY LIFE TOGETHER
WITHOUT HIM

I dropped the day's mail onto the kitchen table, started the coffee brewing, and got out of my clothes before I even looked at the envelopes. As I stretched my tired legs out on the other chair, I shuffled through the bills and junk mail with little interest. My eye was caught by one envelope that bore the crest of a famous inn. The letter had been sent to my parents' home and forwarded by my mother to me here in San Diego. I ignored the rest of the mail and tore into that one.

My heart skipped a beat as I read the salutation: "My Only Love," I held my breath as I turned to the last page of the rather long letter and read the closing. Yes, it was from Derek.

It took me a moment to gather my wits before I cold even begin to read his letter.

"I hope you will forgive me for addressing you in this way," his letter began. "but the truth is that I have never stopped thinking of you as my only love. Hilary, if you are married or happily involved with someone else, please don't bother to read any further. If I don't hear from you, I will understand."

I stopped reading and thought about

throwing the letter away without going on. I wasn't married, and there weren't any other men in my life--unless you counted the men I taught dancing to or the few guys I worked with at the studio--which I didn't. Derek had been--and still was--the only man in my life. So this letter from him after almost a year of silence had shaken me up badly. I wasn't sure I could read on.

I had met Derek on a Saturday night over three years before, at my friend Ron's apartment. Ron and I had dated some in our first year of college, but the romance had fizzled out quickly when I made it clear to him that I was dead serious about having no intimate relations before marriage. He had kidded me about it for a few weeks, probably hoping that I would change my mind, but when I made it clear that I wouldn't, he decided to be my friend.

So when I needed a place to be alone to study or just to think, Ron was the one safe person I could turn to. His 'spare room' was always available to me. It's sparse furnishings--a mattress on the floor in one corner, a small reading lamp on the wall behind it, and bare wooden floor everywhere else--were ample for me. I sprawled on the mattr4ess to read or used the floor to practice dance steps I was working on.

My mother had wanted a 'classical scholar' in the family, so I was majoring in English and History, but dance was my true love. Ron wanted to be an artist but was forced to cook for a living at that time, so we understood each other well.

Derek was a casual friend of Ron's. He was in the Navy and had met Ron at an art gallery. Ron was fascinated by this macho sailor who enjoyed art, and the two of them had struck up a friendship. I hadn't heard of Derek, though, until that Saturday night when he dropped by Ron's apartment with some of his poetry. Ron knocked softly on the door of 'my' room and asked if I wanted to take a tea break.

"Sure," I answered, gathering myself up off the mattress. I had vaguely heard conversation from the front room and was a little curious.

"Hilary, this is my friend Derek. Derek, Hilary."

"Hello Hilary," Derek said, taking my hand.

I was immediately taken with him because when he said hello, his eyes met mine and held them. He didn't give the rest of me the once-over the way most men do.

"I met Derek at the gallery a few weeks ago," Ron was saying. "He writes poetry. And he's a sailor, so be careful."

We all laughed a little, but I noticed that Derek blushed at the jibe and my heart warmed to him.

I can't remember much else of that first meeting except that toward the end of the evening

Derek and I were alone in the 'spare room', and he was reading poetry to me. I fell for him right from the start and decided to ignore Ron's warning. I remember our first kiss vividly. Derek had stopped reading right in the middle of a poem and said, "That look in your eyes is embarrassing me."

"I'm sorry," I told him. "What would you like to do about it?"

"I think I'd like to kiss you," he replied. And when I didn't object, he did just that.

We kissed and touched each other for hours, and I remember that my passion smouted steadily as it became clear that I was not going to have to fend him off as I had with Ron. He never went further than I wanted him to go--in fact, I found myself wishing that he would be a little more aggressive.

I had to be home in time for Sunday dinner the next day, and Derek had to be back at his base that night, so we didn't have much time together after waking late that morning, both of us still fully dressed and wrapped in each other's arms. I explained my situation to him and promised to meet him the following Friday night at Ron's. I knew the week was going to drag by, and it did. I hardly thought of anything by Derek all week.

I got to Ron's earlier on Friday that I ever had and did my best to put up with his good-natured kidding about Derek and me.

"I warned you about sailors," he said with a

twinkle in his eye, "but you just wouldn't listen to me."

"There was no need to warn me. Derek was a perfect gentleman," I said huffily.

Ron continued to teas me until Derek arrived. Then the kidding stopped and our loving began.

Because of my situation, Derek and I couldn't do any normal dating. If my mother found out that I was dating someone--especially a sailor--instead of studying during those weekends I was supposedly staying with my girlfriend, it would have been curtains for me. Once in a while, if Ron had other friends around, we could go out to a restaurant in a crowd, but we had to be careful about public displays of affection lest word get back to my mother. So most of the time we just stayed at Ron's.

At one point during that second weekend, I did have to tell Derek about my resolve concerning sex, but that conversation was the first and last time the subject had to come up between us. Derek respected my wishes without question and never tried to get me to change my mind. That didn't mean we didn't have some very passionate moments. We spent long periods of time together during which we kissed and held each other tight. But it never went beyond that.

The following summer, Derek had a change

of duty status that kept him away a lot more than before, and it was also a little more difficult for me to get out of the house without the usual excuse of studying with my 'girlfriend'. I started hearing rumors about Derek and other girls, and one weekend I confronted him with those rumors.

"True and not true," was his immediate response. "I have been out now and then with the gang, and once in a while I take one of the girls to a movie--when you couldn't get out. But I figured that this was really necessary as a camouflage."

"What do you mean?" I asked, beginning to worry.

"Well, honey, you said your mom was really suspicious of you. I figured that with me being a lone sailor in town, hanging around with some of your friends, she might start to put two and two together. This way, if she does hear something about you and me, you can tell her I date the other girls and that should take care of it."

"I guess that makes sense," I said reluctantly. "But really, do you feel anything for the others?"

"Nothing. You are my only love," he said, taking my hands in his.

He got that faraway look in his eyes that I had come to recognize as his 'poet's gaze', and I knew he was thinking about a poem. I let the subject drop. for a time and eventually forgot about it in my desire to be reassured by him. I was completely surprised the next morning when he read me his latest poem, which he had titled "My Only Love", and in which he vowed to be faithful to me in spirit and body. From that time on, I was his 'Only Love' and I never doubted him again.

That fall, I met a girl named Dottie and we became friends. She had the same kind of problem with her parents as I had with mine--they wanted her to get a 'real' education, and she wanted to learn crafts like weaving, pottery, and woodworking. Like me, she put in her time with the usual academic stuff and spent all of her spare time working hard at her true interest. After only a few weeks of knowing each other, I confided in her about Derek. She was skeptical at first.

"Look, I don't want to ruin a budding friendship," she said, "but it sounds to me like the guy is giving you the royal runaround. I mean, he has you and everyone else, and you only have him. Kind of lopsided, if you ask me--which you didn't, so I'll butt out."

"That's okay," I told her. "I prefer that you voice your honest opinions rather than tell me what you think I want to hear. Maybe you'll get a chance to meet him someday. Once you've seen how we are together, I think you'll understand."

"How long have you known him?" she asked.

"I met him about a year ago at my friend Ron's," I explained. "Hey, that gives me an idea.

Why don't you come over there this weekend? You can meet Ron and whoever else shows up, and Derek will be there, of course. What do you say?"

"Well, I'll check my heavy social schedule and let you know," she said laughingly.

I gave her Ron's address and told her to just drop by any time. For some reason I was really happy about being able to introduce Derek to my new friend. Later it dawned on me--Dottie was the first person I had thought of as a friend since I had met Ron. I had really been keeping myself in seclusion for quite a long time, and I didn't really like the idea after that.

Friday night when Derek arrived, I told him about Dottie and how anxious I was for them to meet. He seemed distant as I described her to him, and I asked him about his mood.

"I was just thinking," he said. "I used to know a girl named Dottie who was into pottery. Wonder if it's the same girl?"

"Wouldn't that be a coincidence!"

"Yeah," he replied in that still-distant voice.

Later that night, as we cuddled on our mat and kissed and caressed each other, I felt a little uncomfortable. It was like Derek was not really there. But I didn't question him any more and I tried not to let it worry me. I knew that he would tell me what was bothering him when he was ready.

The next morning, Derek was still moody, and he spent most of the time sitting on the mat with his pad in his lap. But I noticed that he really wasn't doing much writing--he was just doodling and staring off into space. Dottie came over around eleven, and I went out to meet her and introduce her to Ron and his friend Phil. I felt a little uneasy about taking her into the room to meet Derek because of his mood, but I decided at last to just warn her about it. I was sure she would understand.

As we walked into the room, Derek glanced up and then, strangely, the minute he saw Dottie his mood changed like magic. He got quickly to his feet, a smile on his face, and offered his hand to her.

"You must be Dottie," he said as he took her hand. "Really glad to meet you."

"Well, thanks," Dotty said. "It's good to meet you too, Derek. Especially since you are all that Hilary ever talks about. Now I'll have a face to go with all that information."

"Oh no! I hope it's not all bad information," Derek replied.

"Only about half of it," Dottie joked.

We all laughed, and Derek asked Dottie about her crafts and her other classes. While they talked, I stood there wondering what had come over Derek. I had never seen him change his mood so quickly before. It was almost like he was relieved, or like he was greeting a long-lost friend or something.

At first I thought that he was just forcing himself to be cordial for my sake, because I had really built Dottie up to him. But I realized, as I watched him talk with her, that he was relaxed and truly interested in what she was saying. And he was caressing my back gently as they talked-- another sign of a complete return to normal for us that had been lacking the night before and earlier this morning. But then his tender touch had its usual effect on me, and I stopped wondering about anything just then and simply enjoyed the moment.

Dottie stayed the day and got into a game of chess with Ron that evening, while Derek and I kibitzed and kissed. She and Ron were still playing when Derek and I went to bed, so I didn't get a chance to talk to her until Monday on campus.

"Well, what do you think of him now?" I asked as I joined her there.

"All I can say is, if that's an example of Derek in a blue funk, I'd love to see him in a good mood."

I had already forgotten his strange mood, and it took me a minute to understand her comment. Before I could explain, she added. "Funny thing is, though, he acted kind of, well, relieved to see me."

"I know," I exclaimed. "that's exactly what I thought at first. It was kind of like he needed something new to get him out of his mood. Or maybe like he was worried about meeting you in the first place. Well, anyway, he was in a dark mood until you showed up. I'm sure glad you came. Did you enjoy playing chess with Ron?"

"Oh, he's a doll," she said almost dreamily. "And we are well matched. I'm going to drop in some night this week and play a tie-breaking game with him."

"You played two games?" I asked.

"Four," she corrected. "I think it was about three in the morning before I left."

"I'm so glad you had a good time," I told her. "Ron is very special to me, and it makes me feel good that you to get along."

"Well, not as well as you and Derek," she said with a leer. "I don't think he took his hands off you all night."

"That's how it usually is with us," I admitted. "I can never get enough of him, and when he isn't around, I can't wait for him to come back."

"Sounds like a dangerous obsession to me," Dottie said. "Sort of like putting all your eggs in one baskct."

"Well, that's one way to look at it," I said. "But I prefer to think of it as making an investment in my future. And besides, I feel comfortable with Derek. I don't have to play all the usual games with him, you know? I never get hassled about sex, and I don't have to act any special way for him--"

"Listen, Hilary. I'm really happy for you, and I don't mean to be a nag or anything like that," Dottie cut in. "But just let me say this one thing--I know a few women, friends of my mother's really, who married their first love, and to hear them talk, it is the most miserable kind of existence possible. They complain all the time about being stuck in a rut and not having any experience with the real world. And they are thinking all the time about how it would be with some other man--not that they aren't happy with their husbands, but just because they never had the chance to experiment.

"Now, I'm not saying the same thing is going to happen to you, but what if you do marry Derek? Will you ever wonder, like they do, if you have made the right choice?"

"No chance of that," I told her. "You've seen us together. You know how right we are for each other."

We had to get to classes at that point, and the conversation ended there, but the thoughts lingered in my mind. I knew that Dottie meant well, but my first reaction was that she just didn't understand how it was between Derek and me.

Later, I began to think about how littloe

experience I had with the real world. All of my life had been spent in school so far, and most of the people I met in school were locals like myself. Derek was one of the first people I had met who hadn't been born in my town. He was from Michigan and had already traveled over a lot of the country and into Canada and Mexico--he seemed like a truly cosmopolitan man to me. Dottie was right about my having led a sheltered life and not having much experience, but I knew that Derek would show me the world through his eyes, as he had already started doing with his poetry.

I tried to put her words out of my mind, but she had planted a seed that kept struggling to grow. And to make matters worse, Derek didn't show up that weekend. Dottie and I were at Ron's on Saturday when Derek called to tell me he had pulled weekend duty and couldn't get away. I wanted desperately to talk to him about us, but I just couldn't with Dottie and Ron in the same room, so I just assured him that it was okay, and that I would look forward to the following weekend.

It turned out to be two weeks before I saw him, and the absence had tied me into such knots that I practically exploded into his arms when he arrived that Friday night. My hunger was so strong it even frightened Derek. I held him tightly and kissed him with all my pent-up passion, pressing my body to his. He finally pushed me away gently, looking at me in a kind of trouble way for a long minute before he spoke.

"Hilary, has something happened? Are you in some kind of trouble?" he asked.

"No, nothing like that," I assured him. My heart was pounding so hard that I could hardly speak, and I had to swallow a few times to wet my throat. "It's just that--" I pulled him to me again, more gently than before, and buried my face in his neck before continuing.

"Derek, it's just that I'm feeling scared. I've been thinking about how little I now of the real world. I've spent all my life in one kind of schoolroom or another, and this little room of ours is all I know about the outside world. Derek, will you teach me about the world. Will you help me?"

"Oh, darling," he said, rubbing my back as he spoke, "of course I will. It's not as bad out there as you think. We'll conquer it together, you and I, and I'll never let you down,"

Then he kissed me again, softly and slowly and thoroughly, and soon my fears disappeared. I was so in love with him I didn't even feel silly for doubting him or us. I just felt good.

The next year passed swiftly for me. School was tough in my junior year because I was determined to get all of my upper division credits out of the way and leave lots of time for dance in my senior year. It became easier for me to accept

Derek's occasional abse3nces for weekend duty, and even though rumors about his other affairs still crept through, I didn't let them get to me. Dottie and Ron were developing a very close friendship, and I was really surprised when Dottie told me one day that she and Ron had done some heavy petting, but that the physical part of their relationship had never gone beyond that. I told her about my experience with Ron, and she sort of shrugged it off.

"Maybe he has matured since then," she said.

"Or maybe he is in love with you the way Derek loves me," I replied, thinking about how readily Derek had accepted my feelings about premarital sex.

She gave me a look that said that subject should not be discussed, but I pressed the issue anyway.

"I know you have never accepted Derek, and it doesn't really bother me," I said. "I think our friendship has grown in spite of that. But you must admit that Derek and I are still together and our love is growing stronger. That must count for something."

"Yes, I guess you have a point there," she said. "I wish I could trust him, if only for your sake, but.." She let her voice trail off, and it was clear that she didn't want to talk about it. I decided to let the subject drop.

Spring break of my senior year was a time in my life that I will never be able to forget. Dottie and two of her other girlfriends were going to Mexico for the break, and I managed to convince my mother that I was old enough to start making my own way in the world. She said she would worry about me, but finally gave her approval for me to go with the other three girls. Derek was delighted with the news. He said he would get a week's leave and meet me in San Diego, where we would be staying.

Our first day there, the four of us went to Tijuana and spent too much money shopping in all the little tourist traps, buying silly things and having a good time. Derek called from his base to tell me he had got his leave and would be there the next day. He also told me he had a surprise for me, and I hardly slept that night wondering what his surprise could be.

Derek spent only a few minutes at the apartment were we were staying and then rushed me out, saying we had things to do. The girls had planned to go swimming nearby that day and return to Tijuana the next day.

"If I'm not back in a week, just leave without me," I kidded as Derek and I left.

The first surprise Derek had for me was a friend's apartment. He told me his friend was on a short cruise and had decided to keep his apartment instead of looking for a new one when he got back. Derek said it was just a lucky break that we were able to use it for that week. I glanced around the place while Derek turned on the air conditioner and took his suitcase to the bedroom. I went into his arms as he returned to the living room, and we enjoyed a long and lingering kiss. Then he took me by the arms and sat me down on the couch.

"Hilary, I have a very important question to ask you," he said as he sat beside me, holding my hands. "Will you marry me?"

I was so shocked it took me a minute to answer. But there was no doubt about what my answer would be.

"Oh, yes. Yes!" I said.

He kissed me again, briefly, then said, "Just in case that was your answer, I took a chance on buying this last weekend," and handed me a ring box.

My hands started to tremble as I opened the box. It was a beautiful wedding set, with a single diamond in the engagement ring enclosed inn a kind of half-circle of the gold band. The wedding band fitted against the engagement ring with another half-circle of gold that made a complete circle around the diamond. It was perfect. Derek took out the engagement ring and slipped it on my finger. As we kissed, my heart felt like it would burst, and I'm ashamed to say I even felt a little self-righteous thinking about how Dottie and the others would take the news. All of my doubts and worries left in that moment.

"Now, let's do something really wild to celebrate," Derek said.

"Okay, what?" I asked eagerly.

"Why don't we go to a corrida in Tijuana?" he suggested.

"A what?"

"A bullfight. I've never been to one, and I know you haven't, so it would be something we could share. Kind of symbolic of starting our new life together."

I didn't much care for the idea of starting our new life with an experience that involved bloodshed, but I was too happy to object and I thought it might be kind of exciting. It was. As we sat in the hot sun, drinking beer and eating peanuts, I found myself being stirred beyond anything I had ever experienced in my life. I must have felt enough emotion that day to last most people a lifetime.

By the time we got back to Derek's friend's apartment, I was sure I had used up a year's supply of adrenaline. The air conditioning in the apartment felt good, but I was still feeling soaked. I told Derek I was going to undress to cool off and he said he would join me. After he splashed water on his face, he lay down beside me on the bed.

I had thought that I was physically and

emotionally exhausted, but when he kissed me I learned that I was far from it. I pulled him to me and kissed him with a fervor I had never known before. I don't know whether it was the corrida or our engagement or what, but I knew before I even admitted it to myself that tonight was to be the night. Derek seemed totally surprised when I whispered to him that I wanted him to make love to me.

"Are you sure?" he asked.

Those were the only words spoken that night.

The next morning, it was Derek who suggested that we share our happy news with the other girls. I think he was as eager as I to surprise Dottie--I guess her negative feelings hadn't escaped his notice. He bought a bottle of champagne that afternoon and we went to the apartment where I was supposed to be staying. I turned my ring around and tried not to make any flashy moves. I did my best to hide the glow I felt. The girls had been to Mexico that morning, but had decided it was too hot to stay the whole day.

"Well, I have just the thing to cool things off with," Derek said, pulling the champagne from the bag. "Anyone care to indulge?"

"Champagne! What's the occasion?" Laura asked.

"Spring break," Derek replied easily as he opened the bottle. "That's enough of an occasion, isn't it?"

"Sounds good to me," Dottie said, holding out her glass.

Derek poured glasses for all five of us, and then said, "Well, since it's champagne, we might as well have a toast. Here's to--well, here's to the most beautiful woman in the world--my fiancée, Hilary."

Derek and I took a sip, looking in each other's eyes, and then waited for the news to sink in. Laura missed it completely, and Karen seemed unsure. But Dottie's glass got halfway to her lips and then fell to the floor as she let out a scream of delight and grabbed me. Derek just stood there, sipping his champagne and beaming like a Cheshire cat, while the three girls gathered around for hugs and looks at my ring.

On the drive home the following week, I told the girls that the engagement had to be kept secret until graduation. The other two girls and I had no friends in common other than Dottie, so I wasn't too worried about them, but I told Dottie that not even Ron should know. I said that Derek and I had decided to wait until graduation so my folks wouldn't have too many things to worry about.

Derek didn't show up the following weekend, and I was not able to get a call through at the base. Two more weeks went by without a word, and I was beginning to get frantic. I left many messages for him, but he never called.

Finally the news filtered down through the grapevine. At first I didn't believe it, but Dottie checked it out with a friend of hers who went with a guy from the same base. Derek had been married in Las Vegas just two weeks after our engagement. My whole world was shattered.

When I graduated, I didn't waste a minute moving to San Diego. It was big enough to lose myself in and, hopefully, escape my memories of Derek. I got a job in a dance studio, found myself a place to live, and tried to get on with my life.

Then, after almost a year of silence, Derek's letter arrived. I read through it as he explained that a girl he claimed to have dated only once-- about three months before our engagement-- confronted him with her pregnancy. He wrote that he had wanted to call me a few times to explain but just couldn't. He also wrote that even though his sense of fair play required him to marry this girl, he had never felt the kind of love for her that he had always felt for me. He spun a tragic tale of infidelity on her part (my first thought was that it served him right!) and eventual separation after only four months of marriage. He ended his letter with: "I know that you can probably never forgive me for the wrong I have done to you, but I just had to let you know that through all of this I have continued to love you. I you have read this letter all the way through and feel that we could at least benefit from correspondence, please write to me here at the hotel."

I read his letter through at least a dozen times in the next few days, and every time I read it, I experienced a different emotion. I thought about how comfortable i had been to be with him, and how safe I had felt in his arms. I thought about the difficulty I was experiencing, even then, at making my own way in the world. I thought about how good it would be to have him hold me in his arms again.

I called Dottie a few days later, and we talked for hours. I just poured everything out to her and she listened, mostly. Finally she said, "Listen, Hilary, you have to make a choice. You have to decide what is best for you--based on all your experience and on what you think is likely to happen in the future. Don't let anyone--me, your mother, or Derek--make your decision for you."

I thought about her advice for a few days, and then I called Derek at the hotel. They told me he was the night auditor and asked if I wanted to leave a message. I said I would call later. When I heard his voice answer the phone later that night, my heat went into my throat and I couldn't speak right away.

"Hello, this is the Stonehedge Inn. May I help you?" he asked.

"Derek, this is Hilary," I said.

"Hilary! Oh, Hilary, thank you for calling," he said. His voice was so full of relief and pain and other emotions I couldn't name that I felt I would do anything he asked of me at that point. "Where are you calling from? Are you here in town?"

"No, I'm calling from San Diego," I told him. "I live here now."

And as I said that, I felt a surge of confidence in myself that I had not felt ever in my life before. It was true, I did live here now. And I was making my own life out of the ashes he had left me.

"Just a minute, I have to take another call," he said. Then the line went silent as he put me on hold.

As I sat there with the dead phone at my ear, I felt confidence surging in me, and I knew that I had made my decision. He came back on the line and said, "Hilary, I'd like to see you. Can we meet somewhere? I have Sunday and Monday off--I could come to San Diego."

"No, Derek, I don't think t hat would be a good idea," I told him, surprising myself with the steadiness of my own voice. "I'm putting my life together here and I don't think it would do either one of us any good to be dredging up the past. I ust wanted to call and let you know I received your letter. And I wanted you to know that I don't bear any animosity toward you, but I really don't want to see you and I think it's best ir you don't write to me again. I hope you understand."

"Well, I guess I don understand," he said. "I'm sorry you feel that way, of course, but I understand."

"Good," I told him. "I hope you have a good life."

As I hung up the phone, I felt a new sense of identity and strength within me. I was sad to see the last of my old dreams slip away, but I knew I had made the right decision, one that marked a new beginning for me. Sure, Derek and I had been good together, but I had simply refused to acknowledge the nagging doubts which rose in me as I heard the rumors about Derek's affairs, listened to my friends' warnings, and brushed aside my own flashes of uncertainty. He made me feel good, and I just couldn't give that up.

Now I wanted to feel good about me because of me. I knew it was time to concentrate on myself, and I was glad that I had the chance to experience the real world on my own.

I still look forward to the day when I will fall in love again, but I now that the next time I will have the experience I need to see things more clearly, and the strength to be honest with myself.

"YOU AREN'T FIT TO BE
A MOTHER!"

The worst part is, I agree
with my husband

Mike and I were taking a night class together when we met. I think it was a sociology class. I wasn't even sure why I was in the class except that it gave me something to do on Wednesday nights. The teacher was kind of cute and he showed a lot of movies between his lectures, so it was sort of fun. I was working in a small insurance office as a secretary--the kind of thing I had been doing ever since finishing high school four years before. The teacher had announced a break and six or seven of us headed for the door to get some air. I found my cigarettes and was looking for my lighter when Mike approached.

"Need a light?" he asked, holding his lighter up.

"Yes, thanks," I told him. "I know I have a lighter in here somewhere," I added as he struck the light.

"What do you think of the class?" he asked me.

"It's okay. I like the films and the teacher is not *too* hard on us."

"Yeah, he's not too bad. I sometimes wonder what some of the films have to do with the study of sociology, though. Are you working on a degree?"

"No, not really," I told him. "I'm just kind of taking the class for fun. How about you?"

As he told me about this plans to get a business degree and how it all fit in with is idea of starting a delivery service of his own instead of working for someone else, I really looked at him for the first time. I noticed that his clothes were very neat, but they didn't look too expensive. The serious way he talked about his business plans was kind of cute because he was so intense about everything. He checked his watch as he put out his cigarette.

"Well, guess I have time for another," he observed, reaching into his pocket for his pack. "Want one of mine?"

"Sure, I like a little variety now and then. It's funny, but I really don't smoke all that much unless I'm in a situation like this where I know I can't smoke for another hour. Then I have to have all I can get," I told him. He smiled a response as he lit my cigarette.

"And I'm the same way about drink," I continued, laughing. "I can go all morning without having one, but then I have to have three or four at lunch to make it through the afternoon."

He laughed loudly at this and I joined him, though not as loudly because I realized after I said it that it was really no joke.

"Speaking of a drink," he said when our laughter had died away, "how about joining me for one or two or ten after class?"

"Sounds good to me," I said. And that was the truth, because a drink was something that always sounded good to me--at any time of the day or night.

Stopping at a nearby bar for a dink after class became a regular habit for us after that. Sometimes some of the other people in our class would join us and once in a while even the teacher dropped in. The conversation was usually about the class or about what people were going to do with their lives. I began to feel a little uncomfortable as the crowd grew because it all seemed too academic for me. Mike finally asked me for a real date toward the end of tje semester and I was delighted because I had become fond of him. I was beginning to noticed that I did a lot less drinking when I was out with him and hegan to think of him as a 'good influence'.

I don't remember were we went on our first datc, but I do remember that it was close to the holidays and I decided that he would make a good impression on my family at our traditional clan dinner. My parents, my two brothers, two aunts and their families all got together every year between Christmas and New Year's for a big dinner. I asked Mike it he would like to come with me that year and he readily agreed.

"Shall I bring a bottle of champagne? Or would a side dish be more appropriate?" he asked me.

"No, my mother and aunts do all the cooking," I told him. "Champagne would be nice, though."

Mike did indeed make a good impression. He seemed to be able to hold his own in any conversation and he was careful to compliment every dish on the table. Everyone liked him. But as the day wore on and the wine and liquor flowed more freely I began to feel a distancing between us. That led me to drink a little more, of course, and at some point in the early evening (I was told later) I fell asleep on a couch in the family room. I also learned later that my dad, who always got drunker quicker than anyone, had had a real heart-to-heart with Mike about keeping me away from drink.

We had a strained conversation on the way back to my apartment that night.

"Sure was a lot of booze at that dinner," Mike observed.

"Yes, and I guess I drank too much of it."

"Well, too much is a relative term," he suggested diplomatically.

"When I fall asleep in the middle of a party, I guess that's too much," I said, trying to make a joke of it.

"Yeah," was all he said, but he didn't laugh.

The next day I called him at his place and apologized for my behavior. I told him that being with my family was always a strain for me, and he was a little more gracious than he had been the night before.

"Well, I can understand that. I don't have much to do with my o wn family because somebody always seems to get into a fight with someone else. Not that we get to blows or anything like that, but I do understand."

"I'm glad you understand, Mike. Will you let me make it up to you with a quiet dinner on New Year's Eve?"

"Sure, that would be nice," he agreed. "But this time I'll bring a side dish instead of champagne."

He laughed and I laughed with him, and as I hung up the phone I felt better than I had felt in years. I sang and hummed to myself all afternoon as I got my apartment ready for dinner the night of our date and I really enjoyed planning the dinner--which was a major breakthrough for me because I hardly ever ate at home, even when I was alone.

Mike brought a nice salad and some rolls with him, and after dinner we drank coffee.

Neither of us mentioned alcohol, even on this traditional champagne night, but I was feeling so good just being with him that the subject never entered my mind.

I was taken completely by surprise when he turned to me on the couch and said, "I'd like to make love to you. How do you feel about that?"

I was sure that he must have been able to see my heart pounding at that moment, but somehow I managed to find my voice and tell him that I liked the idea.

He was an excellent lover, very considerate and very appreciative. We made love twice that night and completely missed the coming of the New Year. The next day was the happiest day of my whole life. We didn't get dressed all day, but just lounged around the apartment, talking, snacking out of the fridge, making love, listening to music, and watching the parades on TV.

That evening Mike proposed to me. We h ad told each other about our previous marriages, discussed the mistakes we had made, and had shared with each other or ideas of what makes a relationship work. I knew hours before he asked me that he would. And I knew that my answer would be a very firm "Yes!" We had agreed that my drinking was not a problem unless I was with my family, and it was Mike who suggested that the solution was not to ignore my family but simply to not drink when I was with them. I was confident that with his help I could do that.

Life was wonderful for a time. Se were married a few months later, and within a month after our wedding I was pregnant with our little girl. Mike's job at the delivery service allowed him a lot of free time--he only worked as long each day as it took him to get everything delivered--and he was an eager participant in the birth and caring of our little angel. We named her Linda because we liked the sound of it, and because no one in either family had that name. Mike said it was a symbol of the fact that we were starting our own family.

Our life was idea until Linda was about three months old. I was starting to get bored being around the apartment all day with the baby and, even though she was the most precious thing in the world to me, I really needed a change in my life.

One day, I was fixing her bottle when I heard Mike drive up out front. He had had a very short day and I wasn't expecting him. The apartment was a mess, and so was I. I tried to hurry getting the nipple stretched over the lip of the bottle so I could be feeding Linda when he walked in. It slipped, of course, and the bottle went flying across the kitchen floor just as Mike came in the back door.

"Hey, that's creative," he joked, standing in the doorway with a grin on his face.

"Oh-h-h-h," I wailed as I stomped my foot.

"I can't take any more of this. I have to get out of this apartment or I'll go insane."

"Hey, hey, take it easy," he said, reaching for the mop behind the door. "It's just a little spilled formula. And you know what they say about crying over spilled formula."

Instead of calming me, his light-hearted manner just made me angrier, and I ran to the bedroom and flung myself across the bed. I listened to Mike cleaning up the mess and making Linda another bottle. As he did this, I made up my mind that I was going to go back to work.

"Okay, the pumpkin has her bottle, and the mess is a-w-w gone," he quipped as he joined me m the bedroom. "How are you doing?"

"Mike, I think it's time for me to go back to work. I know we can make it on your income, but I just can't stand being cooped up here all day long. I hope you'll understand, because my mind is made up."

"Okay, I do understand," he said as he sat on the bed beside me. "First, let's see if we can find someone really good to take care of Linda in the mornings when I'm at work. That's the important part. If we can both be satisfied that she'll be properly cared for, I have no objections. The extra money will be nice, anyway."

I was astounded at his ready acceptance of my plan. Of course, it turned out tat it was not easy to find someone who was good enough to take Linda. But we finally did find a nice woman who had only four kids in her care and was willing to take one infant. Mike liked her attitude about not taking any more kids than she cold handle safely, and I liked her because she did not seem to be interested in being a substitute mother to the kids. In spite of the fact that I didn't want to be a full-time mother, I didn't want another woman taking my place, either.

After that it was easy to find a job. I had enough secretarial skills to get just about any job that I wanted, and I found one with a large manufacturing firm that suited me. Mike had tried to talk me into a part-time job, one that would allow me to be home part of the day, but i held out for a full-time job that I could sink my teeth into.

I was on the new job only three days when the trouble with drinking started again. My new boss invited me to lunch that Wednesday, as a 'get acquainted' gesture, and I accepted.

"Would you folks like a cocktail before lunch?" the waitress asked as she seated us.

"Sure," Mr. Andrews said, "I'll have a martini. What will you have, Sally?"

"Oh, I guess a glass of white wine would be nice," I replied without thinking about it at all.

"So tell me about yourself, Sally," Mr. Andrews said. "Not all that stuff that's on your application. Tell me about your personal life."

"Well, there's not much to tell," I began. "I have a four-month-old daughter, and my husband works for a delivery service."

"My, you certainly don't look like you've just had a baby," he said.

"Well, thank you. I feel positively dowdy, to tell you the truth. The past six months out of the field have made me feel a little rusty, but I'm sure I'll get into the swing of things soon."

"I'm sure you will, too" he said, patting my arm. "I have every confidence in you. Is your marriage a happy one?"

"Oh, yes. Mike is a wonderful husband and he is really devoted to or little girl. He's going to school two nights a week to get a business degree. He wants to start his own company some day, and feels it would help to know all the aspects of managing a business before he makes the plunge."

Our drinks arrived, and that first sip of wine made my whole mouth numb. It had been more than a year since I had had anything to drink. And that wine really tasted good to me, and my whole body was aglow with the warmth of the alcohol.

"That sounds really sensible," Mr. Andrews was saying. "Tell me, if things are so rosy for you, why did you decide to go back to work?"

"Well, to tell you the truth, I was getting a little bored with the routine," I told him, too honestly. "I guess I just wasn't cut out for the housewife life."

"I can relate to that," he said ruefully. "My wife bores me, too."

I know there should have been an little alarm bell sounding somewhere at that point, but I guess I was feeling too good with the wine coursing through my veins to notice. Mr. Andrews was not exactly an attractive man, but as sales manager of the company he was a man of position and power and that can cover up a lot of physical shortcomings. And of course, he was my boss and I figured that part of my job was to be sympathetic to his personal side as well as his business side.

"I'm sorry to hear that," I told him.

"Oh, it's no big deal. I'm sure she is just as bored with me. Se have a tacit understanding that we each go our own way and whatever we do is our own business as long as we are discreet about it. It's a workable arrangement."

"Well, that's nice. You are very lucky to have such an understanding partner."

"Well put," he replied with a laugh. "But the truth is, I have always felt my coworkers, especially my secretary, are my true partners. My wife is a necessary social appendage, if you get my meaning."

"Yes, I understand," I told him.

And I did understand. All too well. I had heard it before, of course, from a number of bosses over the years. And if I had had my wits about it I would have left that job right then and there. But I guess I felt I could handle him, and I really wanted the job, so I kept playing to his ego, pretending to play along with his game. My shame is that I overestimated my ability to juggle his ego, my fidelity, and the alcohol at the same time.

The Wednesday lunches became a regular feature of the job, and only once in the first few weeks did I find it necessary to fend off an invitation to extend the lunch hour at a 'more comfortable location'.

Mike seemed happy with the new lifestyle my extra income was creating for us, and I was glad I'd made the decision to go back to work. Linda was well cared for, and as it worked out she only spent about four hours a day at the sitter's. I didn't have to drop her off until just before nine in the morning, and Mike managed to get off most days around one in the afternoon. Of course, that meant he had to get started a little earlier each day on his deliveries, but mornings had never been our favorite time of day anyway, so it worked out fine for all of us.

I don't remember what the occasion was, but one day on the way home from work I stopped at the grocery store and picked up a bottle of white wine. I was developing a taste for wine again, thanks to my lunches with my boss, and it just seemed like the natural thing to do at the time. Mike, as usual, took it in stride when I announced that I had bought the bottle for dinner that night.

"This is very nice," he said, eyeing his glass after his first sip. "You have excellent taste, Madame."

"Why thank you, sir," I replied with exaggerated graciousness. "I selected it with special attention to your delicate palate."

It was the first alcohol we had shared since my pregnancy and it should have been very special for both of us, but for me it was just a welcome relief to be able to drink in the evening.

It wasn't long before our evening meal was always accompanied by a glass or two of wine, but it happened gradually enough that Mike didn't think to object until it was too late. He did refuse a glass one night, but said nothing as I poured myself a glass. I was careful not to offer wine to him or take a glass myself the next night, just to let him know I was not obsessed by it. But of course, I was. I didn't know it myself then, but I began to spend more and more of my time planning my days around when I could get a drink.

Things between Mike and me got worse the more I drank, but I didn't even care after a while-- all I cared about was when and where I could get my next drink. I was drunk at work, and I was usually drunk again by evening. Eventually I lost my job, which made me more depressed, and I began to spend my entire day drinking. Mike would come home to a sloppy house and a drunken wife, but by that time it didn't matter to me.

Finally he couldn't live with me any longer. He insisted that we divorce. He gave me a chance to prove that I could take care of Linda, by staying sober for the time between our breaking up and the final split.

I swore I didn't need to drink, but Mike didn't believe I'd be a good mother, so he took me to court to fight for custody of our daughter. She was all I had left and I was determined to win.

I hired a good lawyer and he felt we had a good case, since it is hard in our state for men to gain custody.

I sat in the defendant's chair in the courtroom and watched my whole life pass before my eyes. Most of the time I was not even aware of what was being said, because as each new witness was called in to take the stand, another part of my past came into my mind and I went off on another flight of memory and shame. I was fighting for my little girl here in this room and I still couldn't stop trying to figure out how I had gotten into his mess in the first place. I don't think I once looked at Mike sitting on the plaintiff's side of the room during the three days of the hearing.

"Did you leave your daughter alone in the house the day of the accident?" my attorney asked in a whisper.

"No," I said immediately. "I don't think so."

I wasn't even sure which accident he meant until I looked up and saw our former neighbor, Carol, on the stand. I couldn't remember anything she had said, but I knew that she would be testifying about the time I had rear-ended a car at the stoplight.

Mike had had to work that Saturday and I was left alone with nothing to do. I had gone to Carol's house late that morning with Linda, and I'd taken a six-pack of beer with me. She and her husband, Harry, and I sat in the backyard, drinking, while the kids splashed around in their little plastic pool. The beer ran out at about noon, and I remember that I volunteered to get more. The next thing I remembered was waking up in the hospital.

Carol was recounting the story on the witness stand. "Then Sally left with Linda," she was saying, "and we thought she was going to feed Linda and bring back more beer from home, but evidently she had had left Linda at home and--"

"Objection!" my attorney called.

"Sustained," the judge said. "The witness will confine her testimony to only the facts as she knows them. Please refrain from conjecture."

"Please continue, Mrs. Lane," Mike's attorney said.

"Well, she left with Linda," Carol began again, "and we didn't see her again for a couple of hours. My husband and I wondered what was taking her so long, but we figured she got busy and she'd come back when she could. And then, about three o'clock that afternoon, Mike called and asked if Sally was there. I told him she had left at about noontime and then he told me that he had just come home and had found Linda in her crib alone."

"Objection!" my attorney said again.

"I think I'll allow the witness to relate the conversation she was party to," the judge said. "Overruled."

"No further questions," Mike's attorney said "Your witness."

"Mrs. Lane, do you have any direct knowledge of what the defendant did after she left your house, or of what arrangements she made for her daughter's care at that time?" my attorney asked her.

"No, sir," Carol replied.

"No further questions," he said.

Carol gave me a very sympathetic look, but strangely enough I felt more sorry for her at that moment than I did for myself. Now that I had heard her speak of the incident, I remembered it and knew that I had not been truthful with my attorney.

When I had left their house that day, I had gone back to our house and Linda started acting cranky so I made her a sandwich for lunch. But I couldn't find anything in the fridge that interested me. I just sat there until she finished eating, and then put her down for her nap. She went right to sleep as she always did and I puttered around the living room for a while, straightening up. Then I remembered that I had promised to get more beer for Carol and Harry.

I really thought it would only take me about ten minutes to get to the store and back with some beer and chips, and then I could wake Linda up and go back to Carol's for a while until Mike got home.

I didn't know then how the accident happened, and I still don't. I just plowed into the back of a woman's car when she was stopped at a light. I cut my forehead, on the steering wheel evidently, because the police had taken me to the hospital. Mike kept calling around when he got home around three that afternoon and finally he found out where I was. He came to get me there, and I heard the policeman tell him he wasn't going to jail me for drunken driving because I had a little girl at home. I remember being grateful that Mike had brought Linda with him. I am ashamed to say that at that moment I gave no thought to the danger I had put her in when I left her alone in her crib. Mike drove me home in silence and didn't speak to me until later that night after Linda was in bed.

I had gone to bed myself as soon as we got home, hoping I would go to sleep, but the painkillers they had given me in the hospital were warring with the alcohol for control of my body and I couldn't sleep at all. I tried to fake it when Mike came into the room, but he wasn't fooled for a minute. I had never heard such coldness in his voice before.

"Well, you really blew it this time," he said, leaning against the dresser and folding his arms across his chest. "I want to talk about it right now."

"Mike, I feel just awful and I'm not sure I can talk."

"That's too bad, Sally. Patience is one quality I have run out of. I've put up with your drinking and your obvious lack of interest in me, but this is something I can't turn my back on."

"I'm sorry, Mike," I told him. And I really meant it. "I'll do anything you say."

"I don't think you have any choice about that," he replied. "I have been thinking about this for a very long time and my mind is made up. I've tried working with you, I've tried being stern with you. I've even tried getting you some outside help; but none of it seems to help. You keep drinking, no matter what. If you can't do it at home, you go out. You drink at work, you drink with your friends. I've wanted to make our relationship work, but I just don't see any way it can.

"What we're going to do is this," he continued as my heart started to freeze up. "We are going to put this house up for sale, and when it is sold we will divide up the money and go our separate ways. I'll keep Linda for the time being. If you can convince me between now and the time we split that you can control yourself and your drinking, I will let you keep Linda with you, and ask only that you give me the right to visit her as often as I like. But if you can't get it together in that time, I'll take Linda away from you permanently."

I knew from his tone and the look in his eyes that he meant every word of it. I knew that everything he said was true and that I had to turn my life around or I would lose my daughter. I also knew there was nothing I could do or say right then that would change anything. So I let my tears fall in silence and begged God to let me make it right. And I knew that it would take more than praying.

A noise in the courtroom startled me back to awareness of the present, and I saw Mike's sister on the stand.

My attorney whispered to me, "Can she hurt us?"

"I don't think so," I whispered back.

"They probably just called her as a character witness," he suggested. "It won't help them all that much."

"Mrs. Lester, will you tell the court your

relationship to the plaintiff, please?" Mike's attorney was saying.

"He's my brother," she said.

"And are you acquainted with the defendant in this case?" he asked.

"Yes, she's my sister-in-law."

"And when did you first meet the defendant?"

"At their wedding."

"And will you tell the court if you have any personal knowledge of the defendant's use of alcohol?"

I saw my attorney stiffen at this question, and I held my breath waiting for her answer.

"Well, the only time I can personally say I saw her drinking was the time she came to visit us about two months ago."

My attorney let out a groan at this which I'm sure was heard by everyone in the room. He had told me to tell him everything and I had tried, but there was so much to remember and I was concentrating on things Mike had done which might be used against him in the custody battle.

"Can you be more specific about the time?" Mike's attorney asked.

"Well, it was just after she and Mike had sold their house. I remember that she said that she wanted to celebrate. She and Mike were separated at the time, but we had remained friendly."

"Was she alone?"

"No, she had Linda, their daughter, with her. Mike had let her spend the day with her."

"Did she say or do anything that let you know she had been drinking before she arrived?"

I was surprised that my attorney didn't object to that because he had tried to stop people from drawing conclusions before, but he just sat there listening.

"Well, not really. She had a bottle of wine with her that wasn't opened and she had a six-pack of beer with one bottle missing, but I don't know if she had been drinking or if she just bought it that way."

"Okay, please continue. What happened?"

"Well, she said she had bought the beer because she my husband drank beer and that she had bought the wine for me and her. I opened the wine and we had a few glasses. When the wine was gone she helped herself to one of the beers. We just sat and talked while the kids played in the bedroom. Then she seemed to get a little sleepy and just kind of stretched out on the floor and dozed off."

"Did she spend the night?"

"No, she only slept for about and hour and then she got up and said she had to go. I told her she should stay with us because the weather was bad and it was a long drive home for her. I thought she had slept off her drinking, but I wasn't positive."

"Is that the only reason you suggested she stay?" his attorney asked.

"Well--" she hesitated, as though she wasn't sure about what to say. "--she seemed a little, uh, disoriented. I mean, she was stumbling into things and she seemed to have forgotten that she had Linda with her. And then, once she did get into her car, it was a long time before she actually left."

"And was that the only time you had ever seen her drinking?"

"Well, yes, that was the only time I had ever actually seen her. Mike had told me about other times, but I hadn't been there on those occasions." Mike's sister looked like she wanted to say more.

"Thank you. I have no further questions."

My attorney asked her a few questions, but I could see that his heart wasn't in it. That crazy, stupid night came back to me. I remembered how proud I was of myself that I had stayed completely away from alcohol since we had separated. It was not an easy time for me because even though Mike tried to be casual and even friendly, I knew he was watching me like a hawk. But I made it and I was real proud of myself. I even told myself a couple of times that I might get lucky and get Mike back if I made a good show of it.

Why I had been so stupid when success was so near I will never know. And why I chose to go to Mike's sister's house--of all places--I'll never know. Maybe I wanted to be caught. Maybe I knew somewhere inside that we would all be better off if Mike took Linda permanently. I must have known the truth about myself.

The hearing was all but over at that point. I knew we didn't stand much of a chance, but I held my breath when the judge returned from her chambers and announced her verdict. I was so afraid to hear what she had to say, I couldn't look up when she started to talk, and I felt my hands begin to tremble. I was afraid I might start to cry.

"I do not find that the evidence shows any willful neglect of the minor child on the part of the defendant in this case," she began, "but given all the testimony heard, and even considering the sincere efforts of the defendant to end her dependency on alcohol as evidenced by her active participation in the AA program since separation, I find that the plaintiff has demonstrated a greater likelihood of providing a good home for their daughter. I therefore award custody to plaintiff."

I will be celebrating a year of sobriety next month. Drinking led me to lose everything, but I have to think also that it took that loss to bring me to my senses. I live each day one day at a time now, and I am beginning to bring a measure of self-respect back into my life. Mike has been good about keeping the visitation schedule set down by the judge, and I have the chance, at least, to watch my little girl grow up. I trust that one day

I will be able to make her understand why her mommy can't be with her every day, and maybe I'll be able to help her avoid the kind of horrible mistakes I made.

ONE TOUCH AWAY
FROM TROUBLE

I got into my present career by accident--literally. I was a senior in high school and as rebellious as anyone else, I guess. But I wasn't a bad person.

One weekend a couple of girlfriends and I decided to have some fun. One of them had a car and we thought we'd find ourselves a party somewhere and have a good time.

Jessica, the one with the car, was one of those girls who managed to let you know, without actually saying so, that she was a little better than you because her dad had enough money to buy her a car while your dad didn't. You know the kind I mean. She wasn't exactly stuck up or anything like that, but she made the rest of us in the crowd feel a little beneath her. I sometimes wonder if maybe it wasn't just us and not Jessica's attitude at all, but I never did get that figured out for sure. I guess it doesn't really matter where the feeling came from, it's where it led that counts.

That Friday afternoon, somebody--I don't even remember who--made a comment that got it all started.

"We have to find a way to make Jessica

come down off her high horse, you know?" she said.

"Yeah, it would be fun to see her get real for a change," I agreed.

We all talked over ideas about how to put her in her place, and by the time our last class was over, a plan had been hatched. We would take Jessica out--in her car, of course--and get her drunk or stoned or both and see what she was really made of underneath all those fancy clothes.

Four of us were in on the deal, and it didn't take much to get Jessica set up for it. All it took, really, was planting the idea that we knew where the guy she was hung up on was going to be partying that night, and she was hooked.

Well, we made the rounds of a few parties, always telling Jessica that we were just one step behind her guy. She kept swallowing the story the way she was swallowing the beers, and pretty soon we were headed for trouble. But none of us were sensible enough to know it. We were all having a good time, enjoying seeing Jessica with her hair let down.

We were on our way to the fourth or fifth party when the trouble we were headed for found us. Jessica ran a red light without even noticing it, and we were broadsided by a pickup doing about forty.

They told me later that the pickup hit us right where I was sitting in the back seat, and that we were lucky that we didn't a pole or a building or a tree before we stopped spinning. The other girls were banged up a bit, and Jessica got a cut across her face from the steering wheel, but I was the one who caught the worst of it.

It was Monday or Tuesday before I learned any of this--I was so badly injured that on Sunday they told my folks I had only a fifty-fifty chance of pulling through it all. I did pull through, of course, but the rest of the school year was shot. Graduation was out of the question. I was in the hospital for about two months before I could go home and begin my struggle back to physical independence.

It was while I was in the hospital that I was introduced to physical therapy. The doctors explained that because of my lengthy stay in traction, and then all the time I would be bedridden after that, that my muscles were in danger of becoming permanently weakened. So I had to have regular sessions with a masseuse.

I learned a lot of technical jargon from Marla, the masseuse who worked with me, because I kept asking her about what she was doing and why. I learned that Marla made a pretty good living in her business, and the longer she was with me, the more I started thinking of massage, or physical therapy (P.T., as she called it), as an interesting career.

One day I asked her directly what she thought of my going into that line of work, and her answer was very encouraging.

"Well, Carrie, there are lots of levels of physical therapy," she told me. "Some people start out as amateur masseuses, or masseurs if they're men, and sort of work into the profession gradually. Others get into it because they find they don't really care to continue their nursing or medical studies. And there are some who actually set out to get a degree in P.T., or just a certificate."

"Which one of those do you fit into?" I asked her.

"Well, two of them, I guess," Marla said. "I got into the two-year P.T. program at the city college about the same time I started charging people for a massage. We were warned against doing that kind of thing until we were really qualified, but I needed the money and I thought it would be better that waiting tables. And then, too, the licensing laws in this state aren't too strict, " she explained, "so it was pretty easy for me to call myself a masseuse as long as I didn't do any advertising. I sort of built up my clientele by word of mouth. By the time I got my certificate and my license as a physical therapist, I already had a pretty good practice going."

"Do you have to finish high school to get into the college program?" I asked her, thinking about how little I cared to return to high school once I was back on my feet.

"Not really. You need to pass your G.E.D. exam. Then they test you for high school competency at the college as part of the admission requirement. Most people with enough smarts pass easily."

I found Marla's information pretty encouraging, and it wasn't long before my mind was made up about just what I was going to do with my life. I started studying for my G.E.D., and I kept pumping her for as much information as I could get about her work. Toward the end of my convalescence, I even started reading some beginning texts on anatomy and physiology that she said I would need.

It was really tough reading at first, but I found it went a lot better when Marla started helping me. I would read as much as I could, then ask her about what I had read the next time she came for one of our sessions. She was coming twice a week at that time, so it was almost like being in a college class. I remember Marla laughing about that in our last session.

"I never would have pictured myself as a teacher," she said. "I usually disliked my teachers."

I thought about some of the teachers I hadn't been too crazy about and joined Marla in her laughter. It felt good to laugh--it had been a long time since I'd had anything to laugh about.

Just then my mother stuck her head into the room and said something about being sorry if she was interrupting anything. She then added, awkwardly, that she had heard the laughter and wondered what was going on. Then she was gone as quickly as she had come.

The next day, Dad told me that he'd had a talk with the doctor and that the doctor had told him it was time I started exercising my muscles on my own. I started to object, but then I realized he wasn't being honest with me anyway. So I just kept quiet.

You know how it is when parents get very reasonable with you? I mean, they get so very reasonable that you know they're covering something up. Well, that's just how Dad was being about my massage sessions.

I didn't understand it at the time, but I got the picture later. I don't know whether it was the fact that Marla and I seemed to be having too good a time, or my mother's first look at me nude with just a towel draped across my buttocks. But it was real clear to me that the decision had been made, and no arguments about my body or my studies or anything else I could think of would have changed their minds. Instead, I kept my mouth shut and became very, very determined to finish the book, no matter how long it took me.

I spent the rest of the summer reading and

exercising. Plus, I passed the G.E.D. exam. By the time fall rolled around, I was ready to take on the world, and I had enough confidence in my understanding of anatomy to enroll in college. I decided to take it easy at first, and signed up for the anatomy class, thinking it would be a breeze since I had already read the book--or most of it, anyway.

Meanwhile, I started practicing my massage technique on my friends. Some of them were a little nervous at first, but I soon found that if I suggested they wear a two-piece swimsuit instead of their bra and panties, they were much more relaxed. It was really funny to me to notice which people felt embarrassed and which ones didn't. I got a few surprises along the way, though Jessica's reaction was no surprise at all. I put her refusal down to a combination of guilt for getting me injured in the first place, and anger at the part I had played in getting her drunk and careless-- though as I remember that night, nobody forced her hand to her mouth.

Anyway, by the time classes had started in September, I thought I had pretty well mastered the technique I had experienced so long as a patient. I was feeling very confident about myself.

Then I met Pauline and things really started changing for me. Pauline was in my class and we got to talking one day on break. I asked her what she did for a living, because I could see that she was older and was probably on her own.

"I'm a masseuse," she said.

I nearly choked when she said that. I couldn't believe my luck at running into another professional.

"Me too!" I said. "Well, I'm not really a professional yet. I mean, I have been getting in a lot of practice, and a nurse friend of mine is helping me with my studies," I fibbed, figuring it wouldn't hurt to stretch the truth just a little bit for the sake of making a good first impression.

"That's nice. What do you charge?" she asked me.

"Well...it varies," I said, thinking really hard about what the going rate should be. "Since I'm just starting out, I'm pretty much using a sliding scale kind of arrangement. How about you?"

"I get forty-five a session," she said off-handedly, "sometimes more."

"Oh. Well, I've charged close friends as little as twenty-five," I told her with a straight face, even though I had never taken any money from anyone. "But I figure that's not bad for a beginner."

"You're right," she replied.

I breathed a sigh of relief. "How many classes are you taking?" I asked her quickly, to change the subject.

"Just this one. I usually take one class a year so I can say I'm still studying. Saves a lot of questions."

"Yeah, right," I replied, not having the slightest idea what she was talking about.

Throughout that semester, Pauline said a lot of things that left me clueless as to her meaning, but I did pick up a lot of tips along the way about how the business worked. When we finally agreed to exchange massages one night, I got some really good pointers, and a bit of an ego boost.

We had both stripped down to our panties and she told me to take the table first, which was fine with me as I was looking forward to picking up some new techniques before I showed her my stuff. She was good, but long before she was done I had concluded that she couldn't hold a candle to Marla. I was pretty confident when it came to be my turn.

"Hey, you're good," she said after only about three minutes under my hands. "That feels real nice."

"Thanks. I really owe it all to my friend."

"Well, let me tell you, I plan to steal some of your techniques," she told me.

"Feel free," I offered with a bit of a swelled head.

"You know, you ought to charge a lot more than twenty-five," she said a few minutes later. "You have fifty-dollar hands."

"Uh, thanks," I said--at a loss for words again."

As I think back on it, that night marked the beginning of my true change from an amateur to a professional. It was a couple of weeks after that before I actually received money for a massage, but where it really counted--in my own head--that was the night.

One of the girls I had been practicing on before I met Pauline asked me to give a massage to a friend of hers who had hurt himself playing basketball. I told her that I charged for massages for anyone else but her, and the next day she called me and said her friend would be glad to pay for a good massage.

I chickened out at the last minute on accepting Pauline's evaluation of my 'fifty-dollar hands' and told her it would be thirty. She said that was fine, so I showed up at her friend's house that evening with my satchel of oils and cleaners-- a necessary beginning kit I had learned from observing both Marla and Pauline. I didn't have a table of my own, of course, but as soon as I saw that first real money I began to dream about buying a real nice one like Marla had brought with her to my at-home sessions.

I didn't tell Pauline about my first paid session because I'd decided to keep up the fiction that I had been getting money for a long time-- especially after her compliments. But I did mention to her one day that that I was going to save my money for a table, and her reaction seemed a little odd to me, though I didn't give it much thought at the time.

"Hey, that would be a nice touch," she said. "What a great gimmick."

"Yeah, one of the good tricks of the trade," I replied, trying to match her flippant attitude with an equally blasé response.

"Oh, cute pun there, Carrie," she said.

Before I could ask her what she meant, we had to get back to class and I forgot about it until much later.

I passed that first class we were taking with good grades and told Pauline I was going to take the next class in the series the following semester. "Are you going to take it?" I asked her, hoping we would continue to be classmates.

"Nah, I've had enough of this for one year," she replied. "I'll catch up to you next year, maybe."

I saw a lot less of her the following term, but we still kept in touch. Once in a while we would get together for a session. But I was starting to make some serious progress on getting new clients, and I didn't have as much free time as I had before. My first client--the basketball player--had told a friend of his about me, and pretty soon I was taking care of practically half the team.

I usually did my massages in their own

homes or apartments, so my parents were still in the dark about what I was doing with my time. They knew I was taking classes at the city college, and they were happy about that, but we didn't talk much about what else I did. In just a few months I had enough money saved up to put a substantial down payment on the table I wanted, and when I brought it home their questions about it finally brought the subject into the open.

`   "What the devil is that?" Dad asked as I came through the door with the table.

"It's a massage table," I told him. "Here, I'll show you."

I unfolded the table like the salesman had shown me, but found that it was not quite as easy as he'd made it look. When I finally got it set up, I thought it really looked quite handsome there in our dining room.

"Well, that's real nice, Carrie," he said when I finished. "But what on earth do you want with a massage table? Planning to use t as a sewing table? Or do you have some strange new hobby we don't know about?"

"No, Dad, I'm not going to use it for sewing. I'm going to use it for massage," I said.

"What do you mean, for massage?" he asked warily.

Mom was interested now and was standing in the kitchen doorway, watching and listening. I guess I got a little nervous, and my carefully prepared speech about my new career went out the window under their curious stares.

"I've been taking classes and practicing on my own," I told them, "and I bought this table with the money I've earned doing massages."

"Doing what?" Dad asked. His voice was getting louder.

"Doing massages," I repeated. "I have earned over two hundred dollars already this month," I added proudly.

The silence in that room could have been cut with a knife, and I started getting a sinking feeling in the pit of my stomach as I looked from Dad to Mom, searching their faces for some clue as to how they were taking this news. Mom was the first one to speak, and she had that 'very reasonable' tone in her voice.

"Now, honey, why do you want to get involved in something like that?" she asked. "Surely there are other kinds work you could do if you want to earn a little extra money, though I can't understand why you need any extra money at all. Your father and I take good care of you, and I can't--"

"That's not the point," Dad interrupted. "What you're doing is not a game for amateurs. It's dangerous. What if you hurt someone while you're doing one of these back rubs?"

"That's why I'm taking classes in anatomy, Dad," I tried to explain.

He didn't let me finish because he had a lot more to say, and as he talked I flashed back to the day he had told me Marla wouldn't be coming any more. I knew right then that he was not telling me the truth about how he was feeling, and that he hadn't been telling me the truth then, either.

But I was so confused and upset by their reaction that I didn't stop to try to figure them out, I just got out of there with my new table as fast as I could. I didn't promise to quit giving massages, and they didn't actually forbid me to continue with them, so I made up my mind I would just keep quiet about it until I could find a place of my own.

Fortunately, I had a client to do that night-- another one of the guys from the team--and I was soon able to put my parents' attitudes out of my mind. You see, I had made an important discovery about massage soon after I started practicing on my friends. It feels almost as good to give a massage as it does to get one. There is something very soothing about the steady rhythm of your hands working on knotted, unused muscles, and one's own muscles get quite a workout, too.

My client that night was Rick, a pre-law student at the college. He like to talk about his studies and his plans while I worked on him, so both my mind and my body were busily engaged in wiping out the feelings I'd been left with by my parents' negative reaction.

"I sure like your new table," he said as I worked on his thighs and calves. "It's a lot more comfortable than my floor."

"Yes, I'll bet it is. And it helps me, too," I told him. "I can get much better leverage standing than I can get kneeling on the floor. I think it was a very good investment."

"Speaking of investments, Carrie, I've been thinking that maybe we could work out some long-term financial arrangements." Rick remarked.

"What do you mean?" I asked him.

"Well, I was thinking that if this gets to be a regular session--like say, once a week--you might be willing to give me a cut rate."

"I'll give it some thought," I promised him.

And I did give it some thought. I liked Rick. Of all the guys I was working on at that time, he was the nicest. And it wasn't that he had a good body--most of the jocks were in fairly good shape. The thing about Rick was that he had a mind, too. A good mind. And there was something else that I couldn't quite define, but it had to do with his attitude toward me. It wasn't that he was more friendly--a lot of the guys were just a little too friendly at times. I couldn't quite put my finger on it, but Rick was special.

I was real glad when I ran into Pauline the next day, because I was still thinking about Rick's suggestion and I couldn't really make up my mind. I laid my problem on Pauline and asked her advice.

"Well, Carrie, I'm not in favor of discounts as a general rule," she said at first. "But sometimes you have to do it to keep a good client. I have this one guy who's a little short on cash now and then, and I usually let him get away with it. Of course, he's the kind of guy who doesn't mind leaving a generous tip for the 'extras' when he has money, so it all works out in the end. You see what I mean?"

I understood the general idea of what she was saying, and even though I had no idea what she meant by extras, I didn't want to appear dim, so I just nodded my head.

"What are you charging this client now?" Pauline asked.

"Well, he was one of my first, from way back," I lied. "So I only charge him forty a session."

"Carrie, you're underselling yourself," she commented. "If I were you, I wouldn't give that bozo any more of a discount than that. Like I said before, you are good for fifty, easy. But if you decide to ignore my advice, at least put him on a monthly. That way, you won't lose too much if he turns flaky on you."

"What do you mean by a monthly?" I asked her.

"You said this guy is a regular weekly client, right? Okay, you tell him you'll charge him the regular fee for the first three weeks of each month, and then give him a discount on the last week," Pauline explained. "So he pays you forty for the first three weeks, and you give him the fourth for only twenty. That gives him a little better than ten percent off on the month, see?"

Pauline was real funny that way. She'd had a hard time in our anatomy class, but she had a good head for business and was quicker with figures like that than I would ever be. I used a calculator for even the simplest kind of math.

"Yes, I see," I told her. "That sounds like a good idea. Thanks, Pauline."

"Don't mention it. And you be sure to let him know he's already getting a cut rate to start with. You should be charging him fifty a session anyway."

"Right," I lied, thinking there was no way I was going to do that. I had already worked my way up from thirty to forty, and some of the guys on the team were still getting sessions for the lower rate. I figured I would scare too many of them off if I went or another raise so soon. But it felt good to be talking business with Pauline, so I wasn't about to blow my cover with her. I did start thinking that if I got any new clients who didn't know the guys on the team that I would try going to fifty.

"So how's it going otherwise?" Pauline

asked.

"Oh, not so good. My folks threw a fit the day I brought home my new table," I told her. "You'd think I was going in for back-street surgery or something, the way they went on about how I could hurt someone and get myself into a lawsuit. And some of my old friends are giving me the cold shoulder, too. I'm going to have to find a place of my own, I think. I'm not exactly making enough money to afford my own apartment, but I'm going to have to do something."

"How much are you making now, if you don't mind my asking?" Pauline questioned.

"No, I don't mind," I told her honestly. "I'd say something in the neighborhood of four to five hundred a month."

"That's not very much," she remarked. "What do you pay for your car?"

"Oh, the car's paid for," I told her. "My folks got a nice little settlement from Jessica's insurance company after the accident. That more than paid for all my medical bills, so they gave me their old car. It's not much, but they said it was mine. And I plan on keeping it even when I move out. I figure it's probably good for three or four more years if I take good care of it."

"Find yourself a good mechanic and work out a trade," she suggested. "It will last even longer, and it won't cost you anything."

"Hey, good idea. Gosh, you are just full of

good ideas today, Pauline."

"Yeah, well I have another one," she said. "If you want to move in with me till you find a place of your own, we could work something out."

"Really? That would be great. Are you sure you have the room?" I asked, not wanting to impose.

Pauline seemed sincere, so when she offered to take me over to her place to check it out, I accepted. I followed her over there, and when she showed me around, I saw that she did have a big enough place for two--I'd never been past the living room before. There was a lot of junk in the second bedroom that would have to be moved or thrown out, she said, but the room was plenty big enough for me.

"You'd have to get a phone of your own. It wouldn't work out for us to have the same number," she told me. "But other than that, I think it would be fine. And I sure could use a little help with the rent."

We talked about details, like how we would split the rent and who would get what shelves in the kitchen and stuff like that, and when we had worked everything out, I drove on home. I'd figured that if I could keep making five hundred a month, I would have enough to keep me going. And if I could increase my income by even two hundred a month, I would be able to afford some luxuries like new clothes and eating out once in a while. Pauline didn't cook much at all, so she'd told me that the kitchen would be practically all mine. It was going to be great!

I had a little bit of trouble at the phone company the next day. The woman taking my order told me at first that they would have to have a deposit to install the phone. She said it was standard procedure for students, and I started thinking that this was going to be more expensive than I had planned. I jokingly suggested that I would be happy to trade a few massages for the deposit and told her I got fifty dollars a session.

"Oh, you're going to be working while you go to school?" she asked.

"Yes, I've been working for about four months now," I told her.

"Well, that's different. Who is your employer?"

"Myself. I'm self-employed," I said, and got an immediate rush of pride at saying those words aloud for the first time.

"And what do you do?" she asked as though she hadn't heard me offer the massage.

"I'm a masseuse."

"Oh," she said.

She wrote a few more things down on the application, and I started getting that funny feeling again. It was like a little curtain had dropped down between us when she said 'oh' and suddenly she was treating me with a coolness that I hadn't noticed before. It was the same kind of feeling I got when I told some of my friends I was studying to be a masseuse, and close to what I felt from Mom and Dad when we first talked about massage. It bothered me a lot, but I noticed that she hadn't said anything more about the deposit, and that was all I cared about at the time. I let it go and left the office with the appointment slip clutched tightly in my hand. My new phone number was written on the slip, and I couldn't wait to call my clients and give it to them.

After that, I went back home and packed my things. I left a few things behind in my room, just in case, and told Mom I was going to be staying with a friend for a while. She was strangely quiet about it, and just said something like she hoped things worked out for me. I didn't get any argument about the car, like I had expected, and I was feeling pretty good.

The good feeling lasted through the rest of the week. But on Saturday morning I realized that since I'd skipped my Thursday class, I would have to do some extra reading that weekend.

Appropriately enough, Rick was the first person to call my new number. He said he wanted to confirm our Sunday evening session and asked if I'd given any thought to the discount idea. I told him I had, and explained Pauline's 'monthly discount plan' to him as though I had been doing that kind of thing for a lot of my clients for years. He said it sounded like a fair arrangement, and I told him I would see him at the regular time.

As I was setting up my table at Rick's apartment that Sunday night, I started to get a funny feeling about him. There was something different about the way he was walking around, fussing with little things and straightening his pictures on the walls. And he seemed embarrassed when he got undressed--which was not like him. I managed to calm myself down and stop worrying about it as I began to work on him, but I noticed that he was really tense in the shoulder and neck area. He cleared his throat a couple of times while I was working on his lower back. Then finally he spoke.

"Carrie, there's something I've been wanting to talk to you about, and--well, I don't quite know how to put it. Will you forgive me if I just speak bluntly?" he asked quickly.

"Sure, Rick," I told him as I continued working on him. "I like talking with you, so anything you have to say, just spit it out."

"Great. As a matter of fact, that's sort of what I mean. I mean, we do talk easily with each other, and I guess you could say we have a good physical relationship. Wait. That's not what I meant to say. I mean, I like the way you work on my body. I like you. Carrie, would you be interested in a more involved relationship with me?" he finally said.

Rick had caught me completely be surprise, and I was at a loss for words I liked Rick a lot, and we did get along well. And as I mentioned before, there was something special about the way he treated me.   Rick wasn't overly friendly, and he didn't treat me like a servant as some of my clients did. He was just--real, if you know what I mean. But I'd never thought about having a 'relationship' with him. I guess I wasn't really sure what having a relationship meant other than making some kind of commitment, and I was sure that I wasn't ready to do that. So I asked him a question of my own rather than answering his.

"Just what kind of involvement do you have in mind?"

"Well, I don't know really," he said. "I just thought maybe we cold take it one step at a time."

"What would be the next step?" I asked him, holding my breath and forgotten to work on his muscles for the moment.

"Well, how about dinner? And maybe a movie, or the theater?" he suggested.

"Oh." I breathed easier, and went back to work on his back. "Well, that sounds nice."

"Great! Can we set a date now, or should I call you later?"

"You'd better call me. I'll need to check my phone messages to make sure I don't have an appointment. I'm sorry, but business has to come first."

"Sure. I understand. I'll call you in the morning, if that's okay," he added.

He reminded me that he would call in the morning as I left his place later, and hummed a little tune to myself as I drove back to the apartment. I'd noticed that the tension in Rick's neck and shoulders had decreased dramatically after I had agreed to the date. I realized that his nervous behavior earlier that night was mostly due to his interest in me as a person rather than simply as a masseuse. It was the most positive reaction I had received since Pauline told me I had fifty-dollar hands.

Pauline was at our apartment when I got home and was anxious to talk to me about something. I noticed the same kind of tension in her that I had seen in Rick earlier. It turned out that she wanted to ask me something, too. What Pauline wanted, though, was a favor.

"Listen, Carrie, I have to go out of town for a few weeks and I'm in a really bad spot. The girl who usually covers for me is all booked up. I was wondering if you would mind taking my clients. It will only be for about two weeks, and it would be a bit of extra money for you," she pointed out.

"Well, sure," I told her. "If you think I can handle it, I'd be glad to help out. And you know I can use the extra money."

"Oh, that's great. You're a peach, Carrie. Okay, here's my book. You shouldn't really need it, but in case someone leaves a message and you don't quite get the number, most of my regulars are in here," she explained.

Pauline went on to give me a few more details, but they weren't the kind of details I expected her to be giving me. In my book, I note special problems that some of my clients have-- whether they prefer scented or unscented oils, and things like that. But Pauline didn't seem to have anything but addresses and phone numbers in her book, and some of the addresses were motels.

I was flipping through the book as she was stuffing a few things into a big bag and trying to convince me that she wouldn't have asked me to do this if it weren't a real emergency. I tried to stop her for a minute to tell her it was really all right, but she was talking a mile a minute while she packed. Then, suddenly, she was out the door and gone.

The reason for her many apologies became quite clear later, of course, but right then I was just too stunned by her whirlwind behavior to realize what was going on.

It wasn't until after I got into bed that night that I realized this favor for Pauline might interfere with my first date with Rick. I wished, for a second, that I had thought of that earlier so I could have told her about it. But I realized that I owed Pauline for helping me into the business and for sharing her apartment with me. Rick would just have to understand that our date might have to be put off for a few weeks until Pauline got back. I thought that maybe Rick and I could have lunch real soon so that he wouldn't think I was putting him off.

Rick was more understanding that I'd hoped. He seemed genuinely happy to make a lunch date for Wednesday of that week. While I was talking to him, Pauline's phone rang and I could hear the whir of her answering machine taking a message. After I hung up my own phone, I rewound her tape and listened to a man name Clayton asking for a Tuesday night session at his home. I checked her book, found Clayton and the address, and wrote the appointment in her book as well as in my own so she would know I had taken care of him.

I kept that appointment for Pauline with Clayton and got more of an education that I expected. I was quite surprised to discover that he was a pretty old guy--like over fifty, maybe--and he looked like he hadn't used any muscle in his body for years. And the way he looked at me! Some of the jocks I worked on had tried to be cool and come on to me, but I always knew that they were just 'practicing' and were also embarrassed about getting undressed for their massages. This guy wasn't embarrassed at all.

I asked him where he wanted me to set up my table, and he made some comment about that being a kinky idea before telling me to put it in the bedroom. He didn't waste any time undressed. He was ready before I got the table set up, and my confusion began turning to distrust when he started asking me why I wasn't taking my clothes off, too.

"I don't need to get undressed to give you a massage," I told him as he pulled himself onto the table.

"Oh, a massage. Good, I like that. This should be fun," he said, lying on his back.

I was really starting to get worried now, but I told him to roll over and started working on his back. I figured I had an obligation to Pauline, and I was determined to carry through with it.

I cold die when I realize how stupid and naive I was. I hadn't been working on him for a minute when he started asking me when we were going to get to the 'extras'. That's when it finally hit me. I had heard Pauline talk about the bonus money some men paid her for the extras, and everything fell into place all at once. I stopped the massage right then and told him I thought there had been a misunderstanding, and that I should probably leave. He tried to grab me, but he was no match for me, and suddenly he was on the floor rubbing his head as I beat a very fast and very scared retreat.

I can't remember how I managed to get my table out of his house without folding it up, but I was all thumbs trying to get it folded on the sidewalk so I could get it into my car. I finally managed to get it into the trunk and then I burned rubber getting out of there. I was still shaking when I got out of the shower, even though I had stayed there until the water turned cold.

There were times in the long night that followed when I blamed my parents for not telling me what they were really thinking, now that I realized what it was. Maybe if someone had bothered to talk plainly to me, had taken the time to tell me that masseuse is often just a pretty name for prostitute, I might not have started giving massages in the first place. But that's not true. I probably would have done it anyway, but at least I wouldn't have fallen into the mess I was in now. If just one of my friends had said something to me instead of just giving me the cold shoulder, I could have made better decisions.

I spent all night thinking everything through, and first thing in the morning I packed up my stuff and moved back to my parents' house. I knew what we needed was an open, honest discussion of the whole thing, and after hashing it all out, we realized that our problem had been a lack of communication. My parents now understand how much I love being a masseuse, and they are supporting me in pursuing my Physical Therapy Certificate so I can get my license and work with a private organization or a hospital. Hopefully, that will make it clear to people that I am a professional and will put any 'ideas' that they may have out of their heads.

Things with Rick are just great these days. On that first lunch date, I told him the whole story, and he was very understanding and supportive. Rick and I have continued to date often since then, and our friendship has blossomed into a wonderful romance. But for now, we're taking it slow and easy. We want to keep our minds on our career goals. It will take Rick much longer to achieve his, but I can wait. Because believe me, he's really worth waiting for!

MAYBE THISTIME
I'LL SAY YES WHEN HE ASKS ME

The first time Walt asked me to marry him, I gave him a very firm no for an answer. We were both still in high school at the time, and even if I had been inclined to get engaged to anyone (which I wasn't), I probably still wouldn't have said yes. It's not that Walt wasn't a nice kid. He was. It's just that that's exactly what he was--a nice kid.

I guess he must have changed a lot since then, because now he doesn't seem at all the way I remember him. As I remember, he was kind of thin and had a habit of being pretty goofy. You know, the class clown kind of guy. He was fun to be around because he had a way of making people laugh no matter how bad they felt, but no one ever took him seriously. And I didn't take him seriously when he asked me to marry him.

Now he seems a whole lot different than he was then. He still has a way of making people laugh, but it's more like a person with a good sense of humor rather than a clown. And he's not nearly as skinny as I used to think he was. Maybe he changed. Maybe we both just grew up. Some of the things I went through sure aged me a lot, and I guess it was the same for Walt.

I used to think I was quite a grown-up little

lady because of the way it was at home for me. Mama had left us when I was thirteen. She just walked out on Daddy, the two younger kids, and me. Daddy tried his best to put up a good front about it, but I knew a lot of it had to do with her drinking, though I didn't say anything about it to him. He called all us kinds into the living room that afternoon and had us sit on the sofa. Then he paced up and down for a few minutes before he sat down in his chair and gave us the news.

"Kids," he said, "your mama is going to be away for a while. I don't know how long she'll be gone, so we're just going to have to do the best we can until she comes back."

We all started yammering at the same time, but he held up his hand for us to be quiet and continued. "It might be a little rough at first, but I want everyone to pitch in and help as much as possible. I'll try to fill in the gaps, but need your help.

"Nina," he said to me, "you're the oldest, so I'm going to have to ask you to take on some of the more difficult tasks like shopping and cleaning the house. Not that I expect you to do it all alone--you two younger ones will have to help out as best you can. We'll start by finding out just how much responsibility you can really handle, and once we've established that, we can assign you some regular jobs."

Daddy was clever that way. I guess it sort

of came with being a salesman. I remember reading once about how Tom Sawyer had talked another boy into painting a fence for him by making him think it was a great privilege to do it, and that's just how Daddy was with Davy and Lynn. Davy was ten at the time and Lynn was only eight, but they both got looks of determination on their faces and I knew it wasn't going to be as bad as I first thought.

And it wasn't. The kids were really good at keeping their rooms pretty clean, and Davy soon took over the laundry and dishes. Lynn liked playing with the feather duster and made a great show of dusting the furniture every so often-- though I usually had to finish up after her. But cleaning was the easy part for me. The hardest jobs were shopping and cooking. Daddy tried his best to help, but Mama had always done those things herself, and some of the meals we had in those first few months were positively terrible. We survived though, and pretty soon I felt a lot more confident about my ability to 'manage the house', as Daddy put it, than I probably should have.

It wasn't until my senior year in high school, long after we had accepted the fact that Mama wasn't ever going to come back, that I began to realize the extra work had kept me from learning the kinds of things all my girlfriends were learning about how to make it in the 'real world'. I knew a lot more about housework than any two or three of them put together, and someone was always asking my advice about one thing or another along those lines. But I hadn't had time to take those extra classes in business skills, or work part time jobs like the other girls did. By the time I realized all that, though, it was a little too late to change anything.

I was talking about this with a couple of friends on one of those rare Saturdays when I had a few hours to myself. We were all sitting in a booth at Burger Heaven when somebody threw out the usual question: "So what are you guys going to do when you graduate?"

"I think I have a good job lined up at the Easy Shop," one of them said.

"I'm going to go to Mission to get a degree," Sarah announced. "I'm going to be a dental hygienist."

"You mean you're going to try to snag a rich dentist," Debbie teased. "What about you, Nina?"

"Darned if I know," I said. "I guess I just haven't thought about it. I've been too busy taking care of the house and the kids. The only think I know how to do is clean and cook."

`   "Sounds like you better clean houses for a living. Or find a husband quick," Debbie suggested.

I was just about to say that I didn't care for either alternative when Walt, who was walking by our booth at the time, stopped and made his proposal.

"Say, this sounds like my big chance," he said with that grin of his. "Nina, will you marry me?"

"No," I told him. "Now go away."

Everybody laughed, including Walt, and he left. I didn't give the conversation any more thought until I was walking home later that afternoon, but when I did I found myself taking Debbie's suggestion a little more seriously. I mean the one about cleaning houses. Daddy was home when I got there, and he was in a good mood, so I told him about the conversation. He started to say something right off, then closed his mouth and thought for a minute.

"You know," he said at last in a serious tone, "that may not be such a bad idea. We frequently need the services of house cleaners in the realty business--to clean houses people have vacated, or do the finish work after a new house is built. It pays pretty good, too. Maybe I could get you a few jobs that would give you some spending money of your own. I'm not suggesting that you make a career out of it, but if you want to try it out, I'll see what I can do."

"I would like to try it out," I told him. "I especially like the part about the money. How much does it pay?"

"Oh, it varies," he said. "Depending on how

dirty the house is, how quickly we need it cleaned, and what kind of job is done on it. But I don't think you'd be disappointed with the pay at all. Davy is getting responsible enough to take care of himself and Lynn on the weekends if I'm not here, so you could start off with whatever weekend jobs come up."

`   "That's great, Daddy! Can I start next weekend?" I asked eagerly.

"You can start as soon as we have a job available," he told me.

At first it was really great. The first place I did was a small, two-bedroom house that had belonged to an older couple. They had decided to give it up and move to a retirement home, and one of the realtors in Daddy's office got the listing. The house had been kept pretty neat, but it was far from clean. I guess the old folks couldn't get down on their hands and knees very well to clean all the little nooks and crannies.

`   It was a tough job, but when I was through and had hung the freshly cleaned curtains back on the windows, that little house shone! Daddy and the other realtor went with me to inspect it, and I got handed a check for more money than I had ever seen in my life--of my own that is. I told Daddy I wanted to spend most of it on some better cleaning equipment, and he patted me on the back so hard it almost knocked me over.

"Spoken like a true professional," he said. "But don't get carried away, honey. Remember that you may not stay with this for long, and you don't want to invest too much in your business. Have a little fun with some of your money, or you'll go sour on the business real soon."

I promised him I would spend some of it on myself, and I did sort of do that. I mean, I put some into a savings account so I could start saving for a car of my own. But I spent the rest of it on better cleaning equipment to make my next job easier. And the very next weekend I was sure glad I had.

The second house I did was a real mess. It had had renters in it for about a year and they hadn't cared one little whit about cleaning up the place. I found dried food--at least I hoped it was food--on the floor of almost every room, so I was really happy to have the little plastic scrapers I had found. Lots of other things I had bought came in handy on that job, too.

I'll never know how much the fact it was Daddy's listed affected how much I got paid for the job, but I figured that even if he did give me a little more, I had earned it. That Sunday night I was so exhausted that I went to bed at eight, and still managed to sleep through my alarm on Monday morning.

I don't think I heard a word in my classes that day--the one's I went to, that is--and when

Debbie asked me later how I did on the test, I could barely even remember any of the questions. She gave me a real razzing about that, but I was just too tired to care.

Daddy asked me on Thursday if I wanted to do another house, and I had to think a minute before I answered. "Could I look it over before I say yes?" I finally asked him.

"Sure, Pumpkin," he said. "The Lawson place was a toughie, wasn't it?"

"Yes, I was really bushed. I'd rather not take on another house like that. Not without help," I told him.

"Well, that shows you have a good business sense," he said encouragingly. "I'm glad to see you're using your head about this."

I didn't realized it until later, but I think he was secretly pleased that I hadn't found my second experience as easy as the first. I don't think he wanted me o do this on a full-time basis but I also don't think he was aware of how unprepared I was to do much of anything else. I never told him about the 'fun' classes I hadn't been able to take, and I also forgot to mention how I had wangled the shorter school day for myself so I could get home early and be ready for the kids.

Anyway, it was all water under the bridge now. Besides, I was having second thoughts about this housecleaning business myself. But when I went to check out the latest job, it looked like it would be closer to the first house I had done than to the second one, so I wound up taking the job.

I finished the job on that third house in one day, thanks to my improving skills and my better equipment. Sunday was all mine, and after I calculated how much of my pay I would put into the bank, I still had enough left over to buy myself some new clothes. So I took myself on a shopping spree.

Funny how things workout, though. I had every intention of buying myself a pretty dress, but as I walked through the department store, my eyes was caught by the uniform shop. I found myself trying on some sensible-looking cotton pants and shirts. I was surprised at how nicely they fit. Every person I had ever seen wearing those 'service' outfits looked like they were wearing something three sizes two big or two sizes too small for them. I was also surprised to learn olive drab and white aren't the only colors they come in.

"Say, that blue is a real nice color on you," the salesman said as I admired myself in the mirror.

"Thanks," I mumbled, blushing a little. "I like the fit."

"Sure looks good on you. What kind of work do you do?"

I hesitated a second before answering him. I had never given a thought to describing my occupation to anyone outside of my girlfriends at school, and I wasn't sure just how to put it.

"I work for a real estate firm, doing prep work on houses," I finally answered, remembering the phrase one of Daddy's friends had used.

"Hey, that sounds like it might be interesting," he said. "You get to see all the latest models that way."

"Well, sometimes," I lied. "I also do older houses. I guess you could say I get to see all kinds. Do these come in any other colors?" I asked him quickly, anxious to get off the subject.

As it turned out, pale blue was about the only 'new' color they came in, so I bought two outfits in that color.

"Would you like me to have name tags sewn on for you?" he asked me as he carried the outfits to the cash register.

I hadn't really thought about putting my name on them, but once he mentioned it, it sounded like a good idea. Then I had another thought before I answered him.

"No, thanks. I think I'll embroider them myself."

"Hey, a woman of many talents. Well, okay, I'll just ring these up for you. Will that be cash or charge?"

"Cash," I told him, taking out my wallet.

"Say," he said a moment later as he took my money, "do you have a business card you could give me?"

"Uh, no, I don't have any with me," I fibbed. "Why?"

"Well, you got me thinking. Cleaning house is one of my biggest headaches. I'm divorced and I have two kids at home. Kitty's four and Jerry's five. And, well, I thought maybe we could talk business."

My mind immediately went into high gear at that. I hadn't paid him too much attention--he was just another salesman. I had noticed he was in his late thirties or early forties, but not much else about him had registered. Now I took a more careful look at him.

I had some idea of how little money he must make, from conversations I had listened in on between Daddy and his real estate friends about what other salesmen made as compared to realtors, and I immediately figured that he probably couldn't afford to pay me as well a s Daddy's office paid me. But then I also figured that he was probably talking about a different kind of house-cleaning than what I did for Daddy and the other realtors.

I decided that it wouldn't hurt to at least talk to him about it, so I told him to give me one of his cards and promised to call him when I had a free moment. He scribbled his home phone number on one of his department store cards and handed it to me with my package.

I decided to drop by Burger Heaven after I left the store, since I hadn't spent nearly as much money as I'd planned to. I found a few of the gang there.

"Been shopping?" Debbie asked as I slid into the booth.

"Yeah, I just picked up some work clothes," I said.

"Work clothes? Hey are you serious?"

"Sure, my new job is working out so well, I've decided to go into it in a more professional way," I said with a surge of pride.

"Well, get her," Debbie said to the other girls in the booth. "One day she doesn't know she's going to do with her life, and the next she's beating all of us into the work force. Making any money?" she asked.

"Well, I have a little in the bank," I bragged. "Won't be long before I have a car of my own at the rate I'm going."

Debbie joined the others in offering her congratulations. She talked hard and brassy, but we all knew she didn't mean anything by it. Her abrasive manner came in handy when a particularly aggressive guy needed a brush-off, so we liked having her around.

And speaking of guys, Walt took that opportunity to lean over from the next booth and offer his second proposal.

"Did I hear someone say 'money in the bank'?" he said with that silly grin of his. "Can't pass up an opportunity like that. Nina, will you marry me?"

"No, Walt. Go away," I told him again.

Everyone laughed, including Walt, of course, and we girls returned to our conversation. That turned out to be the last time we were together as a group, at least for me. I got really busy after that, and pretty soon graduation was upon us and summer had arrived. And I was getting busier than I ever had been. I didn't even go to the class party. Once in a while I saw one or two of my friends as I was driving to a job in my little station wagon, or taking the kids somewhere, or just out doing some shopping. But hardly ever had time to just sit and talk.

I had started working for Don, the salesman at the department store, about two weeks after he first suggested it. I found the work a welcome change from the 'deep cleaning' I did most of the time. Daddy didn't like the idea of my taking on the job at first, but Don's offer had been hard to refuse. I did his house on Tuesday and Thursday nights, for two hours each night--at first.

When summer started, I told him I would prefer to work during the day, and he said that was okay. It was more like the other work that I did, with him and the kids gone, and I was just getting into the new routine when things started changing. One morning I arrived at his house and found him still there.

"I took a few hours off this morning so I could talk to you, Nina," he said as he met me at the door.

"Is anything wrong?" I asked, fearing that he wasn't satisfied with my work.

"Oh, no. In fact, I'm very happy with your work. It's nice to be living in a clean house again. And Jerry and Kitty like it. They like you, too. In fact, it's the kids that I wanted to ask you about."

He asked me to sit down on the couch before continuing. "The things is," he said, sitting next to me, "since you're here two mornings a week, I was wondering if you would mind having Jerry and Kitty here while you work?"

"Of course not," I told him. "They're both cute, and they never got in my way when I was working evenings."

"Well, that's good. And do you think you could take them to the daycare center after you finish? It's just three blocks from here, so it shouldn't be out of your way."

That didn't seem unreasonable, so I agreed to do it for him.

Well, one thing led to another, and pretty soon I found myself giving a lot more of my time to Jerry and Kitty than I was getting paid for. I really started to resent the way Don was taking the little extras he kept asking me to do for granted. Like the time he asked me to take the kids to the dentist instead of the daycare center when I was through with his house. I agreed, even though it meant a lot of extra driving for me. And when I got them to the dentist, the receptionist told me that I was to call Don at work.

"Nina," he said when I reached him. "I can't get away from work like I'd planned, so would you mind waiting for Jerry and Kitty and then taking them to daycare when they're through there? I'd really appreciate it."

I was too mad to tell Don just how much I minded, and before I could say anything at all, he added that he had to run because he had a customer waiting for him. Then he hung up on me. I sat there in the dentist's office until the kids were done, and I was still burning up with the way Don was using me as his personal slave. I tried not to let it show--for the kids' sake--but it was a big effort.

Then, as if I wasn't already tight-jawed enough, the car started acting up on me, stalling out at lights and sputtering when I tried to accelerate. I looked around to see where I was-- between Jerry and Kitty and the car and my anger, I hadn't been paying too much attention--and I realized that I was only a few blocks from the dealer where I had bought the car.

"Kids, we're going to have to make a

detour," I told them. "I've got to find out what's wrong with this car before we go any further."

They were delighted, of course, the way little kids always seem to enjoy anything new or exciting. So I drove to the dealer and gratefully let the car die out again right in front of their service door. A mechanic came over to the car as I got Jerry and Kitty out, and I explained the problem to him. He said he would check it out and let me know what the problem was.

I took the kids to the showroom, figuring the shiny new cars would keep them interested for a while. As I was sitting there, I still couldn't stop clenching my teeth, and I darn near jumped out of my skin when a voice at my left said, "So! You wouldn't marry me, and went off and got yourself a ready-made family, huh?"

I spun around and there was Walt, looking surprisingly grown up in a suit and tie. I just stared at him for a minute, vaguely waving my hands at Jerry and Kitty, trying to think of some way to explain how I happened to be there with two towheaded youngsters. All of a sudden I just burst out crying, like seeing Walt was the last straw or something. He took me gently by the shoulders and led me to one of the little offices off the showroom.

"You want to talk about it?" he asked, handing me a second or third tissue for my eyes.

His words and even the tone of his voice were so unlike the Walt I knew, that I forgot I was sitting with the 'class clown' for a minute and just started to pour out my feelings to him. He listened with such interest that before long I found myself telling him about how much I had missed out on at school because of Mama leaving.

"Boy, you've had it rough," he said. "When I think about all the teasing I did--well, I feel like a jerk!"

"Oh, Walt, don't feel that way," I told him. "I never minded your clowning around. Neither did anyone else that I know of. In fact, it was good to have a laugh now and then."

"Well, thanks," he said in a tone that suggested he didn't believe me. "But listen, why don't you just tell this Don to buzz off? Sounds to me like you don't really need the money, with all your other work. And you sure don't need the aggravation."

"Oh, I suppose I should," I admitted. "But I just can't bear the thought of Jerry and Kitty being stuck. Oh, my gosh, the kids! I completely forgot about them. I hope they haven't gotten into any trouble."

I went back into the showroom, in much better control of myself after my talk with Walt, and found the kids sitting in a Jeep, pretending to drive it. Another salesman assured me they were no trouble, and just as I was getting them out of there the mechanic came in and told me they had adjusted my carburetor and that there would be no charge. Between that news and running into Walt, my day had totally turned around. I was feeling a lot better as I got Jerry and Kitty back into the car. Walt followed me out, and as I walked around to my side of the car to get in, he took my arm and stopped me.

"Nine, I just want to say one other thing. What you said about feeling sorry for that jerk's kids sounded a lot like what you used to say about your own brother and sister. Well, what I mean to say is, someday you're going to have to start living for yourself instead of everybody else."

I was about to tell him that I had begun to realized that myself, but he held a hand up to stop me and continued. "All I want to say is that if you decide to do that soon, my proposal is still open."

I waited for the grin, but it didn't quite show up on his face as I'd expected it to. Instead, there was a sincere and hopeful look in his eyes. I finally managed to mumble, "Thank you, Walt," and got quickly into the car and drove away.

On the drive tot he daycare center, I tried to put his words out of my mind as I had done before. Funny things was, without that big grin it was harder to dismiss Walt as a clown. And I had this fluttery feeling in my stomach.

Anyway, but the time I got the kids to daycare, it was time for me to get to my next job.

Soon, I had forgotten about my anger as I scrubbed floors and polished furniture for the old couple who had hired me a few months back. That was one of the nice things about my job. I could either do it on 'automatic' and leave my mind free to wander, or I could really throw myself into it and clear my mind completely as I concentrated on each little task. I chose the latter course that afternoon, and by the time I got home I was bushed, by feeling a lot better emotionally.

By the time the following Tuesday rolled around, I had made up my mind to tell Don that I wasn't going to take care of Jerry and Kitty for him unless he was willing to pay me my regular rate for the time I spent doing that. I was pretty sure that would put a stop to his using me, but I was ready to flat quit the job if he didn't see it my way. I wasn't prepared for the note tacked to the front door of his house when I arrived that morning.

I let myself in with my key and started to work right away, wondering if the note meant that Don had realized that he was using me, too. I started feeling a little foolish at the way I had exploded with Walt, but that feeling didn't go a far as making wish I hadn't run into him. In fact, I was discovering that the more I thought about Walt, the better I felt. By the time I was nearly finished with the job that morning, I was humming silly tunes to myself and feeling positively good. I was so engrossed in my own thoughts that I didn't hear Don come into the house. I didn't even realize he was there until I turned to leave the bedroom I had been putting finishing touches on.

"Nina, I'm glad you're still here," he said as he approached me, apparently unaware that he had startled me.

"I'm--I'm just finishing," I stammered.

"I need to talk to you," he said, again ignoring my nervousness. Then he put his hands on my shoulder and said, "There is something I have to tell you."

I tried to twist out of his grasp, but he gripped me more firmly and looked at me with such intensity that I started to get really scared.

"Don, I--"

"No, please listen to me, Nina. You have been a part of this house and me for a long time now, and I have to say this. I want you, Nina. I need you," he said huskily.

I could smell alcohol on his breath, and I knew that he'd had a few drinks to bolster his courage. That scared me even more. Maybe he wasn't even aware of how much he was hurting me. I thought about hitting him in the gut to make him let go and then running out of there, but I decided to try to reason with him first.

That was a mistake. Another mistake. My first mistake had been in not taking Walt's advice and quitting the job the previous week. I had been lulled into a false sense of security by Don's note and his apparent change of heart. And now I realized that this scene had probably been planned much earlier. Maybe even as long ago as the first time I had let him know he could use me without complaint.

Suddenly I found myself being pushed backward onto the bed, and then it was too late to think about hitting him because he was on top of me, pinning my arms to my sides.

"Don, stop it! Stop it right now!" I screamed at him.

"Nina, Nina. Just let me love you," he moaned. "You'll see, you'll see."

Terror started to grip me, and I felt my muscles turning to jelly as I began to fear the worst. Then, just at that moment, something my friend Debbie had once said to us in our booth at Burger Heaven came to my mind.

"Never mind spitting and scratching," she had said. "If he's that close, bite him!"

We had laughed ourselves silly at her typically aggressive advice, but this was no time for laughing. And it *was* time for biting. My head was about the only thing I could move at that moment, so I closed my eyes, opened my mouth, and lifted my head off the bed until I felt my mouth come in contact with something. Then I bit down as hard as I could.

My memory of the next few minutes is

really strange. I can remember things happening like they were in slow motion, yet it felt like everything was happening real fast. I remember hearing a scream that sounded like it was coming from very far away. I don't remember how long I lay there on that bed before I realized I wasn't pinned down anymore. When I did become aware of it, I was out of that house like a shot.

Don's car was blocking my little station wagon in the driveway, but somehow I got around his car and was driving away fast. I think I drove right across his front lawn. And all of a sudden I was parking my car in front of my house, and then I was inside--in the bathroom, being sick.

Hours later Daddy knocked on my bedroom door and asked if I was okay. I really wanted to talk to somebody, but I didn't think Daddy would understand. Or worse, he would understand and would want to do something about it right then. So I just told him I was tired and I heard him say he'd fix dinner.

Then I started feeling guilty about not taking care of Davy and Lynn and I got up and took off my work clothes and went to the bathroom to wash my face. I glanced at myself in the mirror, and suddenly I heard Walt's words ringing in my ears.

"Some day you're going to have to start living for yourself instead of for everyone else."

I wanted to talk to Walt. That's what I wanted to do for myself right then, instead of pretending that everything was all right and trying to be brave. I sat on the edge of my bed and looked at the phone book on the shelf of my nightstand, wondering if I should just call him, when suddenly the phone rang. It scared me out of my wits, and I let it ring three times before I answered.

"Hi Nina, it's Walt," he greeted me.

I couldn't believe the coincidence, and I just sat there, speechless.

"Uh, well, I see you're real happy to hear from me, as usual," he joked.

"Oh, Walt, thank you for calling," I said at last. "Would you believe I was just about to call you? I really am glad to hear from you."

"Well, that's a relief. I thought for a minute there--but anyway, the reason I'm calling is to ask you to dinner this Saturday night. And I don't mean that greasy burger place. I just closed a big deal, and I want to celebrate. And since you didn't tell me to go away the last time I proposed to you, I thought that I might stand a chance of at least getting a date with you. What do you say?"

I almost giggled at the way his words came rushing out. And suddenly I felt a whole lot better just knowing he was there and that he cared.

"Well, Walt," I said after a few seconds, "you told me a few days ago that I should start living for myself, and I can't think of anything I would rather do for myself than let you buy me dinner."

We talked for a while after that, about everything and anything. And as we talked, I felt the pain of my encounter with Don ebbing away from me. I realized that I had Walt to thank for that.

I took the day off Saturday so I could take my time getting ready for our date. I was pretty sure Walt would propose to me again--but this time he'd be serious. And I'd answer him in a serious way. We'd both know my answer couldn't be an unqualified yes, just yet, but it would be an enthusiastic maybe! Then we'd take it from there...

I WANT TO GO WHERE YOU GO...

Wade and I had been together for as long as I could remember. We grew up together--went to the same schools, the same church, and our families were very close. We had never been like each other, though. I came from a small family. My folks were quiet and reserved, and I grew up shy and untalkative. Wade, however, had eight brothers and sisters, and everyone in his family were very outgoing.

Wade took care of his brothers and sisters a lot, and I guess it was just natural that he wound up taking care of me, too. When we were kids, he would keep other kids from teasing me, and as we grew up he was always giving me advice about everything from schoolwork to handling my parents.

Wade is two years older than me, but he was only one grade ahead of me in school. When we got to high school, he started giving me advice about boys, but I didn't listen to any of it because I knew he would be the only boy for me.

One day in my sophomore year, I was with a group of kids at the drive-in near school, and some kids a little older than us started teasing me about my freckles. I tried to ignore them, but one boy kept it up until I felt I had to leave before I started crying.

Just as I was reaching for my books on the table, Wade came in and saw what was happening. He walked up to the boys and said in a quiet voice, "Leave Becky alone. Right now, and forever."

The other boy was a lot bigger than Wade, but he didn't even turn to look at him. There was something about Wade's voice that had that effect on people. You just knew when he said something that he really meant it. I guess it came from always being in charge--he knew how to talk to people.

"Come on, Becky, I'll walk you home," he said to me after the boy and his friends had left.

"How long am I going to have to take care of you, Becky?" he asked me as we walked along the street.

I had to think about it for a minute--I was never as good as Wade at talking to people--but I finally realized that the time had come to tell him how I felt. So I said, "I guess like you told that boy--forever."

He didn't say anything for a while, which was unusual for him since he always seemed to know what to say. But after a bit he took my hand in his and we kept walking. When we got to my house, he just kept walking right on by and took me to his house instead.

From that time on it was 'Wade and Becky'. No one ever commented on it that I ever heard, and everyone seemed to accept it. Even our folks just took it like something that like it had always been, and that's the way it stayed. My life didn't change all that much right away, though Wade started coming to my house after evening chores a little bit more. We'd sit together and talk about things like we always had, and he would cuddle me like my Mom had when I was little. But that was about all that was different.

Then, about two years after that, Wade started to change. I noticed that he was getting restless or something, and I tried to ask him about it but it took a long time before he'd answer any of my questions. Wade always liked to talk, but I had become aware that what he talked about was things and other people--not about himself. So when the day came that he started talking about his own future, I really took notice. And I listened very carefully.

"Becky, I don't know what's going on with me," he said, "but I feel like something is beginning to bust loose. I don't know why, but I think I have to get out of here."

"Do you mean out of my house or out of this town?" I asked him.

"Maybe even out of this state, or this country," he answered.

Then he seemed to think about what he had said for a minute before he continued. During that minute I got a little scared, because I began to think I might lose him. But I calmed myself down and just waited. I knew he would do the right thing, whatever it was.

"Yeah, maybe even this country," he repeated. "I guess it's just that I can't take this life much longer. I don't see any future here for me. The only thing I can see is me working in some restaurant or something like that for the rest of my life, and I figure that if that is what I'm going to do I might as well get out of here and see what the rest of the world looks like."

"Okay," I said, not knowing what else to say.

"Okay," he said back. Then he took me in his arms, and we cuddled for a long time.

Later he stood up, and I walked with him to the door. It was already dark out, and we stood on the front porch to kiss goodnight, like we usually did.

"I'm going home now," he said unnecessarily. "You have a bag packed. Just one. I don't know when we'll go, and there may not be time to pack when the time comes."

"Okay," I said again, doing my best to keep myself calm to match his mood.

As soon as I was back inside the house I let out a little cry of joy. I had been so scared that I was going to lose him, that I didn't even think about the fact that I had just agreed to go with him on an adventure that was going to lead to who knows where. Maybe even out of the country, he had said.

I started planning immediately what to pack in my bag, and never gave a thought to what might lie ahead for me. Within less than twenty minutes I had backpack loaded with extra socks and panties, some jeans and sweat shirts, a toilet bag, a half box of granola bars I found in the kitchen, a notepad, and two pencils. Then I strapped my heavy coat to the outside. I put a fresh outfit on top of the backpack in the back of my closet, hoping I would have time to change into it when Wade said he was ready. I took what little money I had saved and stuffed it into the pocket of my jeans.

I looked around my room slowly and carefully, trying to memorize each little part of it, and hoping--though I didn't admit it at the time-- that I would be seeing it again soon. Then I took the picture of Mom and Dad off my dresser and added it to the stuff in my pack. Now I was really ready.

"Tonight's the night, Becky, I'll come by around eight," Wade told me about three days later.

"Okay," I told him.

I was grateful that I would have time to change before we left, even though I had been careful to have an acceptable traveling outfit on each day since Wade had first told me about this plan. Mom had been surprised at my sudden conscientious attention to washing and drying my own clothes, and I felt guilty accepting her praise knowing that I was going to leave her soon.

I had already written my parents a letter which I planned to leave on my bed so they wouldn't worry about me. I didn't think Wade would mind. I didn't tell them anything about where we were going or how we were going to travel because I didn't know any of that anyway. But I did tell them I was going with Wade and that we would be careful and that I would keep in touch with them. Then I added a PS, saying that I really loved them but that I had to go with Wade and I hoped they'd understand. I rewrote that latter six times before I finally got it right, then I quickly sealed it and put it in my dresser drawer until the day came when I'd need it.

And the day was here. I was dressed and ready when Wade's knock came at the door. He had picked a night when both our parents were out and his little brothers and sister were being baby-sat by his sister Daphne, who was my age. He knew our parents would not notice our absence until the morning--and we would be far away by then, in case they objected to our leaving.

"Ready?" he asked me. "Got everything you need?"

"Yes, I'm ready," I told him, slipping into my light spring jacket and backpack. I patted the pocket with my money in it, just to be sure, and walked out the door.

Wade walked us briskly to the highway and stuck out his thumb. We got a ride after only about six cars, and were soon headed toward Washington.

"I want to start off from the Capitol," Wade had told me as we waited for our ride. "I went there once on a field trip, but I want to see it for myself."

"Sounds good to me," I told him, delighted that we were starting off and looking forward to our adventure. Though I was a little worried about hitchhiking because I had heard how dangerous it could be.

We had to wait about an hour for our second ride, and I was getting cold and hungry. I thought about the granola bars I had packed in my knapsack, but I didn't want to start eating them so soon. I don't know what I was saving them for, but I just had a feeling that this was too 3early to be raiding my stash. I started having doubts about this adventure right then, but I didn't say anything to Wade. Finally we got a ride. The guy was going right near where we wanted to go, so I settled in against Wade's shoulder and fell asleep.

Wade woke me just as our driver was pulling up in front of a big building with stone columns in front of it. Wade thanked him and helped me on with my backpack, then put his on.

"Well, here we are," he said. "Now we can see things for ourselves."

"Could we eat first?" I asked him. "I'm kind of hungry."

Wade said sure, and we walked for about six blocks before we found a restaurant. I don't ever remember food tasting so good. I don't know if it was the spirit of adventure or what, but it was really a fabulous breakfast. By the time I was finished, I was ready once again to follow Wade anywhere he wanted to go.

We walked everywhere that that. By the end of the day I had seen enough monuments and stone buildings to last me a lifetime. It was exciting, sure, but it was a lot of work, too. We had lunch at a hotdog vendor's stand, but as it began to get dark I started worrying about something other than food.

"Wade, where are we going to sleep tonight?' I asked him.

I didn't know what plans he had--whether we were going to stay in motels or what. The weather was still a little too chilly to be camping out, but if he had suggested it, I'm sure I would have made the best of it. He didn't, though.

"I heard about a youth hostel where we can get a bunk and breakfast for only a couple of dollars," he told me. "I guess we could head that way now."

Once again I found myself being reminded to place my trust in Wade. He had always known what to do up to now, and I began to realize that he probably always would. Even when it meant a lot of pain to him, he always did the right thing.

When I think about pain, I'm reminded that I really don't have anything to complain about. There were lots of times that I was scared, and even a few when I was flat terrified, on that trip, but I never felt pain. Wade, on the other hand, never seemed to be scared, but he sure felt a lot of pain.

Like that time we were in Ohio. We had just left Pennsylvania and were headed for Detroit. Wade had finally told me he just wanted to see some of the big cities. I said that was okay with me, but truthfully I felt that if Pittsburg was an indication of what we would find in the 'big cities', I couldn't care less about visiting them. Anyway, we had hitched a ride with these two guys who said they were headed for Cleveland, and Wade said that was right on our route, so we climbed into the back seat of their car and we were off.

Sometime in the middle of the night we woke up and found the car was stopped alongside a quiet country road. Wade asked the diver what was going on, and he said his buddy needed to go to the bathroom, so he had stopped for him. I was just about to cuddle up to Wade again and go back to sleep when the other guy came back and got in the car. Before he closed the door, though, he looked over the seat at me and then said to Wade, "Say, how about us sharing your honey--you know, to pay for the ride?"

I didn't get what he meant at first, but I guess Wade did, because he told the guy that nobody touches me.

"Aw, c'mon, just a little funnin' won't hurt," the guy said He reached into the back seat and put his hand on my knee.

Wade knocked his hand away and repeated what he had said to the guy. I started getting a little scare because we were trapped in the back seat of their car, and there were two of them. The driver said something to his buddy about forgetting it, but the other guy was getting mad and was grabbing for Wade, calling him greedy and ungrateful, and a few other names I don't care to repeat.

Then all of a sudden Wade's left hand was moving fast, and his fist connected with the guy's face. It was suck a solid hit that the guy went flying out of the car. Wade pushed the seat forward and jumped out after him, and called for me to follow. I grabbed our packs and then looked at the driver. He looked at me for a time, then looked at his buddy and Wade who were going at each other beside the car.

"Go on, get moving," he growled at me finally. I could tell he was angry, but I didn't know if he was angry at me or Wade or his buddy. He just sat there while I got our things out of the car, and then he turned to watch the fight.

It wasn't much of a fight, really. The other guy landed a few punches, but it was mostly Wade who was doing the hitting. I had never seen him move so fast, even when he was playing basketball in the gym, and he was punching the guy everywhere. Finally it stopped, and Wade was standing there with his fists clenched, breathing heavy. The other guy was sitting on the gravel, holding his head with both hands.

"Wade, let's go," I urged him.

He looked at me then, and with a quick glance at the driver, grabbed his pack from me, took my arm with his other hand, and marched me down the road back the way we had been traveling.

"Where are we?" I asked him after a while.

"I have no idea," he admitted. "I'm so mad at myself!" he added a few seconds later.

"I should have seen that coming. I should have refused that ride and kept you out of danger. Boy, that hurts, he said, touching the knuckles of his right hand.

There was a half moon out at the time and it was enough light for me to see that two of his knuckles were cut and bleeding.

"Let's stop here so I can fix that. I have some first-aid cream in my pack," I told him.

He stopped without a word and waited until I had cleaned the wounds with a tissue, and was applying the cream, before he spoke again.

"Becky, maybe you should go back home," he said, sending my heart into my stomach. "I don't want you to be hurt, and this kind of traveling is too dangerous for you."

"Nonsense," I told him. "I'll go home when you do, and not before. That's final. Besides, who would bandage you up if I left?"

He grinned at that, and it was good to see him smile, but his face got serous again right away. He was about to say something else when we noticed headlights coming toward us from the direction where had had the fight.

"Quick, into the bushes!" he said, pulling me after him.

We crouched down in the bushes beside the road and watched the car we had been riding in drive past. They weren't driving slow like they were looking for us or anything, and I breathed a sigh of relief.

"Just as I thought," Wade said. "This road wasn't on their route at all. They probably pulled off here just to see what they could stir up. So we'll keep going in the same direction, and we should get back to the highway soon."

As it turned out, Wade was right again. In

less than a mile we were back on a three-lane blacktop. Once we were headed west again, we could see the lights of a good-sized town ahead. We hadn't walked very far and we were in Canton. We found a gas station where Wade could wash up, and I re-bandaged his hand. After a sparse breakfast, we were back on the road.

Wade had learned caution after our experience, and now, as people stopped for us, he would ask them where they were headed and size them up while they were answering. He told me that the first guy who stopped was looking at me when he was talking to Wade, so that's why he had turned down the ride, even though it sounded like a good one.

That's how we decided to skip Detroit and head for Chicago instead. A nice older couple stopped and said they were going to Lima, and Wade said okay. We could still have gone north from there to Detroit, but Wade said the "signs" suggested we head west. I wasn't sure what signs he meant, but I didn't question his decision. I was just so grateful he hadn't insisted on putting me on a bus home that I didn't care what direction we took.

The old couple talked just about the whole way to Lima. They talked mostly about their kids and how successful they were, and how they were real good to their parents and stuff like that. It was kind of boring, but they bought us a good lunch, and they didn't ask us any questions about where we were from or where we were going. It turned out the be the best ride we had had so far. And we did get to see a lot of pretty country. But by the time we got to Lima I was pretty tired, since I hadn't even had a chance to nap with the old folks talking all the time.

"There's the bus station," Wade said after the old folks had let us out. "Let's wash up there and find a place to sleep."

As we walked into the bus depot, Wade noticed a "Help Wanted" sign in the window. He went to the ticket counter and asked what kind of help they needed, and the guy told him their janitor had quit. Wade told him he would clean up the place for a ticket to Chicago, and the guy said that Wade had a deal. Then Wade winked at me and told the guy I would clean up the bathrooms for my ticket. The guy didn't care much for handing out two tickets, but he finally agreed after Wade told him between the two of us we would make the place sparkle. It only took us about an hour to do the job, and the stationmaster was real happy with the way the place looked. Wade actually cleaned the men's room while I did the ladies', and we worked together on the waiting room and the office area.

"Not a bad deal," he suggested as we settled into our seats. "We have a place to sleep and a ride to downtown Chicago for just an hour's work.

If I can work more deals like that, we'll have plenty of money left when we get to Seattle."

"Seattle?" I asked, a little taken aback.

"Yeah, I figure Seattle is about as far away from home as we can get. Maybe we'll stay there a while, or maybe we'll just keep on going into Canada."

I couldn't think of anything to say to that, so I just went to sleep. It was early in the morning when we pulled into the Loop in Chicago. When I saw the size of the station, I knew that we were in for an experience that would be unlike anything ever. And I was right. Chicago was like a giant amusement park. The local train system there runs at ground level, then above the ground, then under the ground. It's as much fun as a roller-coaster, but it doesn't cost as much. And the food! They have a restaurant in the Loop which serves more different kinds of hamburgers than I could imagine. And you can buy foods that they eat in Thailand, or India, or just about anywhere. And right on the same street you can get hamburgers and hot dogs.

We stayed there for two days, just walking around, looking at people, riding up to the top of the Sears Tower, and riding the train. Finally Wade said it was time to move on, and I reluctantly agreed. I had written a postcard to my folks our first night there, and when we left the hotel I gave it to the clerk with our room key and asked her to mail it for me.

Wade and I took a commuter train our to the suburbs, and then walked to the highway, and we were soon on our way to Iowa. Once we crossed the Mississippi, the land got really boring. No more interesting river valley or big cities, just lots and lots of flat land in every direction.

About halfway through Wyoming, things looked like they would get interesting again, but soon we passed through Salt Lake City, and the promise of the Rocky Mountains gave way to a disappointing desert. I caught a look at Wade's map and asked him why we were so far south if we were going to Seattle. He said he wanted to see San Francisco on the way.

That trip across the desert was the worst ever. It was hotter than anything during the day and freezing cold at night. We got stuck in some small town in Nevada one afternoon and evening, and if I never see that place again I won't mind a bit. Mosquitoes bigger than anything I've ever seen attacked us near sundown as we tried to bed down in a park in town, and between the itching and the cold I don't think I slept for five minutes that night. I was hot and tired and cranky by nine o'clock the next morning, and if we hadn't gotten a ride right away I really believe I would have told Wade to forget the whole thing, and taken a bus for home myself. But we did get a ride, and soon we were in Reno.

Wade wanted to have some fun at a casino, but all I wanted was a bath and some sleep. As Lady Luck would have it, we both got our way. Wade hit a hundred dollar jackpot on a quarter slot machine, and immediately got us a room with the biggest bathtub I had ever seen in my life. It was darn near as big as some of the swimming pools I had seen back home. Wade took a twenty out of his winnings and said he was going to play with that, left me to my bath, and was gone. I soaked in that tub until my skin was all puckered up, then slipped between the sheets of the big bed and went contentedly to sleep.

When I woke up the next morning I found Wade, still in his clothes, sleeping on the other side of the bed. I watched him sleeping for a while and wondered why he never made a move to make love to me. We hugged and kissed a lot, and he was usually really affectionate when he wasn't worried about something, but that was it. If the truth were known, I wouldn't have said no if he had ever asked me. But he never did, and for some reason I was thinking about it that morning. Maybe it was the bath and the good night's sleep.

I got out of bed and found the room-service menu. I was hungry enough to eat everything listed, but the prices were too high to suit me. So I fished a granola bar out of my pack and made do with that. Wade and I had been through about three boxes of those bars on our trip so far, and I was sure glad to have them.

While I was munching away, Wade woke up. I asked him if he had had any more luck the night before, and he told me that he hadn't.

"I broke even, at least, so we still came out the hundred ahead. And this room only cost us about forty, so I guess this town is okay," he said.

Wade asked me if I wanted to stay another day, and I told him the sooner we got out of the desert, the better. He said okay and took a shower while I packed our things.

We got a ride to Sacramento right off, with a guy and his girlfriend. He was about forty and the girl was about twenty. They didn't pay much attention to us, which was just fine with me because I was so taken with the scenery. Almost immediately after we left Reno we started into the mountains, and every little turn of the road presented a new vista to us. I guess the couple we were riding with was used to it, but for me it was the most breathtaking part of our trip so far.

From Sacramento, we got another ride into San Francisco, and I almost clapped my hands with glee as we topped a hill and saw the city for the first time. The sun was just beginning to drop into the ocean (the ocean!) and the city sparkled like a crown of jewels across the bay. Our driver kept up a running dialogue like some kind of tour guide, pointing out places he thought would be of interest to us, but my eyes were constantly on the watch for another look at San Francisco. Fortunately, I had not even the least suspicion about the trouble we were headed for, so I was able to enjoy the sights without concern.

Wade found us a hostel to stay in, and even though it didn't look like a very clean place, we were too tired from hiking up and down hills to look further. Wade didn't like the idea of us having to be separated, but the hostel had a hard-and-fast rule about men and women sleeping together. I was shown to a dormitory with about thirty bunk beds in it, most of which were occupied. I just kicked off my shoes and flopped on the bed without undressing. And it was a good thing I did.

Sometime in the early morning I woke up to find a very hard-looking woman kneeling beside my bunk. When I started to get up, I got the scare of my life. She put a hand on my breast and shoved me back down on the bunk, then flashed a knife right in front of my face.

"Keep your mouth shut or I'll cut you," she said in a husky whisper.

I closed my eyes, and then immediately opened them as I felt her hand squeeze me. She said something like, "This one's a little cutie," and then asked another woman what she'd found. I realized then that there were two of them, and the other one was going through my backpack.

"Nothing but clothes and some chocolate bars in here," the other one said.

I had an insane urge to correct her about the granola bars--I guess I was so scared I wanted to do something normal. The woman with the knife still had her hand on my breast, and every once in a while she'd give a squeeze--maybe to remind me she was still there, though I didn't need any reminders.

"Where's your money, cutie?" she asked me.

"My boyfriend has all the money," I lied. Our money was in the pocket of my jeans. I just closed my eyes again to keep from looking there, and I started to cry.

"You gonna cry, you better cry quiet," the woman hissed at me. Then she gave me another squeeze that really hurt, and said, "Don't move, or you bleed."

When I dared open my eyes again, the two of them were gone. I was shaking so much I could hardly move, but I finally got out of the bunk, stuffed my things back into my backpack, and walked cautiously to the lobby. There was no one in sight except for the sleeping attendant. I woke him and asked him to wake Wade for me. He was pretty surly, but I was scared and mad, and I stood my ground until he got up and walked to the men's dorm. I stood in the doorway and pointed out Wade's sleeping form to him. Then I waited impatiently while he shuffled toward the bunk and shook Wade. Wade didn't respond at first, so the attendant shook him again, harder, and then suddenly he straightened up and came back to me.

"Was he bleeding when you got here last night?" the man asked me.

I must have got white as a sheet, because I could feel myself go cold all over. I brushed past the attendant and ran to Wade. There was an ugly blue mark on his forehead, and a trickle of blood running down his temple and into his hair. I shook him myself, calling his name, and then I put my head on his chest to listen for his heart. But my own heart was pounding too loudly in my ears for me to hear his.

"He ain't dead," the attendant said. "I guess I'd better call the cops."

"No! Wait! Get me a wet towel first, okay?" I asked him, trying to sound reasonable.

Talk of the police had brought me back to my senses in a hurry. I got this picture of the two of us being asked a lot of questions about where we were from, and I knew I didn't want that. Mostly, I didn't want to chance having my folks find out we were in trouble. Besides, I knew the police would never catch the people who had done this. Even if Wade had seen his attackers before they knocked him out, it wouldn't do any good.

The attendant came back with the damp towel, and started to leave, but I asked him to help me. He held Wade's head up while I wiped away the blood and bathed his face. That brought him around, and somehow I managed to get him out to the lobby and out of the hostel. The attendant was still protesting, telling us we had to wait there while he called the police; but I ignored him as I got the two of us to the street. We walked away, and turned a corner, and I spotted a taxi. I led Wade, still stumbling a little bit, to the cab.

"What are you doing?" Wade asked groggily.

"Don't worry, it will be okay," I told him. "Golden Gate Bridge," I told the driver.

"Which side?" he asked me as he put down his flag and started off.

"Other side," I told him, having only a vague idea of where I was taking us, but anxious to be away from there in case the cops had been called.

I hoped it wasn't too far, and that I wouldn't be spending too much of our money; but I figured we were lucky to have any money at all. I put some first aid cream on Wade's cut and left everything else to the driver.

It was getting light as the cabbie let us out at the rest stop on the north side of the bridge. It was supposed to be a very nice view of both the bridge and the city from there, but even if there'd been anything to look at besides fog, my mind was on getting us away from there, so I didn't bother. I told Wade to sit on a bench, and I asked people in t he parking area for a ride north. Luck was with me and we were soon headed for Oregon.

Two days later we headed inland from the Oregon coast towards Eugene. Wade's head was healing nicely, and we had both met enough nice people all along the coastal route to get the images of our brush with danger out of our minds. I hadn't told Wade about what happened to me, because I knew that his need to protect me would just add to the pain he was feeling already. But I had learned something very valuable from that experience. I'd learned that I was able to take care of myself if I had to. I guess that doesn't sound like a whole lot, but for me it was a major accomplishment. It didn't really change my relationship with Wade in any big way. In fact, I found it even easier to let him make the decisions once I realized that I didn't have to.

I was beginning to regret Wade's decision to head inland, though, after we had been sitting beside the freeway outside of Eugene for more than three hours without getting a ride. It was a hot day, I was sweating like crazy, and I wanted a bath.

I was just about to tell Wade how I felt when

a guy driving a station wagon pulled onto the shoulder, and started backing toward us. We were both so grateful for the ride that Wade didn't even bother to check the guy out. He just opened the back door for me, got in the front seat, and thanked the guy for stopping.

The guy was going to Salem, which I knew from the road signs was only about an hour or so away, but the car had air conditioning, and being cool for even that short a time felt like a blessing to me. The driver and Wade talked about the road to Seattle, and hitchhiking and stuff, but I just sat back and enjoyed the cool comfort.

"Say," the guy said at one point. "why don't you two come to my place this evening? My ex is coming by to take our daughter for the weekend, and you could bunk up in her room tonight. Dinner and a shower, breakfast in the morning, and then I'll bring you back to the highway. What do you say?"

Wade looked over his shoulder at me, and I could see the guy glancing first at Wade and then at me in the mirror. He looked like an okay guy, so I nodded, and Wade told him we'd like to do that.

"Good," he said. "I have to make a few stops in Silverton, then we'll head for the hills. My name is Charlie Austin, by the way."

I almost cried when Mr. Austin pulled into

his driveway. The area reminded me of home--green, rolling hills of woods and pasture land. There was a creek running right by his house, and I could see a horse munching on the g rass out behind a little shed.

"You have horses!" Wade exclaimed.

"Yep. I thought I'd keep that as a little surprise, since you told me you like to ride. There's a saddle in that little shed over there," Charlie added as he parked the car.

One thing for sure about Wade--he wasn't shy about horses at all. In no time he had that little mare saddled, and trotting around the pasture. He was grinning to beat the band. Charlie sat there on the fence, watching, and grinning almost as much as Wade was.

We met his daughter later when she got home from school. The four of us had a nice dinner, and then she left with her mother for the weekend. Charlie showed us around the house, and suggested we shower while he cleaned up the kitchen. He told us we could just leave our dirty clothes in a pile, and after we'd had our showers, he'd wash and dry them for us. I couldn't believe the way he was taking such good care of us, and I kept waiting for the 'catch'. It never came, though.

After our showers, Charlie handed us a list of movies he had on VCR tape, and asked us to select one. Wade picked one out while Charlie was loading the washer with our clothes, then he put the tape on for us and sat in his chair, drinking brandy, or something, while we watched the movie. I felt so comfortable I fell asleep on Wade's shoulder halfway through the movie.

The next morning I heard Charlie talking to someone on the phone as I was getting dressed. I heard things like "couple of kids" and "headed for Seattle". I shook Wade awake, thinking we might have to get out of there fast, and told him what I'd heard. Charlie come down the hall as Wade was dressing, knocked on the door, and told us breakfast was ready.

Scrambled eggs, melon, toast, coffee, and milk awaited us in the kitchen. I felt like I was being torn in half. One half of me wanted to sit down and enjoy that meal, and the other half wanted to get us the heck out of there before whoever Charlie had been talking to showed up. Fortunately, Wade decided in favor of the breakfast half. As we took our seats, Charlie told us about the phone call I'd heard him making.

"Talked to my brother just now," he said around a mouthful of toast. "He lives across the bay from Seattle. Place called Bremerton. He told me to send you on up there, and he'll help you find a place to settle, and find you some kind of job to get you started. Here's his phone number." He slid a card across the table toward Wade. "Just call him when you get near Seattle or Bremerton, and he'll come and get you. Soon as you're through with breakfast, we can get you back to the highway."

My heart was so full I could hardly swallow my food. We had met some nice people on the road, but no one had gone out of his way like Charlie had. On the drive back to the freeway, he sort of explained why he'd helped us.

"I left my home in Michigan when I was sixteen," he told us. "In Florida, I met a plumber who gave me a place to stay, a clean pair of socks, and a few tips on how to find the right job. I'm grateful to you two for giving me the chance to return the favor. Maybe you can pass it along sometime, too."

When we finally got ourselves near Bremerton, we called Charlie's brother, Jim. He and his wife came and picked us up at the gas station we'd called from, and took us to their house. We got the same treatment from them that we got from Charlie, and better. On our second day there, they introduced us to a couple at their church who worked with kids. It was some kind of service they did as volunteers, but I never did quite understand exactly what the service was about. In our case, they gave Wade a couple of job leads, and gave us a place to stay as long as we needed it. They didn't ask us a lot of questions, and they didn't insist that we go to their church, tough they made it clear we were welcome.

The second night we were there, Wade and I had a long talk about our future. He didn't seem very sure about what he wanted to do yet, so I helped him a little bit by telling him that for me there were only two choices--either we stayed here, or we went back home to Virginia. He was a little surprised at the way I put it to him, and made some comment about how things had changed between us ever since San Francisco.

"Yes, they have," I agreed. "I realized there that I want you more than I need you. Up until then, you see, I had only known that I needed you. Now I know that I could make it on my own if I had to. But I also know that I don't *want* to make it on my own. I don't want to be without you-- ever. And I know that I've had enough of traveling. I want to settle down someplace, and start a family of our own, and start meeting nice people like we've met here."

I guess that was probably the longest speech I had ever made in my life. And it led to two very wonderful things. Wade and I made love for the first time that night, and for me it felt like our honeymoon had started. The other wonderful thing was that Wade said we would wait until we got home before we got married so our families could be part of it.

So that's what we're going to do, but we're

going to stay here until we earn enough money to buy train tickets home. While our trip out here certainly was a great experience for Wade and me, we both realize now that we were very lucky not have gotten into any worse trouble than we did. Hitchhiking is dangerous, particularly for a girl or a woman, and though Wade was able to protect me in that one incident with the two guys, that was just dumb luck. Another time...

But there isn't going to be another time! From now on, Wade and I are going to play it safe with our love.

THE THINGS HIS EYES SAY TO ME

If anyone had told me that my future happiness would come out of the most frightening experience of my life, I probably would never have believed them. My life had been very carefully planned and supervised by my mom to be nice, normal, and safe. Any time there was the least hint of trouble, Mom was always there to smooth things out. Not that she always made things easy for me, or anything like that--I had to earn my rewards along the way. But when difficult situations arose, I could always count on Mom to be there with assistance, or advice, or whatever was appropriate.

When I graduated, Mom and I talked about what kind of job I wanted to get, and it seemed natural that I should try for a job at the bakery where she worked. I had been in the bakery quite a lot--just to say "hi" to her after school, or to check in with her about what needed to be done around the house, so I knew most of the people who worked there. Mom said she would talk to Mr. Behrn, the owner. The next day she told me that he wanted to interview me.

There wasn't any application to fill out since it was a family operation. I just talked with Mr. Behrn in his little office for about twenty minutes, and I had the job.

The bakery was mostly a wholesale business. We made croissants and turnovers and similar items which were then frozen and sold to people in retail businesses, like restaurants and some grocery chains that had in-store bakeries. I was surprised to find out how many businesses were selling pastries that were made in our bakery, and just baked in the other stores each morning.

Mr. Behrn was a really nice man to work for. He came from Switzerland where he'd been a baker's assistant. He'd started his little business in a small shop that was located in a light industrial area. There wasn't a regular retail front to the place, but as his reputation grew, so many people started asking him to bake some of the pastries he made, and other things, like cakes, and eventually he wound up doing a little retail business on the side. But he never put up a sign, or did anything to advertise the business. People just knew about it by word of mouth, and they'd drive up and knock on the big overhead door on the loading dock.

He told me during my interview that some day he was going to do something about the retail end of the business, but I soon learned that he had been saying that to everyone for years. In fact, it was sort of a joke among all the workers, and when Mr. Behrn wasn't around they liked to imitate his accent and say things like, "Vell, ve are going to haf to do zomething about zis mixing machine zomeday zoon."

When I first heard people clowning around like that it made me kind of mad, but Mom told me it was all good-natured fun. I soon realized that everyone really liked him, and that they weren't being malicious about it. I learned to join in the laughter, but I never got to the point of being able to make one of the jokes myself.

One bad thing about taking the job that I hadn't anticipated was that it hurt my relationship with the guy I'd been dating for most of my senior year. Well, it wasn't just the job, but that was what sort of set everything off. I guess I was growing up a little faster than him, and our petting sessions were becoming more annoying than anything else to me. We would go to a movie or a dance, and then we would drive home--nearly--and park the car to make out.

When we were in school I had enjoyed his attention, and actually welcomed his slightly clumsy groping and kissing. But after I started working at the bakery, I found myself becoming less and less interested in that kind of nonsense. I suppose if I had let him go all the way it might have changed things, but I just didn't love him in that way, so I never did. And I was more tired afer a day's work than I had been after school, so I was a little less patient with him than I had been before.

One night we were parked in his car after the Friday night movie, and I just told him to give it a rest.

"What the heck's the matter with you?" he asked me, angrily.

"I'm just tired, Andy," I told him, expecting him to understand that things had changed for me.

"What do you mean, *you're tired?* You never got tired of this before! Don't you love me?"

Andy was always trying to get me to say I loved him. I think he figured that if I told him I loved him, I would let him do anything he wanted.

"Andy, you know I like you a whole lot," I told him, scooting over on the car seat and casually buttoning my blouse. "It has nothing to do with that. It's just that I'm working now and I don't feel like wrestling with you all the time like I used to."

"Well, I work, too, you know," he said, trying to set his jaw and make himself look important. "Maybe being a grease monkey isn't as glamorous as working in a bakery, but it's hard work and I'm good at it. And I don't get too tired to give you what you want."

I don't know what made him think that working in a bakery was glamorous. I guess he was just so unsure of himself that he was defensive about being a mechanic and gas jockey. And I was about to tell him as much, until I got the meaning behind his last words. That made me mad, and I told him so in no uncertain terms.

"Give me what I want?" I snapped. "Listen, mister, if you think you're some kind of great lover, you have another think coming. I like making out with you sometimes, but if you're going to take that kind of attitude about it, you can just keep your hands to yourself!"

"Fine! If that's how you feel about it, fine. So why don't you just take a hike!" he yelled back.

He leaned across me, and I got a little scared because I thought he was going to hit me. But he opened the door on my side, and just sat there glaring at me. We were only two or three blocks from my house, so I didn't even give it a second thought. I got out of the car, slammed the door, and walked home.

The next day was Saturday, and I had the day off. I spent a lot of time in my room, thinking about the incident, and I almost called Andy a couple of times. But better sense prevailed, and I finally decided that it was time to end the relationship anyway.

When Mom got back from shopping that afternoon, I talked to her about it and told her what my decision was. She agreed with me totally, as she frequently did, and convinced me that I had done the right thing. I think I did a lot of growing up that weekend, and I went back to work on

Monday morning with a little more confidence than I'd had before.

Mr. Behrn had started me off doing the easy jobs, like packing the pastries in boxes and putting them into the freezer, or keeping the tables cleaned off and ready for the next batch of dough to be worked. But he soon started showing me other jobs that required a little more skill. Once he saw that I caught on quickly, he accelerated my training. I learned how to mix the doughs, roll them out on the rolling and folding machines, add the butter, work the croissant cutter, and eventually I started training under Mom at cake decorating. Of course, I found that the easiest thing to learn, because I had watched Mom do it for years at home. It was even easier at the bakery with all the right equipment.

One day Mr. Behrn was up to his elbows in grease, working on one of the dough mixers that had slipped a gear or something, and he asked me to take care of one of our customers. That was the job he always handled himself--putting the order together, helping with the loading, and collecting the money--and I considered it quite an honor that he trusted me to do it for him. I double-checked everything, determined to make no mistakes, and put our copy of the invoice along with the customer's check on his desk when I was sure I had it right.

A few hours later, another customer

knocked on the door and Mr. Behrn asked me to handle it again, even though he was finished with the mixer. I opened the heavy door and was greeted by Mike, the Mouth-watering Morsels man. I knew him because of the tee shirt he always wore that read "Mike's Mouthwatering Morsels" on the front, and "Mike Himself" on the back.

"Well, hello there, beautiful," he said when he saw me. "If I had known it was you, I would have helped you with the heavy door."

I was a little miffed by this and told him I could handle it alone.

"I'm sure you can," he replied in a more reasonable tone of voice. "I've watched you in the bakery now and then, and I know you're competent enough. Is Fritz busy?"

"Yes. He asked me to take care of you," I said.

"Well, great You're really getting around in this business, aren't you?"

His attention was a little flattering, and I guess if it hadn't been for that overly familiar way he had of using pet names instead of my own name, I would have warmed to him right away. I mean, he was kind of good looking, and I felt attracted to him for some reason. But I wanted to be taken a little more seriously--especially after what had happened between Andy and me. I tried my best to be businesslike and get Mike's order filled, but I found myself looking at him in a slightly different way.

He stopped in the middle of writing out his check and caught me studying him. His eyes met mine and I wanted to look away, but I found that I couldn't. I began to feel a little weak, and then he totally surprised me by saying, "Ellen, I want to apologize for my comments earlier. You are a very competent person, and I have a feeling you'll go far in this business. You're also a very beautiful woman, and I guess that makes me a little nervous. I hope you'll accept my apology and not let my attitude interfere with our working relationship."

I was so stunned I could do anything but nod my head. He finished making out the check, handed it to me, and then left with a "See you next time, Ellen." I just continued to stand there with his check in my hand until he had driven out of sight around the building.

Fortunately, there was still a lot of work to be done, and I didn't have much time to think about the encounter until much later. By then I had forgotten about the funny way my heart beat when he looked at me, and the way my fingers tingled when he handed me his check. But I hadn't forgotten that he had called me a "beautiful woman", and I found myself taking an extra careful look in the mirror as I undressed for bed that night. The mirror told me that I hadn't become more beautiful than I was the day before, but I felt a pleasant glow deep inside me as I tucked myself into bed.

Weeks passed, and everything seemed to be going along pretty smoothly. Every time Mike came to the bakery to get his order of frozen pastries, he managed to find a way to say a few words to me, but he was always very formal. I began to think that I had scared him off with my remarks that first time, and I started finding ways to let him know that I was interested in him. I asked him about his business and things like that, and he would answer, but I often felt like there were things left unsaid between us. I spent a lot of time thinking about ways I could let him know I was interested without appearing to be too eager, but I just never seemed to say the right thing. Mike started spending a lot of time with Mr. Behrn in the little office when he came to get his order, and I didn't have much opportunity.

Another thing that made conversation difficult was that Mr. Behrn was hiring a lot of new people, and the place was getting really crowded. Some of us who had been around for a long time began to get a little nervous about that, but Mom told me one night that she knew that none of us were in danger of losing our jobs. I asked her how she knew that, but she just gave me one of those little smiles of hers and I had to be content to just trust her.

Then one day Mr. Behrn called me into his office and asked me to close the door. I tried to remember what Mom had told me about not worrying, but I was still a little nervous as I sat there, waiting for him to speak.

"Ellen, I have something to discuss with you, but I have to ask you to keep our conversation confidential," he finally began. I just nodded my head, and he continued. "We are getting ready to make some changes in the business, and I'm going to tell you about them. But you mustn't tell anyone else until the time is right."

"Okay," I managed to say. My head was spinning with curiosity, and I couldn't figure out why he was telling me this. But I soon found out, because he got right to the point.

"Ellen,, I want to ask you how you would feel about managing this bakery."

I was stunned. If I hadn't been sitting, I'm sure I would have fallen down. I knew I could handle any job in the place--thanks to the training Mr. Behrn had been giving me--but then I started thinking about all the new people he had hired, and I wasn't sure I could manage that many. I could see he was waiting for a reply, so I said the first thing that came to my mind.

"I'm very flattered that you have such confidence in me," I told him, "but I don't think I could manage this many people."

"Oh, no," he said, interrupting me with a little laugh. "I don't mean manage these people. Wait, I'll tell you more. We are going to open a new plant on the other side of town. All of these people will be moving there. My partner and I want to keep this place open because we have a lot of customers who wouldn't like to change, and we don't want to lose them. Also, we might still use this place for something else."

He was being pretty vague, and I suspected that he wasn't telling me everything, but I was beginning to get a clearer picture of what he had in mind.

"What we want you to do," he continued, "is to stay here and handle the business from this end. There will be some wholesale customers who will still pick up their orders here, and there will also be some cakes and other special orders that will be picked up here. You would be working alone. At first."

"Oh," I said, kind of lamely. "Well, I think I can handle everything we do here," I finally added. "I mean, I do know how to do it all, but--"

`   "Good!" he said, interrupting me again. "We can discuss the details later, but I just wanted to sound you out on the idea. Remember not to discuss this with anyone," he said, ending our conversation.

Needless to say, my mind was filled with a confused mixture of questions, thoughts, and fantasies for the rest of the day. I could hardly do the simplest job as I thought about what he had told me, and when Mike came in that afternoon, I practically ignored him. He seemed a little hurt at first, but after he came out of the office following his usual chat with Mr. Behrn, he seemed more tolerant of my absentminded behavior. I should have been smart enough to put two and two together right then, but I wasn't and I didn't.

The very next day, things started changing. I quickly found out that the new bakery, which had been under construction for quite some time, was nearly finished. Some of the new people were put to work installing machinery and moving some of the stuff from our bakery, and there was quite a lot of activity.

About a week after our little talk, Mr. Behrn announced to everyone that I would be in charge of the bakery from now on, and asked them to check with me when moving something to make sure nothing essential was taken. When he made the announcement, Mom gave me a wink and a little salute, and I felt more proud than I could ever remember.

Mike came in later that day, and when I told him his order was all ready for him, he said, "Well, I see you are starting off on the right foot."

It took me a minute to realize that he had somehow known about my promotion before Mr.

Behrn announced it, and when it did hit me, I stopped and turned to him.

"I take it you know about the changes taking place," I said, handing him another box from the freezer.

"I know a great deal more about the business than you imagine," he said with a straight face. "And I'd like to know more about you, too."

My heart started pounding, and I'm sure my face turned red. It was the first time in a while that Mike had said anything that even suggested he was interested in me personally, and now I couldn't think of anything to say to let him know that I was in favor of the idea. I guess he sensed my embarrassment because he turned away and got very businesslike again. But I remembered the way his eyes had looked at me for the rest of the day.

The one thing I was not prepared for in my new position was the loneliness. There had always been other people around at the bakery, and I hadn't realized how few people came into the place. Mr. Behrn came by at least once a day at first, and there were those occasional customers who would come by to pick up their orders, but I was alone most of the time. I found myself watching the clock quite a bit, wondering when the next customer was due to come by just so I could have someone to talk to.

Mike's visits became more frequent, and I

expected that he would be asking me out soon. Still, it didn't happen right away. I tried to let him know I was interested, but I didn't have much practice at that sort of thing. Our conversations were a strange mixture of business and personal topics, and I remained unsure of just how interested he really was. After a while I began to doubt that he had called me beautiful or that he had said he wanted to get to know more about me. I tried a few different hair styles and makeup techniques on the days I knew he would be coming for an order. I was also careful to look fresh and clean as I could around noontime each day when he usually showed up.

And then that day came that totally changed everything. There was really nothing unusual about the beginning of the day--nothing to let me know that it would turn out to be the strangest and most memorable day of my life. I opened the bakery as usual in the morning, and about a half hour later Mr. Behrn came by with a load of croissants to be stored in our freezer. He had a hard time with the big overhead door and mumbled something about fixing it soon. I grinned to myself, remembering the way the other workers would mimic him. Then I was alone again for most of the morning.

Around noon I heard a knock on the door and I checked my hair before I opened it, thinking it was Mike. As I pushed the heavy door upward, I realized it wasn't Mike because the shoes I could see standing on the other side of the door were scruffy looking. When I got the door fully opened, I saw a tramp standing there in front of me. His hair and beard were ratty, and his clothes looked like something he'd found in someone's trash. His hands were shoved into the pockets of the torn coat he was wearing, and he was looking at the ground as he spoke.

"Got any stale bread, lady?"

"Uh, no. I'm sorry, but we aren't that kind of bakery,' I told him, trying to be polite and wondering if I could manage to close the heavy door in his face.

"Well, how about some old doughnuts or something like that?" he asked, as he shuffled forward under the door. He moved lazily into the loading room, but I could see that his eyes were taking in the bakery in a quick, sweeping way.

"No, we really don't have anything at all," I told him. "All our stuff is frozen. And we're not supposed to let anyone in," I added, turning to confront him and trying to make my voice firm.

He turned toward me and his eyes met mine. I got really scared then, because there was a look in his eyes that made me feel chilled. I started to demand that he leave, thinking that I would tell him I was going to call the cops, but before I could open my mouth I found my arms being pinned to my sides and a pair of hands grabbing at me, squeezing the air out of my lungs. The tramp's mean eyes lit up and he straightened and stepped toward me, clearly in control of the situation, and just as clearly not interested in stale bread.

I realized then that he was in league with whoever had grabbed me from behind, and that made me even more frightened. I tried to kick out at the man behind me, but I missed and began to gasp for air as the pressure of his grip increased. I heard a funny buzzing noise in my head and only vaguely heard the first man say, "She's a feisty one. That should make this more interesting."

The world was starting to get a little darker, and I was feeling a helplessness like I had never known in my life, when suddenly everything changed. The first man's mean eyes got very big with surprise as I felt a jolt from behind, and found myself released and falling to the floor. As I fell to my knees, gasping for breath, I saw the tramp running for the door. I watched as a foot connected with his backside in a kick that propelled him right off the loading dock. The other man, the one who had grabbed me from behind, was running after him, holding his hand to his right ear as he ran. If I hadn't been so scared, I might have laughed at the sigh.

Then they were gone and Mike was kneeling beside me.

"Ellen, are you okay?" he asked in a

breathless way.

I just nodded in response, not sure that I could find my voice right then.

"Let me get you to the office," he said, helping me to my feet and holding on to my elbow as though he was handling some respected old invalid. I would have protested, and maybe even laughed at his concern if I hadn't been having such trouble breathing right then. As it was, I let him lead me to the office and sit me down.

Once he was sure that I was okay, he grabbed the phone and dialed a number. "Fritz, this is Mike," he said quickly. "I'm at the bakery. There's been a little trouble here, but everything is fine now. . .yes, everything is fine now, but I want you to bring Ellen's mom over here, and call the police. I'll explain when you get here."

After he hung up, he asked me if there was any tea in the bakery, and I had to think a minute before I remembered the tea bags in the cupboard by the coffeepot. He rushed away to make the tea, and was back in no time at all with a steaming cup. As he handed it to me, he said the strangest thing.

"Ellen, this is all my fault. We never should have left you alone here. If you can find it in your heart to forgive me, I promise I'll make it up to you."

I sipped the tea and started to feel better right away. I thought I could talk at last, but I didn't know what to say. I couldn't figure out what his words meant, but I liked the tone of his voice and the tenderness in his eyes.

Before I could think of what to say, Mom and Mr. Behrn arrived, and one of our local policemen was right behind them. The next few minutes were very confusing, with the three new arrivals asking questions simultaneously and Mike trying to answer everything at once. Finally he took the officer out to the bakery floor and left Mom and Mr. Behrn with me in the office.

After I had managed to assure them that I really was okay, Mr. Behrn said I could go home with Mom, but I told him I would rather stay at work and finish out the day.

Mom shot me a look that said, *That girl of mine!* and I smiled and felt proud. Mr. Behrn was obviously still worried and angry about what had happened, but he finally agreed that I could stay if someone stayed with me.

"I'll stay with her," Mike volunteered, coming back into the office at that point. "We have a lot to talk about, anyway. The cops are going to round up those two men, and make sure they won't bother us or anyone else in town. Now, if the rest of you don't mind, I'd like to have a few words with Ellen."

I got warm all over watching and listening to Mike take charge like that, and just then it hit me that he had saved me from what could have been a very ugly situation. Mom and Mr. Behrn left Mike and me alone in the office, and as Mike turned to me he seemed to be searching for words. Before he could speak, though, I said, "Mike, I want to thank you for saving me."

"Oh, Ellen," he said with anguish in his voice. "First, let me tell you a few things. You should know that I'm Fritz's partner--a silent partner. I helped him finance the new bakery, and I'm going to be taking over this bakery now. I have plans to turn it into a retail outlet for Fritz's products, and for some things of my own.

"I wanted him to get you to take over this place because I thought I would ask you to be my manager when we made the changeover. We had to keep this all quiet because if the word got out it would have jacked up the price of the new place and--well, I'm just sick that this happened."

My head was reeling with all this new information and I was having a hard time taking it all in, but I tried to assure Mike that I didn't consider what happened to be his fault.

"Well, be that as it may," he said, "it wouldn't have happened if I'd had the courage to talk to you myself instead of letting Fritz set it all up. If I had let you know how I feel about you, maybe things would have been different. Maybe we could have started being together right away and you wouldn't have been alone."

"Mike, what do you mean, 'how you feel about me'?" I asked him. "Is there something you want to tell me about that?"

"Look, Ellen," he began. "I've been attracted to you from the moment I laid eyes on you. And every time I came here, I wanted to tell you that, and ask you if you would consider getting to know me better. I guess I could just never think of the right words."

"Well, you're doing fin right now," I told him, surprising myself at my own boldness. "Why don't you keep going and tell me exactly how you feel. It can't hurt, and maybe we might discover that we both feel the same way."

Mike looked at me for a few seconds, then said, "Ellen, I'm in love with you. I want to get to know you, to know everything about you, and I want us to spend a lot of time together. I know you don't know much about me, but I'm pretty sure you like me, and I--" He broke off, looking straight into my eyes, and he put his hands on my shoulders. "Ellen, how do you feel about this?"

"Oh, Mike, I feel the same way. I love you, too," I said as he pulled me into his arms and kissed me tenderly.

Mike and I spent the next few months getting to know each other, happily in love. I feel closer to Mike that I've ever felt toward anyone, and I joyfully accepted when he asked me to marry him. We'll be married in another two months, and Mom and Mr. Behrn have promised us the biggest, most beautiful wedding cake ever.

For now, Mike and I are running the bakery together. He never lets me stay there alone, and we're planning on installing a good security system. Because even though the two men who attacked me were arrested within the week, Mike says he's never taking another chance on losing me. He says that now that we're finally together, we're going to stay that way--forever!

I CAN NEVER TELL MY MOM
WHAT WENT WRONG ON MY
"PERFECT" DATE

Where I ever found the courage to defy Mama and Gram, I'll never know. It wasn't an easy thing to do, and I had to make my decision in the face of a lot of strong opposition from both of them. When I look back on it, I can see that they only wanted the best for me. It's just that they didn't know all the things I knew about Tod. And they also didn't know about my feelings.

I guess that's the important thing--my feelings. Of course, at first I was just as taken in as they were by Tod's charm and the little gifts he gave us, not to mention his handsome face. But while Mama and Gram never saw past those things, I was getting a lot more inside information about Tod's character that I couldn't possibly share with them. And even if I had, I'm not sure they would have listened to me--or even believed me if they did listen.

Take my name as an example. Mama and Gram both claimed that after I was born and they saw me for the first time, the name just popped into their heads. They had named me Jacqueline. How a name like that would just pop into the heads of my mother and grandmother, I can't figure out. My guess has always been that the two of them picked a name that was, for them, foreign and exotic and different. They were determined right from the start that I wasn't going to be ordinary, plain, or poor like they were. So they picked a name that sounded like everything they had wanted to be but never had the chance to be.

Well, that was okay, I guess. But when I started school, there wasn't a single kid there, or anywhere in the county, for that matter, who was going to call me Jacqueline. I became Jackie almost from the first day of kindergarten.

But every time Mama heard someone call me Jackie, she cringed.

"Jacqueline," she would say, "I just do not understand you. We gave you a perfectly beautiful name when you were born, but you insist on using that silly diminutive. What will become of you if you keep lowering yourself like that."

Well, that was Mama's standard speech, and it was just like her. I mean, even to using words like 'diminutive' instead of 'nickname'. I usually got a little embarrassed when a new friend heard The Speech for the first time, but after a while I realized that nobody paid Mama any mind, so I didn't even listen myself. And everyone kept calling me Jackie, so it just sort of stuck.

The fact that Mama and Gram never, not even to this day, accepted that nickname is a perfect example of what our relationship was like.

Once they had their minds made up on a certain subject, there was no changing them. So by the time I was twelve, I had learned to keep my mouth shut on subjects we disagreed on. And that's what made it so difficult for me to talk to them about Tod.

At first, I thought Tod was the greatest. I warmed to him almost immediately. Of course, the fact that he was dressed in a Navy uniform and that he had singled me out of a group of five girls that night had something to do with it, too. I'm not exactly anyone's idea of a raving beauty, but I'm not as bad off in the looks department as some of the girls in our school. I have a pretty nice figure, plus I know how to use makeup without looking like a punk rocker.

Anyway, I thought that at least two of the four girls I was with that night looked better than me, so I was real taken with Tod when he made it clear that it was me he wanted to be with. And he had such a cute way of doing it, too.

We were sitting in a booth at our favorite fast-food hangout when he came up.

"Pardon me, ladies," he had said, looking at each of the other girls as he held his sailor's hat in his hand, "but would you be good enough to allow me to join you so that I might have the pleasure of meeting this absolutely lovely lady?"

And as he said those last few words, he

looked at me for the first time. When our eyes met, I was a goner. My friends all laughed and giggled, and nobody objected to him joining us. I mean, how could we object to such a smooth approach? Two of them slid over in the booth to make room for him, and then those eyes of his zoomed in in closer as he took the place beside me. I moved over a little to make room for him, but I didn't move as far away as I could have.

"If I may take this opportunity to introduce myself," he said, keeping his eyes locked on mine, "my name is Tod Dayton. And what is your name, lovely lady?"

"Well, actually, my name is Jacqueline," I began, "but my good friends call me Jackie."

"Jacqueline." He repeated my name, saying it in a sort of breathless way like he was tasting it rather than saying it. One of the girls on the other side of the booth--I think it was Jane--started making little gagging noises, and some of the others giggled, but I didn't care, and Tod didn't seem to notice. "That is so sophisticated, so European," he declared. "And it suits you perfectly. I can picture you sitting at a little sidewalk cafe on a quiet street in Paris, the envy of every woman and the delight of every man who passes by."

If any of the boys in our school had tried to use words like that, I'm sure I would have joined Jane in gagging. But there was something about

Tod. Maybe it was the way his eyes seemed to laugh at his own silly charm that made it seem perfectly okay. I mean, you just knew he knew he was feeding you a real line, and that he realized you knew it, too. And that made it all right for some reason.

Anyway, I was sure flattered, so I continued talking with him for a while, answering his questions about who I was and where I went to school and where I lived. We had only been talking for a few minutes, though, when two other sailors walked up to the booth and Tod looked up at them as though he was surprised to see them there.

Suddenly Tod and I were leaving the booth, and the two new sailors were taking our place. Then he invited me to take a walk in the moonlight with him. Well, it was just barely dark and there was no moon, but I agreed anyway. As we walked along the street, he told me a little about himself, but mostly he told me how much he wanted to get to know me.

Before we had gone two blocks, I had agreed to a date. I gave Tod my address and he said he would pick me up at eight that Saturday night. Then he walked me back to the restaurant and said good night. I could see that the other two sailors were still sitting in the booth with two of my girlfriends, so I just left without going inside and went home.

I decided not to say anything to Mama about my date until Saturday afternoon, because I knew she would give me the third degree about who this young man was, where he came from, and stuff like that. I just didn't want to get into it with her. I figured she could meet Tod on Saturday and I'd take my chances that he would be able to handle her.

Boy, did he ever handle her! Gram, too. He showed up promptly at eight and I met him at the door. Mama and Gram were doing their imitation of 'interested but not nosy', but I knew they were a bundle of nerves. Tod wasn't wearing his uniform. He was dressed in slacks and a sport coat and looked real nice. And the car at the curb was nice without being too flashy, so that was a good sign, too.

But all that meant nothing as he stepped inside and took his hand from behind his back, revealing flowers. He handed me a pretty little bouquet and then, still holding two roses, he turned to Mama and Gram.

"Ah, I see that I was right to bring roses," he told them. "It is very clear where Jacqueline acquired her beauty. It is certainly my pleasure to meet you. This is for you, ma'am," he said to Mama, handing her one of the roses. "And this is for you," he said to Gram.

I didn't know whether to laugh or groan.

How he delivered those lines with a straight face, especially in light of what I learned about him later, I'll never know. But right at that moment I was just delighted to see Mama stopped in her tracks. As she looked from Tod to the rose and back again she was speechless. And for Mama, that was like saying the sun had forgotten to rise that morning.

Tod was totally in control of the situation. "Jacqueline, why don't you put those flowers in water while I chat with your mother and grandmother for a moment? Then we should be going," he directed.

I was glad to go along with him, since I was afraid my smile would soon crack my face. I hadn't had such fun in years. As I was getting the vase down from the top shelf in the kitchen, I heard Tod telling Mama and Gram that we were going to a movie and volunteering what time he expected to return me to the house. I realized then that he had used my full name, not Jackie. It was uncanny how he seemed to know just the right things to say, and even how to say them, to give my folks the right impression.

Of course, none of these thoughts occurred to me at the time. I was just too happy with how smoothly things were going. I guess that in the back of my mind I hadn't only wanted a date with Tod, but I'd also wanted to shock Mama and Gram with my choice of dates. After all, Tod was in the

Navy, which meant he was a lot older than the boys at school--though I really wasn't sure how much older. I guess I'd hoped that Mama would be upset by that. Well, it wasn't working out like I'd planned it, but it was even better.

When I got back to the living room, Tod was telling them about what movie we were going to see. As I set the vase on the coffee table, he complimented me on the arrangement and then took a bright pink carnation out of the bouquet. With a "May I?" to me, he broke the stem in half and placed the flower in my hair just above my ear.

"Stunning," he announced. "Shall we go?" He opened the door for me and then turned back to Mama and Gram. "Good evening, Ladies," he said as he ushered me out the door.

Mama's eyes were shining and Gram had forgotten to close her mouth. I sure knew what they would be talking about all night.

On that first date Tod was a perfect gentleman. Nothing about his manners or his treatment of me hinted at what was to come. When he took me home that evening, my blouse was unwrinkled, my lipstick unsmudged, and the pretty pink carnation was still in my hair.

Mama had collected her wits enough to invite Tod to join us for Sunday dinner, but he told her graciously that he couldn't make it. "Duty calls," he explained vaguely, just before kissing my hand.

Once Tod left, Mama gave me the once-over, and it was clear that she was happy. "Well, I must say, young lady, that I am impressed with your gentleman," she said. "He is certainly the most well-mannered young man I have ever met."

Gram, who was usually in bed long before such a late hour, put in a word of her own at that point. "And he didn't call you Jackie even once."

"Yeah," I replied. "Well, I like him, too."

I went to my room then, feeling kind of funny. I had been looking forward to seeing what effect Tod's charm would have on Mama and Gram, but now that it was over I wasn't so sure it was what I'd wanted at all. Sure, it was nice not to have to listen to the lectures and the third degree that I usually got from Mama when I got home from a date. And I had had a good time with Tod. But somewhere down in the pit of my stomach I had a funny feeling I couldn't quite analyze.

As I got undressed for bed, I caught a glimpse of myself in the mirror and turned to give myself a careful going over as I slipped out of my bra. I just stood there in my panties, looking myself up and down like I was applying for a position as a model or something. That's when I asked myself why Tod had chosen me. Just what was it about me that made him single me out from my group the other night?

I gave up trying to figure it out, got into my

nightgown, and slipped into bed. But I couldn't get to sleep right away, so I lay there staring at the ceiling, still wondering about Tod. I fell asleep without coming to any conclusions.

The next Monday at school, the gang was buzzing with talk about the three sailors who had picked up on us. Jane had gone out with one of Tod's buddies, and both Anne and Marcy that they would soon get dates with the other one. But mostly everyone wanted to know about Tod.

I told them all about how he had charmed Mama and Gram, and that was a treat for everyone because they had all heard Mama's lectures. But I didn't tell them much else. I guess there wasn't much to tell, anyway, when I thought about it. Carla looked kind of left out of it because she was the only one there that first night who hadn't connected with one of the guys. So, to try to brighten her up a bit, I told her that I'd let her have second crack at Tod when I was through with him, and I was surprised at her response.

"No thanks!" she exclaimed in a voice that made everyone look at her. "I wouldn't touch all that charm with a ten-foot pole."

Someone made a comment that she was just jealous, and the mood swung back to kidding around. But Carla's tone of voice stuck with me for a while, and that funny feeling I'd had after getting home from my date with Tod started coming back. I laughed a little too loudly at a joke someone made to try to shake it off, but it stuck around all day.

Tod called me the following Friday to invite me out for Saturday again, and the minute I heard his voice I felt good all over. That charm of his came right through the phone and grabbed me. When he suggested a late afternoon picnic at the beach, I readily agreed, even though I had a sinking feeling I wouldn't fit into last year's swimsuit. I also wasn't sure if I could talk Mama into buying me another one on such short notice. She usually made me wait until she could find a sale going on somewhere, so I started thinking about how I was going to word my request even before I hung up the phone.

"Was that your young man on the phone?" she asked me before I could rehearse my lines.

"Yes. Tod invited me for a picnic at the beach tomorrow," I told her.

"That's nice. What time is he calling for you?"

"Around four," I said. "But I'm not sure my old bathing suit will fit me," I added lamely, thinking that was *not* the right kind of line to use on Mama.

"Well, certainly you'll have to be properly attired, dear. You can look for a suit in the morning, and I'll put together a nice picnic basket for the two of you while you're out shopping."

I couldn't believe my ears. This was totally unbelievable! I started thinking that maybe the heat was getting to Mama the way it did sometimes in the summer, and then I reminded myself that this was only late spring.

"Oh, you don't have to bother," I told her finally. "I can put a snack together--"

"Don't be silly, Jacqueline," she cut in. "You'll have enough to do between shopping and getting yourself ready. I'll fry up some nice crispy chicken in the morning--men love chicken--and maybe put together a potato salad and some deviled eggs."

Later, as I looked through my closet trying to figure out what I would wear over my new suit, it came to me: Mama had her eye set on Tod for me. That charm of his had gone right to her head, and she thought all of her dreams for me were finally going to come true. I realized then that my little plan to shock her with someone older that the boys I'd been dating was going to backfire right in my face. Unless I missed my guess, Mama was already planning the guest list for my wedding!

The next day I found a real nice two-piece that did wonders for my figure. (It had little ruffles on the top, which added some curves where I needed them.) Plus, the suit was priced low enough so Mama wouldn't scream about it.

Though I was beginning to think that maybe I could take advantage of her present state of mind and get some really nice things, all in the name of impressing Tod, of course. But I decided not to press my luck.

Tod arrived with flowers again, and was just as charming as he'd been the week before. We drove up to Santa Monica and, after spreading the blanket on a fairly empty stretch of sand, we went for a swim. When we'd had enough of that, we ate. It was almost dark by the time we finished, and I expected Tod to suggest we head back. But I was wrong.

As I was packing away the remains of our meal, Tod moved closer to me and said, "Now, how about dessert?"

I started to tell him Mama hadn't packed any dessert, but I suddenly found myself being turned, wrapped in his arms, and kissed. I didn't object. He sure knew how to kiss! He started slow and easy and let me warm up to it, stroking my hair with one hand as he eased me back on the blanket with the other. It was nice, and I didn't mind it too much when his kisses got even deeper.

I was just about relaxed enough to think of returning his kisses in the same way when I felt his hand on my thigh. *Hey*, I thought to myself, *not quite so fast!* I tried to let Tod know by shifting my hips that I didn't care for that, but he didn't get the message. I was getting ready to break off the kiss so I could tell him in words, when his hand left my thigh. I started to relax again, thinking he had finally gotten my message. Boy, was I in for a surprise! Suddenly his hand was back, not on my thigh but where it shouldn't have been.

I grabbed his wrist and tried to pull him away from me. Then I got really scared because he wouldn't move at all. He just kept pressing more firmly. I twisted my head to break the kiss, and he said in a voice that had lost all of it's charm, "Relax, baby. Just relax. You'll enjoy it. Trust me."

"No," I told him. "I'm not ready for that." I was still trying to pull his hand away.

"How do you know until you've tried it?" he asked, finally removing his hand.

"I'm just not ready," I repeated. "Let's just take it a little slower, okay?"

All of a sudden the charm was back. Tod pulled away from me a little and started stroking my shoulder. "I'm sorry, Jacqueline," he said. "You are just so totally beautiful that I guess I lost my head. Please forgive me, and kiss me again to show me you aren't angry with me."

I *was* angry, but when he leaned toward me I let him kiss me, and soon found myself responding again. This time he kissed me on the lips only for a long time and kept his hands on my back. But I noticed that his body moved in closer and soon we were pressed tightly together.

We necked for a long time on the beach that night, and two or three times I had to warn Tod not to put his hands where they didn't belong. Once he caught me off guard and got his hand under the top of my suit, and I almost slapped his face. But each time he did something like that, he would apologize in his charming way and get me all relaxed again. Finally I told him I had better be getting home and he reluctantly agreed.

That night as I got ready for bed I had a serious talk with myself about Tod. It occurred to me that I didn't even know his last name. In fact, I didn't know very much about him at all, and I wasn't sure I wanted to. I knew I couldn't talk to Mama about him. She was already convinced that Tod was the best thing that had happened to me since I was born.

As I drifted off to sleep, I found myself thinking that I wouldn't mind it at all if he didn't call again. Maybe, I told myself, I had turned him off with my refusal and he would just drop me. But that's not what happened.

We went out again the following weekend. Tod told me we were going to a movie, but this time it turned out to be a drive-in. The opening credits of the movie weren't even through running when he started in on me again. It was worse than the time at the beach, because I found out I wasn't dressed for defense. I was wearing a full skirt and a strapless top under a loose blouse. As it turned out, I would have been better off with a full suit of armor!

It was horrible the way Top kept pawing at me. First it was his hand on my thigh. Then he tried slipping it under my top. When I took his hand away to let him know that he'd gone too far, he slid it right up my skirt--which was hiked pretty high with all the wrestling we'd been doing.

"Tod, stop!" I practically screamed at him the second he touched me. Then I did scream as he almost managed to do what he wanted.

He stopped right away when he noticed people in the cars nearby looking at us. "Baby, I'm sorry," he started saying again in that smooth voice of his.

But this time I wasn't buying it. "Take me home this minute," I told him through clenched teeth. "Take me home now or I'll get out and walk."

He immediately started the car and turned off the radio, cutting out the sound of the movie. Then he put the car in gear and started moving out of the space, talking a mile a minute about how sorry he was and how he just got so excited being with me that he kept losing his head. I didn't say a word. I just stayed next to the door and kept my eyes straight ahead.

Later that weekend Jane called me. She'd been dating Tod's friend, the one she'd gone out with that first night at the restaurant. She said she had some news for me about Tod.

"I'm not sure I'm interested," I told her, "but go ahead, anyway."

"Well, I'm not real sure about this, but Bruce let something slip when we were out last night that makes me think Tod has a steady girlfriend," she said. "He might even be married."

"Are you sure?" I asked calmly.

"Well, I said I'm not sure, but I got a real strong feeling. Especially the way Bruce tried so hard to change the subject as soon as he realized what he'd said," Jane went on.

"What exactly did he say?" I demanded.

"Hey, is something wrong?" she asked without answering my question. "You don't seem at all surprised to hear this."

"I'm not. Things haven't been going too well. I don't want to talk about it, though. Just tell me what Bruce said."

"Well, okay. We were talking about people I know, you know? And when I mentioned your name, he said, 'Oh, that's the girl Tod is after'. Then he said something like 'I sure hope his old lady doesn't catch him'. Well, I asked him what he meant, and he just changed the subject. And I mean, he changed it fast!"

"It wouldn't surprise me if he turned out to

be married," I said coolly.

"Hey, what gives, Jackie?" Jane asked. "I thought you were riding high with Tod."

"Well, I was--at first. But lately he's gotten to be...well, never mind. But anyway, I don't think I'll see him again."

"Because of what I said?" Jane wanted to know.

"No, I'd pretty much made up my mind last night," I assured her.

We talked for a little while longer, just gossipy things about girls we knew and who was dating who, stuff like that. It felt good to be talking about normal things and not worrying about how I was going to handle Tod or Mama. I began wishing I'd never met him.

Tod called me in the middle of the week. When Mama told me he was on the phone, I told her I didn't want to talk to him. She gave me a dirty look, went back to the phone, and, polite as you please, said, "Tod, Jacqueline is indisposed at the moment. Why don't you call back later?"

I tried to signal to her that I was going to be 'indisposed' all night, but she wasn't paying any attention to me. And when she hung up, she turned on me and asked me what I meant by refusing to talk with Tod.

"I just don't want to talk to him, that's all," I hedged.

I couldn't tell her what had happened. In the first place, I didn't think I could use 'acceptable' words to describe what Tod had tried to do. And in the second place, I had the feeling she wouldn't have believed me if I had been able to tell her. After all, she was convinced Tod was a perfect gentleman.

I started to go up to my room, but she called me back and gave me the 'Young Lady, You Don't Know What's Good For You' lecture. Only this time it was loaded with praise for Tod, the Gentleman. I let her get through it--I had learned long ago that there was no point in trying to stop Mama once she got started--and then headed for my room.

"When he calls again, you *will* talk to him, Jacqueline!" she called after me.

I was almost to the top of the stairs when she said that, and my first thought was that I would just pretend to fall asleep and get out of it that way. But I realized that would only be a temporary measure--that she'd tell him to call again and I'd just have to go through the whole scene all over again.

So I stopped at the top of the stairs, turned slowly, steeled myself, and said, "No, Mama. I'm not going to talk to Tod ever again. And I'm not going to see him again. And that's final, Mama."

Gram had come in from the living room, where she had been listening to every word, and the two of them just stood there with their mouths hanging open like a couple of flycatchers.

I waited for the tirade, but it never came. After a long minute, I turned and went into my room. I could hear them whispering to each other in hushed, angry voices as I closed my door.

Later, I heard the phone ring, and I was tempted to pick up the extension in my room to listen in. But I knew Mama was too sharp to miss it, so I just laid on my bed and listened to how sweet the tone of her voice sounded. I just knew she was talking to Tod, probably telling him I had a headache or something equally stupid. I didn't really care what she told him. I had made up my mind, and I wasn't going to let her or Gram talk me out of it.

I was kind of surprised the next night when we got through dinner without a word about Tod. Well, I was only too happy to avoid another confrontation, so I didn't say anything myself. I confess I did think about telling at least Mama what the turn-off was all about. But the more I thought about it, the more difficult it became for me to find the right words. She was so hard to talk to about real things. And Gram? Forget it!

Later that night I heard the phone ring, and then Mama called out, "Jacqueline, it's for you, dear."

I almost picked up the phone without thinking, but stopped myself in time. "Who is it,

Mama?"

"Oh, I don't know, dear. One of your friends."

Again, I almost picked up the phone, but stopped myself short. Mama always, and I do mean always, checked to see who was calling me.

I got a brilliant flash. "Mama," I called down the stairs, "my hair is all wet. Find out who it is and tell them I'll call them back, okay? Thanks."

I left my door open a crack and listened carefully. There was a long silence and I could almost feel her standing there in the living room, hating the fact that I had outfoxed her. Then I heard her on the phone again, and I knew from that simpering tone that it was no friend of mine she was talking to. It could only have been Tod on the other end of the line.

Tod never called again. I guess he got the message and went on to other conquests. And I have to say, in Mama's defense, that she didn't bring his name up too often after that. There were a few mild lectures on how I had blown my chance to have a truly fine man interested in me. But she didn't push it. So, to my relief, we were both able to let the subject of Tod die and rest in peace.

I did see Tod one last time. Jane and I were taking the bus out to the pier about a month after his last phone call. Jane was sitting at the window, and as we came to a stop I saw him standing at the curb. He looked as handsome as ever in his uniform. And the woman on his arm, clearly about five or six months pregnant, looked pretty good, too.

"Jane," I said, nudging her. "There's Tod!"

She turned to look out the window as the bus pulled away from the corner. "Yeah," she said as the happy couple disappeared in traffic. "And it looks like he has his old lady with him today."

I don't think we stopped laughing for at least ten blocks. I couldn't have felt better, because no matter what Mama and Gram might have thought of Tod, I knew I'd made the right decision.

I'D NEVER HURT MY KIDS!

Raising three kids on your own is no bed of roses. There are lots of rewards along the way, and there are even a few things about being alone that make life easier than doing it with someone else. Without a man around, there is no one to contradict you when you lay down the law. And there are no conflicts--except with the kids, of course--when it comes time to decide what the family is going to do for fun on the weekends.

Remembering things like that kind of helps to keep you sane. Yet, I still wonder if maybe t he right man came along--a man who could be agreeable and not argue about every little thing, a man who could be a part of his family instead of seeing it as something he had to put up with between work and evenings with his friends--it could be just as easy, and maybe even easier. The six years with Michael, the children's father, and the four years on my own have taught me that, for some people, there is no such thing as 'the right man'.

Anyway, I'm not really complaining about doing it alone. Even if it isn't easy, there are rewards. I guess if I had to do it all over, I'd probably make the same choices. Of course, I'd like to be able to avoid that really awful time last year that frightened me, but I don't see any way I could have known it was coming.

I was working part-time in an office during my senior year in high school when I met Michael. He delivered office supplies for a company in the city and, as the junior gofer in the office, it was one of my duties to check in the supplies he brought us and stock them. He flirted with me the first day, and within a week he had asked me out for a date. I thought he was a nice guy, so I accepted.

He was a little older than most of the guys I knew in high school, and the age difference really showed. He took me to a movie, and on the drive into the city, he told me a little bit about it from reviews he had read. I was pleasantly surprised at how much more I enjoyed the movie once I knew the things I should watch more closely.

He proposed to me on our third date, and I told him that I wanted to finish school before I got serious about anyone. He said he would wait, and when he continued to date me in the same way, I believed that he meant it. I let him make love to me about two months after we had started dating, and I got pregnant that first time. As luck would have it, there were only four months of school left, so I was able to graduate before I even started showing. We got married the weekend after graduation. My folks were happy about it. I think they were relieved to get me out of the house. I moved into Michael's apartment without a honeymoon.

Not that I missed the honeymoon all that much. Michael was really nice that first year, and I was happy enough to be his bride and starting my new life. I stayed at work because I was on the health care plan there, even though I was only a part-time worker. Soon, though, I started working more hours because the company was expanding and they wanted experienced help. After the baby came--Michael was overjoyed that I gave him a boy, Frankie--I went back to work without any discussion. Life seemed to be pretty okay for a time.

Then the following year I got pregnant again with Doug. Right after I told Michael, he started changing. First, it was just little things, like he was an hour late getting home from work and just shrugged it off with a comment like he was talking with some of the guys. But, after a while, he started getting home later and later, and finally I had to have it out with him.

"Michael," I told him as we got ready for bed one night, "we need to talk about our schedules."

"Why?" he asked. "Something going on at work?"

"No, it's nothing like that. I mean about our

evenings. It's getting to the point I don't know when to fix dinner anymore. I think you must have had to eat leftovers at least a dozen times this month."

"I don't mind," he said.

"Well, it's not just you. It's me and the baby, too. I mean, I like to have dinner as a family. Is that too much to ask?"

"Hey," he practically screamed at me. "What do you have to complain about? Don't I help out around the house? Don't I do dishes some times? I have needs, too, you know."

I could see this was not the right time for this kind of conversation, so I just dropped it. I told him I was sorry, and made our lovemaking special that night to show him that I still cared for him. As I drifted off to sleep later, I told myself I would wait for a better time to bring up the subject. Of course, that 'better time' never came around, and by the time Doug was born, we had become set in a pattern that was to last until our divorce.

I took a little more time off work after the second baby--the pregnancy really wore me out. But by the time Doug was four months old I couldn't take any more of Michael's complaining about how little money we had. I still had time left on my maternity leave, but I decided it was easier to go back to work rather than listen to

Michael's constant griping about the bills. My boss was really glad to to see me come back early, and we had a nice talk my first day. She told me that the temp they had hired to take my place hadn't shown half the enthusiasm for the job I did, and my co-workers had been complaining about having to re-do a lot of her work. And when I told her the money was the main reason I came back so early, she gave me a look that said she knew better but wouldn't ask me about it. Two weeks later she told me I was getting a raise.

When I told Michael about the raise, the first words out of his mouth were, "That's great. Now we can get a better car."

I thought he meant we could get a better car for me, but I was in for a surprise. Two days later he came home in a new car of his own, and I was stuck with my old, very-used car. I felt really resentful, especially since my car was four years older than the one he had been driving. And it was my raise that had made the purchase possible in the first place. So I confronted him with my feelings.

As usual, Michael just brushed it off. "Look, we wouldn't have been able to get anything out of your car on the trade," he said. "We're better off just driving that thing until it drops."

Nothing was said about the extra money being mine.

Well, it went from bad to worse in a hurry.

By the time Doug's first birthday rolled around, Michael was in the habit of not only coming home late, but also staying out all night now and then. He would give me some lame excuse like he had had too much to drink and didn't want to drive. But I couldn't help but notice on the few occasions I got to ride in his car--usually when we went to have dinner at my folks' or his--that it smelled more like some other woman's perfume than liquor.

I knew what was going on, but I couldn't think of anything to do or say. I knew that if I tried to confront him with my suspicions that we would just get in a fight, and that I would lose. Michael had a way of turning everything I said into something that sounded very unreasonable, and the arguments he started made me look like some kind of raving lunatic. I was trapped in a rotten situation and, at that time, saw no way out. I kept quiet and tried to make the best of things.

Michael was never actually cruel to me, and if we didn't make love as often as I would have liked, at least I didn't suffer.

My friend Elaine and I got into the habit of spending our evenings together when Michael and her husband were out on the town. She had a way of making me laugh about our mutual problem. She'd tell me about her husband's latest affair, and then make up a story about how she'd get even with him. She had two main fantasies. The first one was about her finding another man, rich and handsome, of course; and the other one was about her husband getting into some embarrassing situation with one of his girlfriends. Sometimes her stories would get a little raw, and I'd have to check to see that the boys were actually asleep or playing in their room and not listening, but she always made me laugh and forget my own sad situation. I don't know what I would have done without Elaine during those depressing years.

Right after Doug turned two, I got another nice raise, along with a small promotion. It was then that I struck the first blow for independence. I didn't tell Michael about the raise, and I started a savings account of my own. What we had been doing was using my paycheck to pay the household bills and part of the baby-sitting, and Michael was supposed to give me something from his paycheck, after he made his car payment. More often than not, there wasn't enough left over to buy decent food. We had a lot of fights about that. Once I told him that if he didn't like the setup he could do the grocery shopping himself and just see how much it took to put meat on the table every night. That lasted about two weeks, then he started giving me more money for groceries.

I began to see that if I was ever going to get a newer car, I would have to save for it myself. So I had opened a savings account at a bank near work, and started putting all my 'raise money' into it. I was delighted at how quickly the money piled up. I began planning how I would surprise Michael by driving home a new car of my own some day. Elaine got more mileage in jokes and stories about my secret plan than I would probably ever get out of the car itself.

About six months later I got a cost-of-living raise and decided to tell Michael about it so he wouldn't get suspicious. He never saw my paychecks, and I thought I could probably have deposited that extra money in my account, too, but I didn't want to push my luck, so I told him about the raise.. But I guess the presence of that special account gave me an added measure of courage. When I told him about the raise, I also told him that I was planning to keep the extra money to buy special things for the boys. He started to object, but I stood right up to him.

"Michael, Frankie will be starting school soon," I reminded him, "and I want him to have all the things the other kids will have. I want him to have new clothes that fit him, and the same kind of lunch box the other boys have. I want that lunch box filled with good food, not just peanut butter sandwiches. And if he needs good shoes so he can play soccer with the other kids, I want to buy him the best. Do you have some objection to your son having the best?"

"No, I guess you're right," he admitted. "But

just don't go overboard."

"I'll go as far overboard as I think I should," I said, surprising myself with my own courage. "You've left all the decisions regarding the boys' care up until now, so let's just leave it that way. If you want more money to spend on your parties and your women, you can just work harder and get it for yourself. This extra money is for the boys."

He didn't have a word to say in answer to that. He just sat down on the couch and picked up the newspaper--which he hardly ever read. I went into the kitchen and started shaking, because I realized that I had mentioned the subject of his fooling around for the very first time, and it hadn't turned into a fight.

For the next two weeks I had a new lover--Michael. I couldn't believe how he was acting. It was almost as it had been before we were married. Of course, it didn't last. I guess the other life he had been building was just too good for him to leave, and soon he was back to his old pattern. And I found I didn't care as much as I had before. As thrilling as his renewed interest in lovemaking had been, I guess I was getting used to my own life, too.

As it turned out, that was the beginning of the end for Michael and me. I got pregnant during that two weeks, and when I told him about it two months later, he hit the ceiling. He told me I ought to get an abortion because we couldn't afford another child. I told him he was out of his mind. I'll never forget his last words to me on that day that was supposed to have been a very happy one.

"Fine. If all you want to do with your life is bring up a bunch of kids, you can do it on your own!"

He walked out of the house, slammed the door, and was gone for four days. By the time he came back, I had made up my mind what I was going to do. The minute he walked in the door I was ready for him. I saw him drive up in his car as I was fixing dinner for the boys. I told the boys to go to their room to wait for dinner, and not to come out until I called them. They were good kids and usually did what I told them, and I guess they knew something was going on. They hightailed it for their bedroom without a word and stayed there. I watched Michael walk around from the garage and met him at the front door and gave him my carefully prepared speech in a level voice.

"If you have come back for your clothes, you are welcome to them. But don't take anything else, don't hang around, and don't even bother talking to my sons. You have fifteen minutes before I call the sheriff."

"Shanna, I--" he started to say. I cut him off.

"No, don't waste my time with any conversation. You have fourteen minutes to pack your clothes and get out," I added, glancing at my watch.

I turned back to the kitchen then, leaving him standing in the doorway. I had a tense moment as he headed down the hall, because I thought he would try to get the boys involved. But soon I heard the sound of hangers being taken off the pole in the closet and I breathed a sigh of relief. I stayed close to the phone in the kitchen, though, ready to dial 911 if it became necessary.

It took him closer to twenty minutes, but I didn't push it because he spent all that time on the move, taking his clothes and personal items out to his car and just piling them into the sets and the trunk. As he drove out of the driveway, I realized his contribution to our home hadn't amounted to much. I couldn't even see much of a pile above the windows of his car as he left with all his possessions.

Then I finished dinner for the boys.

Despite all my carefully laid plans and brave words, I was scared. Soon, I found out I had a right to be. The money I had socked away in my savings account wasn't nearly enough to get me the kind of reliable car I thought I would need. I wound up buying another used car. I got a pretty good deal on the trade-in, though, and I was able to drive away in my "new" station wagon without any additional payments. But with the new baby on the way, things were going to be real tight, and

I had to have quite a few talks with the boys about how we would have to tighten our belts for a while until things smoothed out.

The boys were wonderful about all the changes. I remember hearing an interview on the radio with a psychologist who said that kids have the hardest time adjusting to a divorce situation, but you sure couldn't prove that by the way Frankie and Doug behaved. I couldn't have asked for more. They helped out in little ways that I hadn't even thought about, and except for a few complaints about the lack of ice cream, they didn't seem to mind the new situation at all. Of course, as much as Michael had been out when he had been living with us, there wasn't that much of a change. That same psychologist also reported that his studies h ad shown that it made no difference if kids were being raised in a one- or two-parent home as long as they got lots of love. I'll sure vouch for that. Doug and Frankie got lots of love at home.

Before Michael left it had been my habit to give the boys a snack when they first got home from school, and then plan dinner rather late, in hopes that Michael would be home in time to join us. Afterward, I just cut out the after-school snack and planned dinner for earlier in the evening. Then I would let the boys watch T.V. if they had no homework, while I cleaned up after dinner; or they would sit at the kitchen table with their schoolbooks. After chores were done, we would watch T.V. together or play games that they enjoyed before bath time. When they were younger, I would sit on the stool while they took their bath and read to them; but as they got older, t hey started taking separate baths, so I would hold off reading to them until bedtime.

Our weekends didn't change much, either. I had always tried to find things to do with the kids that were not too expensive but were still fun for them. Picnics were a favorite, especially if they were combined with swimming; and the zoo was a relatively inexpensive way to spend a whole day. The only thing that changed was that I didn't have to bother trying to convince Michael to co me with us on these outings. He hadn't come often, anyway.

Frankie loved being 'the man of the family' and would frequently do his best to act the part. It was hard for me to keep from laughing when he would come to me in the kitchen on a Saturday morning and clear his throat to let me know it was time for a "serious discussion".

"Mom," he would say in a voice that he tried to make sound deeper and more manly, "I think we should discuss what we're going to do today."

"Okay," I'd say, keeping my head turned so he wouldn't see the twinkle in my eyes or the grin that was turning up the corners of my mouth. "What do you have in mind, sir?"

"Well, I think we should consider going to the park today," he would suggest.

Don't ask me where he picked up words like 'discuss' and 'consider'. I'd do my best to answer him in a serious tone, but I usually had to keep my comments to a minimum to avoid bursting into laughter or giving him a big hug to show him how proud I was of him.

I did a lot of hugging, especially in those months right after Michael left, just to make sure the boys knew they were loved. However, I had found that Frankie would get quite upset if I hugged him when he was being 'the man of the family'.

When it came close to the time for the baby to come, I was careful to include the boys in as much of the planning as I could, to be sure they wouldn't develop any jealousy. And Elaine was a great help, taking them off my hands when I was particularly tired.

After the baby came, Elaine surprised me by asking if she could take care of little Holly when I went back to work. She and her husband didn't have any kids, and she said it was beginning to look like they weren't going to have any, either.

"It might be the only chance I'll get to take care of a baby," she said, rocking Holly on her shoulder.

"Well, I just don't know what to say," I confessed. I was flabbergasted, but I guess she took it the wrong way.

"Oh, listen, Shana. I don't mean I'd try to be her mother or anything. I mean, it would be a business arrangement. Say twenty-five dollars a week? And I'm--"

"Elaine, I'd love it!" I said, cutting her off. "You're hired. You just caught me by surprise. And I think it would be great if Holly could grow up with two mommies. She'll be right here so I won't have to worry about packing things for her, and...wow!"

"Well, I'm thinking of myself, too," she said. "I've been wanting to quit that part-time waitress job, but I have to have my mad money, and this is the perfect out for me. And since I'll be home all the time, I can spend more time with my crafts, and maybe even start making a little extra money."

It was a nice win-win situation. And for the most part things were working out very well for us. For a while, life was just great. And then Michael poked his nose back into my life and everything started to go wrong again. He called one night shortly after Holly had been born. I was so startled when I heard his voice, I couldn't think of anything to say.

"Uh, what do you want? I finally mumbled.

"Well, I know it's been a long time, but I

would like to visit my boys, if that's okay with you."

I thought about it so long, weighing the pros and cons, that he must have thought that I had hung up.

"Shana, are you still there?"

"Yes. I'm thinking about it," I told him.

"Well, it's no big deal," he said. "I just thought, maybe, I could take them out for an ice cream cone or something on Saturday."

"I would actually prefer you didn't buy them sweets," I said, grateful that I had something tangible to discuss. "I'm trying to keep them off things that are too sugary. Maybe you could just take them to the park for an hour or so."

"That would be okay," he said, being uncharacteristically agreeable.

We set it up for the following Saturday, and I told the boys to be good and to just visit with him. They weren't very enthusiastic about it, but they didn't voice any objections, either. I hoped it would be all right.

When he brought the boys home--five minutes early--he didn't just drop them off at the driveway, but followed them to the porch.

"Boys, you go in and change now. And be quiet, the baby is sleeping," I told them.

"How about next Saturday?" Michael asked me when the boys had gone inside.

"I'm sorry, we have plans for next Saturday,"

I told him honestly. I didn't tell him I had made those plans that morning, just after he had taken them out, just in case.

"Well, maybe the Saturday after next," he suggested.

"Perhaps. I'll call you and I'll let you know," I said. "But I don't want you thinking you can make a habit of this. I don't mind you seeing them now and then, but you must realize I have three children, and I don't like the idea of the boys going off with you alone, without their sister. It could lead to family problems down the road."

"Okay," he said simply. Then he left.

As I went back to preparing lunch, I realized he hadn't even expressed any interest in seeing Holly, even after I had mentioned her. He probably didn't even know her name. And that was just fine with me. In fact, I would have been happy if he never bothered us again, but I knew that was unlikely.

He saw the boys twice the following month, and once the month after that. But the next month, he didn't wait for me to call him. He called and said he wanted to keep the boys for the whole weekend. I flatly refused, reminding him that he had no visiting rights, paid no child support, and saw the boys only because I felt it was good for them. I also repeated my feelings about having the kids separated, and still he did not offer to take Holly on one of their outings in the park. His tone was somewhat different when he said good-bye, and I wondered if he would try to make trouble.

Trouble struck about two weeks later. But trouble is not the right word for it: horror and humiliation come closer to the truth. I was at work on a Monday, flipping through the stack of priority requests, when the phone rang. I picked it up absent-mindedly and said, "Shana speaking," as was my usual habit. No one except my mom or Elaine called that phone from outside, so I was quite surprised to hear a strange voice.

"Is this Shana Petersen?"

"Yes, this is Shana Petersen," I replied, puzzled at the intrusion. I still did not take my attention away from the stack of requests on my desk.

"Mrs. Petersen," the woman said, "this is Mrs. Laxalt, principal of Jefferson Elementary School."

Now she had my full attention. I dropped my pencil, and tried to talk despite the lump that had formed in my throat.

"Has something happened to Frankie or Doug?"

"Well, not exactly," she said. "I mean, they're fine. They're fine, physically, that is. I'm sorry, this is an unusual situation and I'm saying it poorly. There are two people here from the Children's Services Division, and they are insisting on talking to your sons. I want you to understand that the law requires me to cooperate with them, so I really had no choice. But I felt that I should call you and let you know?"

"What exactly is going on Mrs. Laxalt?" I demanded.

"Well...they said they had received a report of abuse--"

"What!" I shouted, not even noticing that I now had the attention of everybody in the office, including our boss who had a glassed-in office of her own at the end of the room. "What do you mean, abuse?"

"Mrs. Petersen, please understand that I am powerless in this situation. I think I know your boys well enough to say that such an accusation is false, but our hands are tied. When CSD gets a report, they have to follow up on it, and I am required by law to cooperate. I'm sure nothing will come of this, but thought you ought to know about it."

"I appreciate your call, Mrs. Laxalt," I told her, fighting to stay calm. "Are they still there?"

"Yes," she practically whispered. "They're talking with Doug now. They've already interviewed Frankie."

"I'll be there as soon as I can," I told her. "Please have them wait for me."

I hung up the phone and grabbed my purse. I was about to head for my supervisor's office, when I noticed she was already on the way to my desk. I took the time to put a paperweight on the stack of requests I had been working on, then turned to her as she walked up.

"Trouble, Shana?"

"Yes. My kids at school. I have to go."

"Of course. Call me if you need anything."

I only had time for a hurried "thanks" as the elevator swallowed me up and dropped me quickly to the first floor. My heart was still beating like mad as I got into my car and drove away. I made it to the school in record time, breaking about eight or ten traffic laws to do so, but I was still too late to talk to t he CSD people. Just as I turned the last corner, I spotted an official-looking car leaving the school. I gave them a hard look as I passed them.

Mrs. Laxalt was waiting for me as I entered the office, and she beckoned for me to follow her into the library. The library was a glass-walled room that doubled as a crafts room. There were large tables and tiny little chairs here and there. We did not sit.

"They told me as they left that they'd found nothing--which I could have told them was exactly what they would find, had they asked me."

"Did you ask them to wait? Did you tell them I was coming?"

"Yes, but they said they had other appointments and had to leave. I think they were a little embarrassed," she added.

"Well, they're going to be a lot more embarrassed when I get through with them," I promised. "Where did they talk to the boys?"

"Here, in the library," she told me.

"And what about the other kids in their classes? What are they thinking about, Mrs. Laxalt, now that Frankie and Doug have been called out of their rooms and questioned in this fishbowl by officials?"

"Mrs. Petersen, I know that it looks bad from your point of view as a caring mother," she said. "But believe me, it would probably be better--for the boys in particular--if you just forgot about the incident and let it go away quietly. The case-worker told me that they had found nothing to substantiate the accusation."

"What was the caseworker's name?" I demanded.

"She left her card for you. I have it here."

I took the card, thanked her more brusquely than I'd intended, and left. As I drove back to the office I thought about making a detour to CSD and confronting the caseworker, to try to find out who made the accusation. I had a pretty good idea who it was, but I would have liked to have it confirmed. Something told me to go back to work, though, and calm down before I talked to the caseworker.

"Everything okay, Shana?" my boss asked as I put my purse away.

"Yes, thanks. It was a false alarm," I lied.

"Sorry for the ruckus."

"That's okay. Better safe than sorry," she offered.

I went back to the stack of requests I had been processing before the nightmare phone call, and I must confess I vented a little of my anger on that stack.

I waited until late afternoon before calling CSD, and did my best to sound calm and reasonable when I talked to the caseworker. She gave me the same pitch the principal had, about what the law requires, and that it would be best to just forget about the whole thing. And, of course, she wouldn't tell me who made the accusation, except to say it was apparently an anonymous phone call. That got me mad all over again.

"Now just a minute," I said. "I know that doctors have to report any signs of abuse they see on kids, and that's a good idea; but do you mean to tell me that any jerk can just call you up and send you off on a wild goose-chase, stirring up people's lives, and creating who-knows-what kind of emotional problems for little kids? That's really sick."

"Mrs. Petersen, I'm sure that once you have had a chance to think it over, you will realize the law was created to protect children, not to harm them. And in this case, the complaint was about sexual abuse."

"Sexual abuse! This is even sicker than I thought, " I told her. "Maybe the law was created for good reasons, but the way the law is carried out could use a little improvement."

"I'm sorry,"

"So am I," I told her as I hung up.

I got practically the same story from my attorney. I told him I was getting a little tired of everybody telling me to take it easy and forget the whole thing.

"If I could be sure it would stop here, I guess I might be able to give it a try," I told him. "But what's to stop Michael, or whoever it was, from trying it again? And what kind of effect will that have on the boys?"

"Shana, I think you are overemphasizing the effect this might have on the boys. In the first place, they know they haven't been abused, right?"

"Right!"

"Okay. And in the second place, I'm quite sure that if CSD gets any more anonymous phone calls, they will ignore them. They do keep records, and they don't want to waste their time going out on bogus investigations and more that you want your boys to be subjected to same.

"My advice to you is to go home, have a stiff drink, or meditate, or do whatever you do to relax. Make the boys a nice dinner, and get on with your life."

Elaine, good old Elaine, was the only person who understood. She and the baby were at her place when I got home that afternoon. I flopped down on her couch and poured out the whole story. Halfway through the tale, she got up and brought me a shot of something that tasted awful and burned going down, but she listened, and she didn't tell me to forget it.

"Was it Michael?" she asked later.

"I don't know," I mumbled. "It could have been, probably was, but I don't know."

"I have a friend whose husband works for the phone company. He could probably find out about Michael's long-distance calls, and maybe prove he called CSD. That would be something, right?"

Her idea got my attention and brought me out of my stupor. I thought about it for a minute, then I recalled something my attorney had said.

"Good idea, but it wouldn't work. My lawyer said that even if we could prove he visited the CSD offices, it would be proof he made the accusation. And he said no court would order CSD to open their files."

"Oh. Looks like we're stumped," she said.

I hugged her. The way she said "we" made me feel, for the first time that day, that I wasn't alone.

"Hey, I have to get dinner started," I said.

"The boys will be home soon."

"Why don't you leave Holly with me for a while," she offered. "No extra charge."

It felt good to smile again. Elaine frequently asked me to let her take Holly out for walks, or keep her for a few extra hours, a "no extra charge". I even had a hard time getting her to accept our agreed upon fee most of the time.

Evidently her husband was so happy with the change in her since she had started taking care of Holly that he had both warmed up and loosened up. Warmed up to her, and loosened up his wallet. She told me she had more 'mad money' now than she ever had since they were married. So the "no extra charge" had become our little private joke.

I had a nice dinner started when the boys got off the school bus.

"What's for dinner, Mom?" Frankie asked, as usual, the moment he walked in.

"Bread pudding," I answered automatically.

"Great. That bread sure smells a lot like chicken, though."

Well, between Elaine's friendly ear, and the usual afternoon routines with the Frankie and Doug, I got into a better mood. During dinner I mentioned, as casually as I could, that I had heard they'd had visitors at school.

"Yeah, a couple of people asked us some dumb questions," Frankie said in a bored voice.

"With dolls," Doug piped in.

"Oh yes, t he anatomically correct dolls," I said, making it sound like it was something that went on every day. "Was it interesting?"

"Naw," Frankie muttered with a mouthful of chicken and biscuit.

I relaxed a little then, thinking that maybe everyone had been right. The boys certainly didn't seem to be upset by it, so I told myself that maybe I shouldn't be upset either.

Then, later that night, I told the boys to get ready for their baths...and all of a sudden I found myself staring out of the kitchen window, asking myself if I was really guiltless. I thought about the times I had sat in the bathroom, reading to them as they took their bath, and then helping them get dry afterward.

"No!" I told myself violently. Then I realized I'd had said it aloud when Frankie called down the hall to ask me what I wanted.

"Nothing honey," I answered in a voice that trembled a little bit.

After they where in bed I called Elaine and asked her to bring Holly over. We got her into bed, and then I asked Elaine to check on the boys for me.

She was halfway into their room when she said, "No, Shana. You check on them, just like you always do."

She stood there, holding their door open for

me and giving me a look that could fill a book with its meaning. I hesitated a minute, then realized she was right and went to tuck in my children.

Later, in the living room, I told her in whispers about the thoughts I had had earlier. She lit into me the way only a close friend can, and by the time she was through with me I saw that the real danger was that I would start believing the accusations myself and create problems for the boys and me by overreacting.

"Thanks, Elaine," I told her again as she got ready to leave. "I don't know what I would do without you."

"That's what friends are for," she replied as she gave me a big hug and patted me on the back. "Just remember those kids deserve all the love you can give them."

And that's all there was to it. Nothing further was ever said, and after a few days I realized t he principal, my lawyer, and even the CSD caseworker had been right. Maybe if I had gone tearing through the 'halls of justice', trying to right the wrong that had been done, the boys would have become more upset by the incident. As it was, they apparently viewed it as nothing more important than the visiting nurse checking everyone for head lice.

Some months later, after I had all but

forgotten about the incident, Michael showed up at my doorstep unexpectedly. I wasn't going to let him in, but he had a look of desperation on his face.

"Please, I need to talk to you," he said.

Although there had been times when I really hated him, there was one part of me that still loved that old Michael of so long ago. I stared at him for a few moments, and then I hesitantly let him in the house.

The last time before that Michael and I had talked, it was about the children, of course. We'd had a heated argument. Michael had wanted to continue seeing Frankie and Doug, and I didn't object to that; but he wouldn't take Holly on any of their outings. I had repeatedly told him that Holly was our child, too, but he just said that I wanted her so badly, I should be the only one responsible for her. The argument had gotten ugly after that.

"But she's our child! How can you not love her?" I asked.

"She's *your* child! I told you I didn't want another kid. Why didn't you have an abortion like I told you?" he'd shouted.

"I loved you, Michael. How could I get rid of the child that came from that love?" I'd pleaded.

"Because I told you to. That should be enough for any wife."

That had infuriated me. How day he

command me to do anything! Besides, what kind
of husband had he been to me? He wasn't faithful
to me and he never did anything nice for me. He
had been a terrible father. He hardly ever saw the
kids, except when I begged him to go on outings
with us. He never paid any child support, and had
never asked about Holly. How *dare* he make
demands!

Well, I'd had enough. I'd told him that if he
didn't want to spend time with Holly, he'd never
see Frankie or Doug again.

That was the last time I had seen Michael.
And I'd really felt that if I never saw him again
that would suit me just fine. But now he stood in
my living room with his head hung down.

"Shana, we need to talk," he said.

"What is it?" I said without any feeling in
my voice.

"I'm really sorry for what I did, but you told
me I couldn't see the boys anymore. I was going
to sue for custody."

"What are you talking about?"

"The sexual abuse report," he mumbled.

"You! How could *you* do that to us," I cried.

"I didn't want to hurt you, I just wanted the
boys."

"How could you put my life in such an
uproar? And if you really cared about the boys,
how could you upset their lives like that?"

"I just thought it would be better if I had them all the time because I began to realize that I hardly know them."

"Well, thanks for not doing us any favors. But you're right about one thing--the boys don't know you. All the time you spent drinking and chasing cheap women stopped you from getting to know your own kids. Well, it's too late now, Michael. And if you come within a hundred feet of me or the kids, I'll have the police pick you up."

After I said that, he left. He was still mumbling apologies, but I didn't care. I went to the police and told them he had threatened me and the children. They issued a restraining order.

I still feel it's a shame that any jerk can pick up a phone and say a few words that will start a nightmare like I went through. I still feel that CSD could do more background investigation before they go plowing into kids' lives, waving their anatomically correct dolls around. But all in all, things worked out okay.

In fact, I think we are all a little better off since then. For one thing, I've decided that my children not only deserve the love, but they also deserve to hear about it from me. So I tell them now and then, "I love you."

The first few times I said it, I could hear the defiance in my voice. I was making a simple declaration of my love, and I dared anyone to interpret it in any other way. But after a while I came to like the sound of the words all by themselves. I think my boys, and Holly, too, will be healthier and happier for growing up knowing how to say those words without shame.

TWO LOVES - ONE HEARTBREAK

When I first went to work at the diner I was not happy about the changes my new job would make in my life: not having as much time with my kids, and probably having to drop the art class I had been planning to take that fall. But if I had had any idea of the *truly* big changes that job would b ring into my life, I would have found some other way to bring extra money into the house.

My husband, Perry, was in construction. Spring and summer were usually the good times for us. He got lots of overtime, and we were usually able to put a little away in our savings account for the autumn and winter slow seasons. But that summer things didn't go so well. It was toward the end of July that Perry finally talked about what we had both seen coming for some time.

"Well, Lynn, looks like it's going to be a tight winter," he said at dinner that night.

"Yes, we are a little behind in our budget, aren't we?"

"I talked to the foreman about it today.

Asked him what was going on. All he really said was, 'It's slow all over'. I could have told him that--I read the papers, too. Then he said he'd do what he could, but I don't think he'll be able to do much."

I thought for a second about suggesting he try getting on part-time with another crew, but I didn't say anything. Perry had done that once before, when we needed a new car, but that had been a long time ago and we didn't have any kids then. Instead, I tried to let him know it would be fine.

"We'll make it somehow. I'll just start shopping for bargains, and repair the kids' clothes instead of buying them new. We'll do okay."

I wasn't ready for the explosion that followed.

"Be quiet, Lynn," he shouted, pounding his fist on the table so hard it made things jump. "I'm not talking about eating beans instead of hamburger, or patching a pair of pants. I'm talking about serious trouble. I'm talking about maybe not being able to pay the rent or keep up the payments on the car."

Sarah looked like she was going to burst out crying, so I ignored Perry for a minute while I calmed her down. Then I told Timmy he could be excused. The kids were just as upset as I was by this unusual outburst of their father's, and the fact that Timmy didn't object about the lack of dessert as he scooted away from the table really made that clear.

"I'm sorry, honey. I guess I didn't really understand. Maybe you'd better fill me in," I suggested.

I don't know whether it was my attitude, or the fact he'd had a few minutes to think about it, but anyway he was a little calmer. I wasn't so sure I liked the change, though, because now he seemed surly.

"There's nothing to fill you in about. The money is getting tight and it's going to get tighter. We have to make some serious changes. I've been thinking about trading in the car for an older one, so at least we won't have that payment to worry about."

I knew that feeling-sorry-for-myself tone all too well. Perry didn't have many faults, but among the ones he had, that was my least favorite. I had seen him get into a pout that lasted for days on end. We all suffered when that happened--Perry probably more than me or the kids--though I was never able to realize that until later. He never touched me, even in bed, and we hardly talked while it was going on. All he did was come home from work, eat dinner, watch TV, go to bed, get up, and go to work. Period. He didn't play with the kids, the yard didn't get taken care of, the cat wasn't allowed in his lap, and the beer disappeared from the fridge much too fast. I decided right then and there that I was not willing to through another one of his pouts. Especially since I thought this one could wind up lasting for months.

I got Sarah through dinner and took her straight in for her bath, spending a little more time with her than usual while I planned my strategy. By the time I got her into bed and got Timmy settled in his room with his books, I had my mind made up. I wasn't looking forward to the explosion I knew would come when I made my suggestion, but I figured that would be better than a month-long sulk. So I squared my shoulders and marched into the living room.

I had raised this subject once before--I can't remember just when--and I knew what kind of reaction it would get. I waited until the news was over and launched my attack during the commercials.

On our good nights, Perry would turn off the TV after the news, and we'd talk, or read, or play a game of cards until a show we both wanted to watch came on later. Sometimes we just went to bed early. But when he was working up to a sulk, he'd just sit there and watch whatever anyone fed him until he got ready for bed. So I had timed my suggestion for immediate feedback. If he was going to sulk, he'd just watch. If my suggestion angered him enough to get him out of the self-pity space, he'd turn off the boob tube and argue with me.

"Perry, if things are really that bad, maybe I should find a part-time job somewhere."

Well, Miss Smarty Pants had it all figured out. He didn't do either of those things. You could knocked me over with a feather when he finally did react. He just sat there like he was going to keep sulking for a few seconds, then he got up, turned off the TV, sat back down and said, "Yeah, I guess it's come to that."

So that's how I found myself applying for a job at the diner. I had done some waitressing in high school so I sort of knew what I was doing. I got the job, but I was the new kid on the block and I had to take the worst shifts to start. I got something like three hours (lunch) on Tuesdays and Wednesdays, six hours (after lunch and through dinner) on Fridays, and eight hours on Saturdays.

As I said, it cut into my social life like crazy, and Perry wasn't too happy about the weekend stuff: but I pointed out it could have been a lot worse--I could have been stuck with breakfasts and weekends only. At least I was able to be home every morning, and my sister took Sarah on the days I worked lunch, which saved on baby-sitting money. Perry stayed with the kids on Friday evenings and Saturdays, and they liked that even if he wasn't a barrel of laughs at first.

"It won't be long before I'll be able to pick

my own hours," I told him. "They have a very high turnover rate there, and I'll have seniority soon."

My insistence that our life would soon be back to normal didn't satisfy him very much. He wasn't exactly sulking in those days, but he wasn't himself, either. I could tell it tore him up to have me working. Not because he thought 'a woman's place is in the home', but because it bugged him that he couldn't support us on his own.

I kept my eyes open for every news item I could find about two-income families, the state of the economy, the inflation rate--anything that would make him see that it wasn't his fault. Sometimes he'd respond. Once in a while he'd even discuss the issue--in very general terms, of course. But mostly, he'd just say nothing at all. It wasn't exactly depressing, but it wasn't a lot of fun, either.

At work things were different. I was meeting new people, though I didn't have much time to chat, and I felt good about being able to bring in some extra money. And I guess that good feeling spilled over into the job, and made me a little more receptive to people I worked with. At least, that's what I told myself later when I tried to justify what happened.

One of the cooks at the diner was--well, I'll call him Dave. Dave was the kind of guy you just couldn't help liking, even if you didn't like the job.

When he had to ask you about a certain order, or tell you that we were out of something, or running short, or having a special that afternoon, he had a nice way of doing it.

And if you made a goof on an order, he'd make a joke out of it--but the joke would be on him, not on you. Like he'd say, "I stuck my finger in the gravy, then picked up your order, and now I can't read it."

If we ran out of something that was on the regular menu, you'd be lucky to even hear about it from the other cooks. Usually you'd get something like, "We ain't got no turkey!"

And of course, this would be said in a tone that implied you were stupid for not knowing that in the first place, and the line would be delivered at the same time your order slip came sailing back over the counter at you.

With Dave behind the window, you'd get that information when you first came on, before you took any orders from customers, and there'd usually be a funny story that went with it.

"Lynn, we have a small problem today," he'd say. "The guy who was supposed to deliver the turkey misunderstood the order and brought his brother-in-law instead. We would have cooked him anyway, but we don't have a pan big enough."

I always got a kick out of his jokes, even when they weren't very funny, because it was such a contrast to the way the other cooks acted. And it didn't stop at business, either. Any time one of us put in an order and he wasn't busy, he'd have a quickie ready--usually a pun, or something like that. It was a lot more fun working at the diner when Dave was there.

Dave made jokes about everything. Of course, the personal jokes were a little different than the others, but one of the other girls had told me about Dave before I even met him. So when I came in that first night we worked together, and he started in on me, telling me I had the nicest legs in town and things like that, I was ready for him. The warning I had received, and the way he said those things let me know he wasn't serious, so I didn't take offense.

After he found out I was a good sport, he started mixing in real conversation with his jokes and his remarks, and by the time I'd worked there a month, we were getting to know each other pretty well. I guess it was his easy-going manner, combined with his genuine interest, that led me to tell him things I hadn't told anyone else. He was easy to talk to, and it was nice to have someone to listen, so I told him why I'd started work, about my kids, my former plans to take some art classes, and stuff like that.

It was the last thing, the art classes, that kind of turned things around for us. He'd kept bugging me about what kind of art I was interested in, and asking me to bring in some samples of my work for him to see, and after three or four weeks of this I finally did bring in my sketchbook.

"Hey, these are really good. You ever think about drawing cartoons?" he asked. "If you could draw the pictures to go with some of my jokes, we could sell them and split the profits fifty-fifty."

I told him I'd think about it. I didn't realize it at the time, but in the back of my mind I was worried about getting involved with him. Throughout all of this time, he had kept remarking on my legs, and how pretty I was, and how I was the best-looking, most intelligent waitress he'd ever met, and like that. I'd taken his comments with a grain of salt right from the start, both because I noticed he kidded around with all the other waitresses, too; but also because I was married.

This was money he was talking about, though, and that caught my attention. I didn't know how much money I could make drawing cartoons, but I figured anything would be all right with me. And if it turned out to be enough money for me to quit that job and go back to my kids and my husband full time, then I was all for it.

The following Friday I told him I'd give it a try.

I was so excited, that as soon as I got home I told Perry about the idea Dave had for us to make a little money. I didn't tell him I was planning to get rich off the scheme, or tell him that I was planning on quitting my job. I just called it 'a little extra money'. So I guess I shouldn't have been too disappointed when Perry didn't show any enthusiasm.

I knew that he was still worried about his job, about his own income. But it seemed to me that he could have at least shown a little interest in what I wanted to do.

As it turned out, I worked on sketches for a couple of ideas Dave had given me, and Dave liked them. He said he'd take care of sending them off for us. I'd signed them with a contraction of our two names, and he was really impressed that I'd thought of that. Then he gave me a couple more ideas, a little more complicated than the first ones, and I made some note on the back of one of my order slips and stuffed it in my pocket.

I wasn't so successful with those new ideas, though, and I told Dave. He explained that it might take months before we got any word that we'd sold anything. We just had to keep on working and sending our cartoons out regularly, regardless.

"I'll tell you what," he said. "You're free on Mondays, so why don't you bring your rough drafts by my place, okay? We'll look over what you have, and maybe I can give you a few suggestions. That should speed things up and we won't have to wait a week between feedback sessions."

I agreed. I took Sarah with me that first Monday, and Dave let me put her down for her nap on his bed, and we worked at his kitchen table while she slept. I finished those second two, and another one he had thought of, that day and it really seemed like the Monday sessions were a good idea.

Monday turned into Monday-and-Thursday, and a few weeks later I started leaving Sarah with my sister so I wouldn't have to waste time getting her to sleep at Dave's. And it wasn't long after that the trouble started.

We were making good progress and the cartoons were going into the mail at a steady rate. Dave was giving me ideas that were increasingly difficult to render, and I was feeling better and better about how I seemed to be improving each day. One day I finished a cartoon while he was fixing something in the kitchen and stood up to look at it.

"Finished already?" he asked.

"Yep," I answered proudly, with a wave at the cartoon.

He came over and looked at it over my shoulder, then told me it was good, and I said something like, "Yeah, I know."

"Well, all right!" he shouted, grabbing me and giving me a hug.

I was beaming, and I felt good, and it was

nice to be appreciated like that. Nothing else happened that day. I left the cartoon with him and went to pick up Sarah, then went home--walking on air all the way.

At our next session he stood behind my chair and massaged my shoulders for a few minutes after I'd complained about becoming hunchbacked. And when I got ready to leave, he took both my hands in his and looked right into my eyes.

"Lynn, I have to tell you this straight out. I never expected that you'd actually be able to do this. To see my ideas going onto paper this way is very, very rewarding for me. The fact I get to work with one of the most beautiful women I know at the same time is just icing on the cake. Thanks."

I almost gave him a hug after that, but something stopped me. I only wish that the something that had stopped me had gone further-- had sent me running home with a vow never to return to his apartment. Maybe I was blinded by the thought of all that money. Maybe I wanted to believe that our relationship was 'strictly business'. And maybe I was just getting a little tired of Perry's non-stop sulk.

Dave was funny, intelligent, and very charming. He always had something complimen- tary to say, and after we started working together the things he said weren't the same kind of kidding around he'd done with me at the diner. Most of the time his compliments were about my skills as a cartoonist.

Once I got the hang of doing those things, I started adding little extras to the cartoons--things he hadn't thought of since they didn't have anything to do with the joke, but which really made the drawings a lot more interesting.

"You know what it is? You have a way of embellishing the drawing so the reader's eye is drawn to the central point," he told me one afternoon.

With those kind of comments coming at me three or four times a week, plus the occasional suggestion that I was beautiful, it was inevitable that I started thinking of him in a different light. And I guess he knew it because it seemed like the minute I started thinking that way, he began pouring it on even thicker.

I was just getting ready to go one afternoon when he kissed me for the first time. It was chilly out and I had brought a sweater. He was helping me with it, holding it by the shoulders while I put my arms in, and when I had it on, he wrapped his arms around me from behind and said, "You know, Lynn, I'm falling in love with you."

Then he kissed me very lightly on the cheek. I started to twist away from him, but somehow I just wound up facing him with his arms still wrapped around me. He kissed me on the mouth and my legs got kind of rubbery. I didn't exactly kiss him back, but I didn't try to twist away from him any more.

It wasn't a long kiss, but that didn't matter. The damage had been done. I had tasted him and I knew, in spite of everything I told myself, that I wanted more.

But I didn't make it easy for him. I didn't go to his apartment that Thursday, and when he asked me about it on Friday when he came to work, I just told him I had been too busy with Sarah. He let it drop, but I could tell he was thinking about it because he didn't come up with his usual string of jokes that night.

Saturday night was a different story. He was back to his usual self, joking with everyone, and telling me how beautiful I was when no one else was around. I began hoping that maybe the Monday incident would be forgotten and that we could, somehow, go on like before without all the entanglements.

So I went to see him the following Monday. I did have a lot of work to show him--things I'd managed to get done during the previous week-- and I figured that if things got too sticky I could just make it clear to him that I wasn't willing to jeopardize my marriage for a little fooling around with him.

Naturally, he was a perfect gentleman the

whole afternoon. He offered to help me on with my coat as I was leaving and was careful to not even touch me. I walked home feeling a little foolish for all the time I had spent rehearsing the things I would say to him if he tried to kiss me again.

Wednesday night Perry and I had a fight. It was one of those crazy, stupid things that started over nothing and ended only after we had covered everything. He accused me of being an uncaring mother, and in the next breath said I was trying to make him look foolish by making so much money. I told him he was just a pouty little boy, then followed that up with a comment about being sick of his macho attitudes. And of course we did all our 'shouting' through clenched teeth so we wouldn't wake the kids.

I guess every couple goes through that kind of thing now and then, finding the other's vulnerable spots and jabbing where they know it will hurt. It seems kind of insane when you look back on it, but it's very important at the time. In fact, it seemed important enough for us to sleep, or pretend to sleep, on opposite sides of the bed all night. I continued to pretend to sleep in the morning when he got up early and left for work.

When my sister called at ten that morning to ask if I was going to bring Sarah by her place, I just said yes without thinking I hadn't thought about going to Dave's--I had been too upset to work--but I guess I made up my mind on the spot. So I got Sarah ready and dropped her off, then walked to Dave's.

He greeted me at the door, wearing the biggest grin I had ever seen on anyone in my whole life.

"What?" I said, a little irritated at all the happiness he was exuding.

"Come in and see," was all he said, bowing deeply and waving me into the apartment.

There on the kitchen table was a bottle of champagne in a makeshift ice bucket, and propped against it was an envelope, a printed form, and a check.

I stopped in mid-step, afraid to go any closer, afraid to find out what it was. My heart was beating so fast I was sure he could hear it.

"What?" I asked again, my voice sounding strange in my suddenly dry throat.

"Look," was his answer.

I went over to the table and looked. The check was for fifteen dollars, but that didn't really count. The form letter was a release, giving the small magazine mentioned in the heading first publication rights to a cartoon I--we--had submitted.

"We made a sale," I finally said, reading the form for the third time.

"Yes, we made a sale. Now you may hold

the check next to your heart while I open the champagne."

I did as he suggested, and he started twisting the wire off the bottle. I was still holding the check there, like some little kid pledging her allegiance to the flag, when he picked up the filled glasses and turned to me. He looked down at the check, then back up to my face and said, "Lucky check."

Then he handed me one of the glasses, and we toasted our success and drank.

When the bottle was emptied of its bubbles I thought I was probably empty of giggles and shouts myself. I sat down on his couch and propped my feet up on his coffee table and grinned. He stood there pretending to wring the last drop out of the bottle into his glass. I had to close my eyes and lay my head back because I seemed to be getting a little dizzy.

"Unbelievable," I heard him say as though he was in another room. "A world-famous cartoonist *and* the most beautiful legs in the country."

I was already grinning so I didn't have to do anything else. I just sat there. Then I felt something on my leg and I opened my eyes, just a crack, to see what it was. It was Dave. He was kneeling beside me and he was kissing my bare leg just below the knee.

"Oh, Dave," I said. "Don't be silly."

When I felt his lips on my neck, I tried to push him away, but I didn't have much strength in my arms.

"Dave, this is wrong."

"How can something that feels so good be wrong?" he asked.

I couldn't think of an answer right away, so when he kissed my lips, I kissed him back. It felt very, very good; and suddenly I remembered the argument Perry and I had had the night before and decided that it served him right.

Dave didn't try anything fancy that afternoon. We just kissed, that's all. But by the time I got home with Sarah I was starting to feel pretty bad. I kept telling myself that Perry didn't appreciate me, and that I had a right to do whatever I pleased, but all my words sounded pretty hollow in my head.

I drank a lot of coffee that afternoon, though I didn't really need to sober up. It somehow helped to calm my nerves, though, and it gave me something to do with my hands. By the time Perry got home that evening I had at least convinced myself that there was no need to talk to him about any of this. After all, I had reasoned, it wasn't like I was having an affair with Dave--he had just kissed me a little, that was all. And I certainly didn't intend to repeat it.

Perry seemed to have mellowed out a little after our argument of the night before and his storming out of the house that morning. He didn't bring me flowers or anything like that. That wasn't his style, even in the days when our finances could take that kind of extravagance. But he was civil for the first time in weeks and even asked me how things were going with me at work. Fortunately, he didn't ask me about the cartooning, or I don't know what might have come out of my mouth. I told him a few funny stories about mishaps at the diner, and he smiled. But after dinner it was the paper and TV, as usual, and I had the funny feeling things were going to be all too normal around our house again.

I didn't see Dave at work that weekend. Someone told me that he was on vacation, and then another one of the waitresses remarked that she had heard he was going to spend a few days with his ex-wife.

I continued to work on the cartoons. I was getting the hang of it by now and had come up with a couple of ideas on my own that I wanted to try out. I didn't go by his apartment, though I did think about it. Somehow the idea of running into his ex was very distasteful to me, and I wasn't even sure I wanted to see him, either.

Then, on Friday, just as I was about to leave for my sister's and work, there was a knock at the door. It was Dave.

"Hi. Can I come in?"

"I'm just about ready to leave. I have to work today."

"Well, I haven't seen you in so long, I was wondering if you were okay," he said.

I wanted to tell him that *he* was the one who had been on vacation, and I also wanted to tell him that I thought it would be a good idea if we didn't work so closely together, but all I said was that I was fine.

"Well, I guess I'll see you later at work, then. Oh, do you have any cartoons for me?"

"No."

As I watched him walk away from the house, my head was buzzing with a hundred questions. Why hadn't I told him about the cartoons, and why had I been afraid to invite him in?

Fortunately, Sarah started demanding attention at that point and I was able to put my mind on other things.

The same kind of strained feeling between us continued that night at work. He wasn't nearly as funny as usual, and even some of the other waitresses noticed it. I overheard one of them discussing Dave with a regular customer, and from what I heard the gossip had to do with his ex-wife. Strangely enough, that suggestion upset me more than I would have expected.

Saturday was about the same, so I wasn't at all surprised when he took me back into the scullery at one point with the explanation that he had to talk to me. The dishwasher was on a break, and things were kind of slow, so we had the room to ourselves, but I was still kind of nervous about personal conversations there. Curiosity got the better of discretion, however, and I went with him.

"Lynn, I have to see you as soon as possible."

"Why?" I asked him.

"I can't explain now. Please, promise me you'll come by my place as soon as you can. I need to talk."

He stressed the 'talk' and I decided to trust him, so I agreed to come on Monday, as usual. He didn't say thanks or anything, just nodded his head and went back to the kitchen. I didn't know what to make of it.

On the following Monday, I was careful to dress in the most unflattering outfit I could find. Pants, baggy sweater, sneakers, the whole bit. And I didn't put on any makeup. I knew I had done right when my sister asked me if I was sick as I dropped off Sarah.

"No, I just have some work to do," I told her.

Dave didn't waste a minute once I got to his

place. I could tell by the sick look on his face that he was really upset about something--he didn't even seem to notice how ratty I looked. But he took me by the shoulders and looked right into my eyes, and let me have it with both barrels.

"Lynn, I can't take any more of this. I've been strung out for days, trying to think things through, and I just can't. I can't do anything but think of you.

"Lynn, I need you. I want you. I love you."

I just stared at him, dumbfounded, not able to think of a single thing to say. I remember thinking later that if he had talked like he usually did, with lots of flowery phrases and rational arguments, I might have been able to keep a conversation going, and might have been able to avoid what happened next. But what could I say to such brief, and surprising, declarations? I think I started to remind him that I was married, but when I opened my mouth he closed it immediately with a kiss.

I don't have any ready excuses for what happened next. Call it chemistry or whatever, it just happened. No, we didn't make love, but I guess you could say we might as well have.

By the time I got home that afternoon, I was aching and tired...and feeling guilty. The walk to my sister's and then to my house usually woke me up, invigorated me, made me feel good. But on that day I only wanted to slip into a hot tub of water and soak my aching muscles and bruised conscience. Unfortunately, Sarah had had a good long nap, and Timmy was due home from school soon, so I had to make do with changing into my bathrobe.

Then Perry walked through the door, about twenty minutes late, and one look at his face sent guilt, and pain, and some other emotions I couldn't define rushing through my body. My minor ache were forgotten as I watched him slump down on the couch.

"Let me get you a beer, hon," I said, going into the kitchen.

He took the beer like a little kid who was being forced to drink his milk, and just sat there holding it. I just knew he was going to tell me he had lost his job, or something like that.

"You want to talk?"

He just shook his head, then mumbled something that sounded like 'later'. I went to fix dinner.

The stony, stubborn silence continued through dinner and through the kids' bath and bedtime story. The TV didn't go on, and the newspaper was ignored. I was in such a state by the time I joined him in the living room, I wasn't sure I was going to be able to keep from screaming.

I sat down beside him on the couch and waited. After a few minutes, he turned toward me, moving away a little so he could look at me, I guess, then he lifted one hand in the air and opened his mouth like he was going to speak. Then hand dropped and his mouth closed and I just couldn't stand it any more.

"Perry, what is it?" I demanded.

"You," he finally said. You and--the cook."

The ice water in my veins should have made me shiver, but I was too numb to shiver. I just sat there, staring at him.

"You're having an affair with him, aren't you?"

I tried to think of something to say, of some way to deny it. It was true, I thought, that I had never been to bed with him, that I had never let him make love to me. But wasn't it also true that I was having "an affair" with him? My body was frozen in shock.

Then I noticed the two tears running from his eyes down his cheeks. I reach out a hand, wanting to stop the flow with my finger.

"Oh, Perry."

The dam burst then. With a choking sob, he gave in to the tears and they came gushing out. His body started shaking with the short, barking, cries t hat accompanied his tears, and my hands flew to my face, to hide the shame I knew must be evident there.

I wanted to tell him it wasn't so, to assure him that I was still his wife. But then he started talking between his sobs. He told me that he felt it was his fault. That if he had been able to make enough money, I wouldn't have had to work. He told me he felt rotten about keeping a beautiful woman like me cooped up in the house all the time, and confessed t hat he had been scared someone would steal me away from him.

I held him in my arms and let him dry his tears on my bathrobe. And I told him a few things. I told him that he was the sweetest, most loving husband a woman could hope to have, and that no one could ever take me away from him. I told him that I had been feeling guilty about the fun I had with Dave, and that I was never going to see him again. I even told him that we had managed to put enough in savings for me to quit my job.

I didn't tell him any of the details of my relationship with Dave--that kind of information wouldn't have helped either of us. I didn't remind him of his sulky behavior, either, because I had been thinking for some time that I had discovered my own sense of humor, and that it would become my job to get him out of those moods instead of trying to avoid them.

Then he told me some things--personal things--and I told him some. Then we went to bed. He was tender and sweet, and very, very good.

Later, as I watched him sleep, I wondered why I had ever thought that kissing a stranger could compare with the love I had right here at home.

And as I drifted off to sleep a little later I sent a silent prayer of thanks to the unknown person--call him or her a gossip if you want to--who carried the news to Perry, and helped to put an end to a foolish relationship that could have led to nothing more than pain and suffering for everyone concerned.

CAN'T YOU SEE HOW MUCH
I LOVE YOU?

As I look back on it, it seems to me that the day that changed my life in so many ways was a very ordinary day. It felt just like a regular school day to me--time to drag myself through another round of activities that had been pretty much the same for as long as I could remember. Get out of bed, wash myself, have a little breakfast, walk up the driveway to wait for Emma.

I could have had a car of my own if I had wanted it badly enough, but I really didn't need one. All of my friends had cars and some of them hardly ever drive them because we would all wind up riding with Emma or Didi anyway--they had the really nice cars. I rode to school with Emma every morning, as did one or two others. She lived a little farther up the hill than I did passed my house, at least on those days she bothered to go home, every morning and evening. And since we were in the same classes and took the same activities (choral, drama, art) our schedules were exactly the same. So why bother Daddy with a request for a car of my own? I could always drive Maxie's car if I had to go somewhere in an emergency, anyway.

Maxie is my stepmother. She and Daddy married about a year after my mom died and we got along just fine. I thought she was a little scattered and maybe drank too much, but she was nice to me--and to Daddy--so those little things were easy to overlook. And with me having my own apartment in the backyard, we didn't see each other all that much anyway.

My apartment is one of the reasons Emma spent a lot of time at my place. I don't remember how it got to be in our backyard, so far up the hill like that, but it was there ever since I could remember. When I started high school, it became mine. It wasn't a building, exactly, and that was part of the charm. I mean, how many girls could say they lived in a railroad car? Yes, a real one. Daddy was active in community theater, and the car was an old prop. Of course, by the time I had been living in it a year, there wasn't much about the inside of it that looked like a railroad car, but the outside was still pretty much the same. Inside, I had fixed it up to suit myself. Daddy had built a bathroom into one end of it, with a small shower stall and a stool, and the rest of it was just a bedroom, really.

I had lots of room for my painting--I liked doing pen-and-ink drawings mostly--and a desk for writing and studying, and lots of pillows strewn around the place. Emma slept on the carpeted floor with a pile of pillows around her so often I had taken to kidding her about charging her rent. We had a lot of good times together.

Anyway, the day that started changing everything was just like an ordinary day. Emma picked me up at the mailbox right on time, and we went to school

"You want to skip home ec today?" she asked me as we got to school that morning.

"Why?"

"No particular reason. It's just so boring."

"We'll see," I told her.

Of course, if I had known what was going to happen that day, I would have skipped home ec-- and the rest of our classes--and stayed home. But we hadn't been told about the speaker who was visiting our class that day, and Emma had forgotten about skipping when the time rolled around, so we just went to class as usual. As soon as Mrs. Johnson showed up, with a strange woman in tow, we knew we were in for a break in the routine and the class started buzzing with speculation.

The visitor turned out to be Betty Woodward from the USO. She had come to the school to invite us girls to do volunteer work as "junior hostesses" at her club for servicemen. She made it sound like a fun way to spend an evening-- meeting new men and making them feel a little less lonely so far from their homes. It didn't interest me all that much, even though I didn't have a steady boyfriend at the time, but Emma was turned on from the very first.

"Let's do it," she whispered to me while Betty Woodward was still talking.

"Why? What about Arnie?"

"It would serve him right if I find someone else," she said with a pout that almost made me laugh.

Emma had been dating Arnie since the start of her junior year, but everyone knew that he was kind of fickle. Usually she didn't mind all that much (she wasn't exactly True Blue Sue herself) but lately she had been acting like she expected more from him. I guess she saw this USO thing as a way to make him a little jealous.

Emma couldn't talk about anything else the rest of the week, and by Friday afternoon I had agreed to go with her. Two other girls in our choral group had also agreed to go, so the four of us made the drive to the club that Friday night.

As Emma drove into the parking lot of the place, I got a very funny feeling in the pit of my stomach. There were a lot of guys walking around the place and they looked hungry. I mean, the boys at high school go that look once in a while, usually when they were in a group, of course; but these guys seemed older, wiser, and hungrier than anyone I had ever seen before. I guess the uniforms did it. About half of them were wearing uniforms, but you could tell that even the ones who weren't should have been. There was something about their looks that gave them away. And they all swaggered. Yes, really. There was something about their walk that let you know they were exactly as Betty Woodward had described them--scared little boys too far away from home. They didn't feel comfortable and they tried to hide it by acting brave.

Unfortunately, I didn't feel any more comfortable than they looked. I was really nervous about it as we walked through the front door of the place. Someone let out a low whistle, and someone else said, "All right!" in a way that made me want to make a mad dash to the car and get the heck out of there. But the other girls kept walking and I kept walking with them.

Betty saw us come in and rushed out of her office to greet us. She took us back to her office and had us take seats on the couch and chairs there, then purposely closed the door on the many staring eyes that had followed us.

"Well, girls. Thank you for coming tonight. I recognize a few of your faces, but I can't remember your names. If you will fill out these forms, I'll fill you in on your duties."

While we filled in the forms, she kept talking, telling us things she hadn't bothered to include in her presentation at the high school. The one thing she said that first night that really impressed me was that we'd soon learn that most servicemen were long on talk and short on action. She also had a few rules to explain to us--like the fact that we were not allowed to leave the club until we were ready to go home, and we were not to allow any of the servicemen to kiss us in the club. She explained that our volunteer work would be to mix with the servicemen and be companionable--make coffee, play cards with them, dance, or just talk about home.

"That last item is probably the most important of all the things you'll do," she said. "These boys are, for the most part, away from home for the first time in their lives. To get a conversation started with any one of them, you need only ask 'Where are you from?' and they'll take it from there. You'll probably spend a lot of your time looking at pictures of families and girlfriends, and listening to tales of what things are like back in the hills of Tennessee or the wilds of Minnesota.

"If you approach this experience as a way to learn about other parts of the country, other customs, I think you'll find it very rewarding and well worth your time."

Then we were being whisked out of the office and back onto the floor of the club and shown around.

I was about to head for the kitchen, thinking

that making coffee would give me something to do until my nerves calmed down, when a young man asked me to dance. I accepted, and found myself being led to the dance hall by a very sweaty hand. Through the last minute of the song playing from a juke box in the corner, he never once looked in my eyes. When the song was over, I asked him where he was from and, just as Betty had predicted, I spent the next three or four songs sitting on one of the folding chairs listening to him tell me all about his hometown.

I danced with Joe (they had called him "Joey" back home, he had told me, but he preferred Joe) again, and then danced with two other young men before I got a chance to check on the coffeepot in the kitchen.

Emma passed through, clearly having a great time, while I was making coffee, but I hadn't seen much of the other two who had come with us. I was beginning to think that this could prove to be a nice experience after all. Then, as I left the kitchen and began walking through the card-playing area back to the front of the club, I was introduced to Tad.

One of the boys I had danced with was standing in a group of about four or five near one of the tables, and he reached out and took hold of my arm as I passed. Pulling me over to the group, he said, "Tad, this is Pattie. First night."

"Well, hello, Pattie. I'm very pleased to

247

meet you."

He offered his hand and I took it, smiling. His hand was dry, his eye was steady as he looked into my eyes, and there was a warmth about him that made me feel immediately comfortable.

The rest of the group he had been talking with had stepped back slightly and were now watching us, and just as I began to realize this, the boy who had introduced us said, "Tad is our official welcoming committee."

Tad blinked his eyes and seemed to be distracted by this comment. He said, "Oh." Then another "Oh!" I felt like something had been said which I was not supposed to understand, and a second later I found out that was exactly what had happened. Tad took me by the hand he was still holding and led me to empty table, then indicated by raising my hand that I was to climb onto the chair, then the table. Three or four of the other boys had started to chant something, and a moment later I heard someone strumming a guitar in the same rhythm. I looked around the group, wondering what in the world was going on, and spotted Betty leaning on the counter outside her office. She was watching us with an amused smile on her face, and seeing her apparently uncon- cerned about the goings-on, I decided to go along with whatever it was.

What it was, was a ritual of sorts that had been going on for a year or so every time I new hostess came into the club. When I was finally standing on the table, Tad released my hand, then struck a dramatic pose, pointed up at me, and launched into a sort of song about a young girl who was seduced by an older man.

It was supposed to be a sort of a ballad, titled 'Have Some Madeira, My Dear' but he had turned it into a kind of a pantomime, with gestures and looks that drew laughter from the crowd that surrounded us. At one point he climbed onto the chair and put his arm around my waist, urging me closer to him. His head was at my shoulder so I sort of leaned against him, and he nuzzled me in response. When he reached a line that went "she let go her glass with a shy little cry", he looked at me expectantly, and I tried my best to respond. What came out was more of a croak than a cry, but our audience ate it up, and he had to take a few more beats before going on.

When the song was over, he helped me off the table and thanked me rather profusely for being such a good sport, then he asked me to dance. As he took me in his arms on the dance floor, surrounded by a crowd of still-smiling faces, I felt like I owned the world. I think I would have done anything Tad asked of me at that moment. As it was, he asked nothing of me.

"You know, you're the first girl ever who has done that little cry. Most times, the girls are too embarrassed to even think, let alone respond like that. You really made it work."

"I could have done even better if I had known what was coming," I suggested. "But I loved it anyway."

I didn't get to see much more of him that evening. We danced a few times, but he had other duties to attend to, and we were frequently interrupted. He was head of the servicemen's committee of the USO, and spent a lot of time with Betty Woodward, planning activities and doing publicity and stuff like that. But that night, on our way back home, I learned a lot more about him. Emma h ad asked some guy about Tad, and had gotten an earful.

"He's a smooth operator, Pattie," she said. "Apparently there hasn't been one hostess at that place he hasn't been with, and I'm not talking about just dancing. Kevin told me some tales that would make your hair stand on end--without benefit of mousse."

"And how does Kevin know all this?"

"They're in the same outfit," she informed me. "Kevin says all the guys know about his reputation. I'd steer clear of him, if I were you."

I tried fitting Tad into the picture she had drawn, courtesy of Kevin, and a lot of it didn't fit. I was beginning to think of him as a sort of Cool Hand Luke, putting on a bit of a show for his buddies now and then, but really wishing they would just leave him alone deep down inside. I didn't say anything to Emma, though. I just let her go on with her tales and pretended to be convinced.

Emma and Joan and I went back the following Friday. Didi said she wasn't interested. Tad was already there when we arrived, and he asked me for a dance right away. While we danced he told me about a plan he and Betty were working on for a variety show at the club. He asked me if I would help him plan it, and recruit some talent for the show. I agreed, and told him I would sing, and get Emma to play her flute. When the dance was over, he took me to Betty's office, leaving the door open, to talk about it. Hostesses weren't allowed to be in a closed room with any of the servicemen (that's why the TV room was off-limits) but sitting in Betty's office on the couch, we were out of sight of everyone in the place, and I wondered if he'd try anything.

He didn't, and after about twenty minutes of talking about the show, I began to suspect that Emma's warning was totally unfounded. Betty came into the office while we were talking and acted like she didn't even know we were there until Tad spoke to her. I put her attitude together with what I felt, and decided that I had been right to ignore what Emma had told me.

"Pattie is going to help with the show," Tad said to Betty as she was about to leave the office with some papers.

"Oh, good. Have you set a date yet?"

"Not yet. I want to see how many acts we can line up, t hen figure how much time we'll need for rehearsals."

"Okay. Let me know. And thanks, Pattie."

When Betty had left, Tad suggested that we exchange phone numbers so we could talk things over outside the club. I asked him if he was going to give me his office number (he worked in some office on the military base) and he told me he had an apartment in town and that the number he was giving me was that number. I had thought that single sailors stayed on the base, and told him so.

"Oh, I have a bunk in the barracks," he said, "and I stay there on the nights when I have duty. But I like my privacy, and you can't get that in a barrack."

I put his phone number in my purse and waited, expectantly, for him to suggest he show me his apartment, but he never did. My confidence in him was growing. When we danced, he held me close, and feeling our bodies together was very nice. And once in a while he would nuzzle the side of my face and even press his lips to my hair. But off the dance floor he was all business, more concerned with the variety show than anything else. Oh, we talked about personal things now and then, but it was always friendly, not intimate.

Two more weeks went by before things

started changing with us. Emma and I started coming to the club on Friday and Saturday nights-- she was beginning to enjoy all the attention--and sometimes Joan came with us, but not with the same dedication Emma and I were feeling. Of course, I didn't let on to Emma what my true intentions were. She thought the time I spent with Tad was 'strictly business' and I never said anything to let her think otherwise. Truthfully, except for the feelings that were growing in me, that was the case anyway. That is, it was the case until that Saturday night.

Tad had called me at home a few times to ask about girls I had mentioned as prospects for the show, and I had called him once, though I never connected with him. That Saturday morning he called when I was out in my apartment. Daddy had installed a little buzzer in the railroad car that he or Maxie used to call me to the house, and he buzzed me when Tad called. I was changing my clothes when Tad called, and it took longer than usual to get to the house, but Daddy was still on the phone, talking with Tad.

"Here she is," Daddy said. "Nice talking with you."

He handed me the phone and then walked off. I sat down in the chair, and Tad and I talked about the show for a while, and I agreed to try to come early that night. After we were through, I called Emma and told her about Tad's request, and she said she would be willing to go early, so we set a time.

"Nice young man, your Tad," Daddy commented when I was through talking to Emma.

"Yes," I said, kind of surprised. Daddy didn't often comment on my friends, and I was curious. "What did you two talk about?"

"Oh, he just told me a little about this show you're working on. Said you were a big help."

"Oh."

"Why don't you invite him to dinner some night?" Maxie put in. Daddy nodded in agreement.

"Well, I'll see," I told them.

Daddy's and Maxie's acceptant attitude was still in my mind late that afternoon when Emma and I arrived at the club and found Tad waiting there. Emma went on in as Tad led me aside.

"Betty is going to be tied up in her office most of the evening," he told me, "so I asked her if it would be okay for us to have our meeting at my place. Okay with you?"

"Sure."

I told Emma about the arrangement, and she gave me a long, hard look--which I chose to ignore as I hurried back to Tad, who was waiting at the front for me.

Hi apartment was on the outskirts of town,

just about six blocks from the club, and we probably could have walked there, but he drove us. It was a fairly new car, clean and shiny, and I wondered how he cold afford it on his pay, but I didn't ask. The apartment looked just like his car- -new and shiny without much in the way of decor.

"Would you like a glass of wine?" he asked as he deposited his papers on the kitchen table.

I almost asked him if we were now rehearsing his little 'welcome the new girl' pantomime, but I didn't. I just said, "Yes, that would be nice."

When we had the whole show arranged to suit us, he asked me if I could like to dance. I said yes.

We danced for a while, holding each other even closer than we did at the club, and it didn't take much maneuvering on his part when it came time for us to share our first kiss. I was ready. In fact, I had been ready for weeks, but I tried not to appear too eager. It was wonderful. His lips were warm and moist and he didn't rush it at all. He took his time, tasting my lips, brushing my cheek, nibbling at my neck.

We stood there in the almost-empty living room, kissing each other, for what seemed like hours. His hands stayed on my back and shoulders, caressing me with a tenderness that left my body aching for more; but just like that first kiss, he didn't rush anything. The record kept playing over and over, but I didn't really hear the music, anyway. We were making our own music.

Just about the time my legs were beginning to give out, he finally spoke. "I want you, Pattie."

It didn't take but a second of thought on my part before I answered him. "I want you, too, Tad."

He was prepared to make love, and it was wonderful. He was gentle and considerate, just as he had been while we were kissing. There was nothing else in the world for me while I was with him in that bed.

My next conscious thought was that someone had turned out the light, then I realized that Tad and I had fallen asleep. We were still in each other's arms, but it was pitch-black outside. I twisted around to see if there was a clock in the room, but there was none. My movements disturbed Tad, though, and he came fully awake in an instant.

"Oh! Damn! I'm sorry, Pattie."

"That's all right. I was asleep, too. I wonder what time it is."

He found his watch. "Almost two," he said with a groan. "Boy, what are your parents going to think?"

"Don't worry about it. They're asleep by now, anyway. I'll call them in the morning."

"Are you sure?"

I pulled him closer to me for an answer, and a moment later I heard his watch drop to the carpet. I had made my decision.

The next morning he was clearly embarrassed about having kept me out all night, but he seemed reassured after I called home and talked to Daddy. I told Daddy that we had been working late and that I had decided to spend the night at the USO with Betty instead of coming home. Daddy thanked me for calling and asked when I'd be home. Tad had said he would drive me any time, so I told Daddy we would be there around two that afternoon.

"God, I love you," he said, taking me in his arms as I hung up the phone. "I can't believe how...how comfortable I am with you. As you probably heard, I've been around, but I've never been so at ease with a woman in my life."

With that declaration out of the way, Tad returned to his usual confident demeanor, and started making a pot of coffee. He offered to take me out for breakfast, or to pick us up some donuts. I told him the donuts would be just fine, and he rushed out with a promise to be back in a flash. While he was gone I washed up and looked around his small apartment. There was a small gold statue of a Buddha--he later told me a story about how he'd bought it while on a cruise in Japan--on his stereo, and that gave me an idea for a drawing, or maybe a pair of drawings.

I was pouring coffee when Tad returned. He

warmed the donuts in the oven, and we shared the first of what I hoped would be many breakfasts. Afterward, we went back to work on the show, and called a few people to confirm their acts, then we left to go to my house.

Tad and Daddy hit it off right away, and the four of us sat in the living room talking for quite a while before I took Tad to my railroad car apartment. I showed him some of my artwork, just to get his reaction without letting him know what I had in mind, and we talked--mostly about me. He was fascinated by my apartment and the relation-ship I had with my parents, and said he hoped that he would be able to be as free and open with his children some day.

I had finished the new drawings, each depicting a Japanese woman in formal dress and holding musical instruments, by Wednesday of the following week, my fingers moving across the paper with loving inspiration, and I signed them to him, with love. I spent Thursday after school getting them framed behind non-glare glass, in simple black wood frames that would look very nice against his plain white walls.

That Friday night he was very curious as I transferred the wrapped package containing the pictures from Emma's trunk to his car, but I told him he would have to wait until we got to his apartment. When he unwrapped them his eyes filled with tears and he held me so closely I thought he'd crack a few ribs.

I spent that entire weekend with him, and Saturday afternoon when we started rehearsals for the show everyone in the club seemed to have reached an understanding that Tad and I were a couple.

Things got progressively more busy. We held some rehearsals in Tad's apartment and my position as hostess there was recognized by everyone.

I guess that's what made it all the harder for me to take the grim reality that fell upon my head the night of the show. Tad had called for a night of rest for everyone on the Friday before the show, and hadn't even suggested that we get together that night. I stayed home, running through the song I was going to perform one last time, and wondering what life with Tad was going to be like when the show was over. We would certainly have more time for each other, and I fully expected that there would be some changes--in quantity if not in quality--within our relationship.

By an hour before show time, I began to get a little worried about the fact Tad wasn't there at the club. Finally, with just a half hour to go, Tad and Kevin burst into the club in a rush. Tad looked wonderful in his rented tux, but I could tell the moment I walked up to him that something was very, very wrong. Of course, club rules being what they were, we never even held hands unless we were dancing.

The audience out front was noisy and it was hard to hear each other backstage without shouting, but I heard Tad and Kevin arguing about something near the stage. Kevin was urging Tad to do something, and Tad kept protesting. Then Kevin said something to another serviceman nearby, and he and Kevin each grabbed Tad by an arm and literally dragged him on stage. Someone else pulled the curtain, and Kevin held up his hand for a cessation of the applause that was thundering through the hall. Finally, it got quiet enough for Kevin to speak, and we all listened with interest to this unexpected departure from the well-rehearsed opening of the show.

"Before we get things underway, I have an announcement," Kevin shouted. "Tad and I were a little late getting here tonight, because we were in Las Vegas less than twelve hours ago. No, we didn't go there to gamble. We went there for Tad's wedding!"

And with that, Kevin took Tad's hand and raised it, with its plain gold band on the third finger.

I felt as though someone had driven a dagger of ice into my heart. My eyes wouldn't focus, and my legs turned to rubber. I felt a strong arm around my shoulders, and I guess it was Emma who led me to a chair against the wall and sat me down.

"Pattie!--Pattie!" I heard someone call from a long way off.

Finally, I saw Emma's face in front of mine, and the look of concern in her eyes brought me back to my senses. I took a deep breath and tried to smile, not sure if I had actually succeeded, but Emma seemed to relax a little.

"Oh, Pattie, I'm so sorry," she said.

I guess at that point I would have preferred an 'I told you so'. Sympathy wouldn't help me pull myself together. And that's what I needed to do because I decided I couldn't let anyone, especially Tad, see that the news had shaken me. I looked up to see Tad leaving the stage, leading the applause for the first act. He was walking backward toward us, so I couldn't see his face, but the message that picture sent me was loud and clear--the show must go on.

"I'll be okay. I think I'll go to the washroom," I told Emma.

"I'll come with you."

"No, I'll be okay. You get your flute ready. You're number three, remember?"

"You sure?"

"Pucker," I told her as I started for the washroom.

In the washroom I splashed a little cold

261

water on my face, then dabbed at my eyes with a paper towel to do the least amount of damage to my makeup that I could. A few deep breaths calmed the fluttering in my stomach. As I stood there I knew that I had to do something--anything--to take charge of myself. I would not allow myself to be beaten by his betrayal. Suddenly, I knew what I had to do.

I found Tad near the stage and planted myself in front of him. The second act had just started, and I knew I had a minute or two.

"Tad, I'm going to change my number."

The look in his eyes almost ruined my resolve. There was apology there, which was sort of expected, but there was also something else I couldn't quite define. Hurt, maybe. I wasn't sure.

"Sure, Pattie. Anything you way to do is fine."

It was just as well he hadn't asked me what I was going to change to. It would be better, I decided, if he got the full impact of it while I was on the stage. I had planned to do an upbeat number, and I wasn't feeling very upbeat. The other song I had thought of in the washroom was far more appropriate. When Emma went out to do her flute solo I checked with our pianist to let her know about the change and to see if she knew the number. It wouldn't have made any difference--I would have done it a capella if I had to.

It went over well. Just as I started the song,

I could see that Tad had registered the fact that I was singing directly to him, and the look of dismay on his face was reward enough for the pain I was feeling. I sang my heart out and it felt good. I milked the applause at the end, forcing Tad into a kind of hesitation walk back onto the stage. Then I gave him a defiant look as I relinquished my position and walked briskly past him to stage left.

    I learned later--from Emma of course--that the woman he married had never been connected with the club. That was a relief to me. I was grateful that I wouldn't have to remember her face smiling at me during that period I had been taken in by his charm. She told me it was rumored that the woman was pregnant, but that sounded to me like a rather flimsy explanation for the hurry-up nature of the wedding.

    When I told Daddy and Maxie about it, Daddy simply asked me how I felt.

    I think it was about three months after the show that he called. We were just finishing dinner, and Daddy answered the phone. He sounded very amiable as he said, "Well, hello, Tad."

    He cupped his hand over the mouthpiece and gave me a raised-eyebrows look. I scowled and didn't move.

    "No, I'm sorry, but she's not here at the moment, Tad. Don't I remember hearing that you had gotten married? . . .Oh, I'm sorry to hear that.

A divorce so soon? . . .Oh, she did, eh? Well, that's too bad. . . .Another hitch in the Navy, eh? How long? . .Four years. I see.. . . No, I don't know when she'll be back. I'll tell you what, though. Why don't you give us a call when you get out of the Navy in four years? . . . You bet, Tad. Good-bye."

I practically flew across the room into Daddy's arms. And I was laughing so hard I was almost crying. Daddy had always let me make my own way, make my own mistakes, and make up my own mind. I never realized until that moment that he knew me so well.

"Oh, Daddy, I couldn't have said it better myself. Remind me to be in Timbuktu four years from now, will you?"

Maxi joined us and we stood there in a three-way hug for a long time, chuckling and sighing.

There have been times since then when I've wondered how it would have been with Tad and me if he hadn't gotten married. We had been good together, but I realized that we hadn't really had all that much experience. Our relationship had taken place in a very limited world, and I hadn't really known that much about him before I made my physical commitment to him. A little older, and much wiser now, I don't think I'll allow myself to make that kind of mistake again.

ROMANTIC AFFAIR

You'd think that with all the jokes, all the stories, all the plays and movies that have been created around that old like, 'My wife just doesn't understand me', it would take somebody pretty darn dumb to fall for it.

Well, I'm not exactly dumb, but I sure fell for it--hook, line, and sinker.

In my sophomore year in high school my school counselor suggested hat since my math grades were so good, I should take courses in typing and economics and prepare myself for a career in business. That sounded like a really good idea to me at the time, so I did what she suggested. When I graduated, I had a job waiting for me.

We had one of those "Career Days", where representatives from the business community came to our school and held group interviews. I had been impressed by one woman who was the Personnel Manager for the railroad, Molly Howard. At that time I didn't even realize there were different railroads in the country, and to hear her talk, there weren't. She did such a good job of selling that I was convinced that going to work for her company would be the next best thing to being President of the United States.

I didn't bother looking any further after I heard Molly Howard talk. I waited around until everyone else had left, then I went up to the teacher's desk where she was sitting and spoke to her.

She invited me to sit down with her right then. We only had about five minutes before the next group started filtering in, but she made an appointment right there on the spot for me to come in for a personal interview .

The following week I went in at the appointed time, and took a typing test. I probably wouldn't have been so nervous if I'd known that she already had copies of all my schoolwork; but I guess I did okay, anyway, because after the test we had a long talk about the various departments in the company. When she got through with that, she suggested that I would probably be better off starting in the secretarial pool. The way she put it, I would get to see a number of departments up close and personal, and then I could decide which one of them I wanted to go into permanently.

It sounded good to me. Then she said I could start at the end of June. That gave me only about three weeks of summer vacation, but she pointed out that summer was the best time to start because I would get more work, filling in for people taking their own summer vacations.

So, like I said, I had my job--and my career--all lined up before I even graduated. Two other girlfriends of mine, Fran and Marianne, had also been promised jobs after their interviews, and the three of us did quite a lot of strutting around during the last few weeks of school. Of course, the other girls tried to play down our good fortune by telling us we were set in our choices, while they were keeping their options open. But we didn't listen to any of that--we knew we had our careers set for us.

It didn't take me very long on the job to discover that I had been 'railroaded' into the same sort of entry-level position that nearly everyone with little or no experience starts at. The personnel manager, Molly Howard, had made it sound so glamorous and so opportunistic--and that was, of course, her job. But I didn't feel much resentment. I was getting better money than I had hoped for, and there really were lots of opportunities.

My first month was a combination of excitement and drudgery. There were lots of new things to learn, from how to find the cafeteria to the proper formats for various kinds of letters, and that was the exciting part. There were also a lot of hours in which I had nothing to do except some-how manage to look like I was busy. I finally found some manuals on the company and started reading during my slow times, but that was so much like what I had just left in high school that it was hard to get enthusiastic about it.

The high point of my week, during those first few months, came on Saturday mornings. Fran, Marianne, and I had agreed that we would meet at ten o'clock every Saturday at the Burgerworld near school. The purpose of this meeting, we all told each other, was to keep each other up to date on our jobs. What none of us admitted out loud was that the real purpose of those meetings was to impress anyone else who happened to see us--professional women having our little business meeting. We wore our work clothes rather than the jeans and sloppy sweaters we would have normally worn, and which everyone else was wearing, of course, and we drank coffee instead of sodas.

The conversation was very conservative, concerning banks, sales, marketing, and tons of freight.

I didn't realize it at the time, but an even more significant benefit of those Saturday meetings was that we were giving each other support for sticking with our boring entry-level jobs during those difficult early days.

If I had had any inkling of what my professional career was going to be like, I'm sure I would have left that table immediately, put on a pair of jeans, gotten Jerry to marry me, and started raising kids right then and there. But I didn't, of course, and the track I was on kept me right there until it was too late.

We all had boyfriends. Jerry and I had been dating since we were juniors. Fran and Bobby were dating off and on, and Marianne was already engaged to Brent. Saturday nights we'd go out--sometimes even triple dating--and do things that all the rest of the crowd was doing. But even that seemed tame to us after graduation and I could sense we didn't have much time before our jobs, or our relationships, or both,, would be breaking up the gang.

The first time I worked for Mr. Charley I didn't even know who he was. I had come to work one Thursday morning and been told to report to Lisa Smithson on the fifth floor. When I got there, she started showing me where things were in her little cubbyhole office, and it took me a while to catch on that I would be filling in for her. She was taking a one-week vacation and I was to be available to her boss, Mr. Charley, to answer phones, and to try to not get anything out of place, as she so nicely put it. When Friday rolled around, I was so sure I would botch the job I almost cancelled our Saturday morning meeting in favor of sneak-ing into the office to practice the things Lisa had shown me.

Monday morning I was as nervous as I

could be. I just knew I was going to make a mess of things. When Mr. Charley buzzed me I almost fell off my chair, then I made him wait while I tried to decide if I was supposed to go into his office or pick up the phone. I couldn't locate my dictation pad right away, so I finally opted for picking up the phone.

"Would you get me a cup of coffee, dear?" he said as soon as I got on the line.

"Yes, sir," I told him, relieved that I wouldn't have to do any real work. Lisa had left me a little list of important personal things to remember. 'Coffee--black' headed the list. And she had shown me where to get it. Not from the cafeteria where we ate, but from a special coffee cart on that floor.

I took his coffee to him and set it on his desk, then took the chair he waved me into. He was talking into a Dictaphone and I watched in fascination, wondering why I hadn't thought to ask Lisa anything about how he dictated letters and so forth. When he was finished he turned to me.

"I'm sorry, dear. I've forgotten your name."

"Oh! It's Abby, sir."

"Abby. Let me guess. Lisa didn't tell you that I won't be using you for dictation, right?"

I wondered if he was some kind of mind-reader, and I was so nervous, I just shook my head.

"I thought not. Lisa is a very competent secretary. A very goal-oriented girl. She doesn't bother herself with what isn't--too busy focusing on what is. And that suits me. I have many other things that need to be done by her--and by you for this week, Abby--to use you on something as mundane as dictation. That's why we have a word-processing department.

"When you find one of these," he took the cassette tape out of the machine and dropped it into his out basket, "in the out basket, just pop it into an envelope, address it to them, and let the mailroom boy take it from there."

He went on for another ten minutes like that, explaining things he wanted done, some of which Lisa had already told me about. Then he dismissed me and turned back to his desk as though I was already out of the room.

And that's the way the whole week went. By Friday night I was so pooped I just wanted to crawl into bed and sleep for a week. I don't think Fran or Marianne got in three words edgewise during our Saturday morning meeting.

Going back to the pool on Monday morning was a real letdown for me. The boredom was magnified by the exciting time I had had the week before. But I had learned some very important things that soon put an end to the boredom. For one thing, I'd found that I really didn't know the company as well as I thought I did from reading those manuals. So I started finding ways to visit various departments, and I asked a lot of questions. I found out that almost everyone likes to talk about their job if the person asking the questions approaches them in the right way. A few well-placed questions can get you a lot of information in a hurry.

During the next three or four months I got a good education. And every time I got a call to fill in for someone on vacation or out sick, I managed the job just a little bit better than I had done on the one before. I was becoming well known, and I was finally getting a handle on what was going on where in the company. So I wasn't surprised when my supervisor told me Mr. Charley wanted to see me.

"Hi Abby," Lisa greeted me. "Go right on in. He's expecting you."

Mr. Charley, as usual, wasted little time. "Abby, good to see you. I've just been handed a piece of bad news. Lisa will be leaving us soon. I was impressed with the work you did for me earlier this year, and I've also had good reports on you from other departments. Would you like the job?"

I didn't need to think about it for even a second.

"Yes, sir," I said.

"Good." He reached for the phone, punched three numbers, then said, Merry, it's Bill Charley.

Abby Hull will be starting tomorrow morning...
yes, I'll send her down to you right now. Thanks."

He put the phone back, wrote something on
a form sitting in a file that was lying open on his
desk. Then he closed the file, handed it to me, and
told me to see Merry in the personnel office. The
file was my personnel file, and I couldn't resist a
quick scan of it as I rode the elevator down to the
first floor. My salary was going to be four
hundred dollars a month higher--starting the very
next day! Talk about a high! I don't think I
touched the floor with my feet the rest of the day.

I worked with Lisa the rest of that week and
all of the next, making sure I was familiar with the
work in progress. My efforts at learning what was
what in the previous months paid off very well.
Even Lisa was impressed when I frequently interrupted her explanations to tell her what already I
knew about a particular project or procedure. And
at the end of the second week she told Mr.
Charley, right in front of me, that I would not only
be able to do her job, but would probably do it
better than she had. I was moving up the ladder.

Jerry was getting jealous.

"You spend more time talking about Bill
Charley than you spend talking about us," he
complained one night.

"Jerry, my job *is* about us," I told him. "My
success with the company is directly tied to our

future. The more money I can make the be4tter our lives will be."

Fran and Marianne were actually more supportive than Jerry was. Of course, I was more careful not to crow too loudly at our Saturday morning meetings, especially since Fran was becoming disillusioned with the insurance business. Marianne was still in her entry-level position at the bank, but we had all agreed banking was a more sedate enterprise and while advancements came slower, it was more secure when it came.

Thanksgiving week I got my first taste of what it means to be committed to the job. Mr. Charley called me into his office Wednesday morning and told me that the project we had been putting together needed some last-minute revisions. He wasn't due to make his presentation until the following Monday, but he said we had a choice of working late that night or coming into the office on Friday, during the four-day weekend. I had promised Mom I'd help her with the preparations for Thanksgiving dinner that night, but I didn't tell Mr. Charley that.

"Whatever you say," was all I said.

"That's the spirit. Okay, then let's get busy on it right now. If we can get it finished tonight, that would be best."

I went back to my desk and called home,

gave Mom the bad news, and we went right to work. I had to type a couple of pages of calculations that had been changed by updated data we had received, and the two of us did our best to design a graph that went with the new figures. He had his sleeves rolled up and his tie tucked into his shirt and I was working in my stocking feet as the dinner hour came and went. By the time we had the finished product put together, we were both a little weary from bending over the table where the graphs and charts were laid out.

"Okay," he finally said, "let's put this back together and see what we have."

He sat in his chair and I stood behind him, reading over his shoulder, as he turned each page. He found one error and suggested we would have to do the entire page over, but I convinced him I could clean it up and did so. I brought the page back to him just as he finished reading the others. He checked it again, agreed it was better, and inserted it into the stack.

"Let's have dinner," he said, running his hands through his hair and stretching.

I followed him to the restaurant, one I had made reservations for him at, but had never been inside myself, in my little car. All the way there I worried about how ragged I must look to be dining out at such a fancy place.

After we had ordered our cocktails, he

started talking about the presentation he would be making on Monday, and I started thinking this was even better than being President.

Right after he had ordered dinner for both of us, a man I didn't know came up to our table and shook his hand. Mr. Charley introduced me as his "right arm, and the brains of the outfit", and I'm sure I blushed. After the man returned to his own table, Mr. Charley told me some stories about him, but I was so far up on cloud nine I didn't even remember the man's name.

The meal was superb, and I couldn't help thinking that Thanksgiving dinner the next day was going to seem awfully boring by comparison. We had wine with our meal, then coffee afterward. It's funny how you remember little things. His saucer had some coffee spilt in it and when he took his first sip, a few drops fell into his lap. I'm not sure he even noticed, but I had the almost uncontrollable urge to leap up from the table and wipe up the spilled coffee with my napkin. I guess I remember that little incident because of the words he said to me a short while later in the parking lot.

He had helped me on with my coat and kept his arm around my shoulder as we left the restaurant and started walking toward our cars. I was tired, so it felt good in a protective kind of way.

"You know, Abby, the things I said back

there weren't just idle praise," he said.

It took me a minute to figure out what he was talking about, so I just looked up at him and smiled.

"On Monday, I'll make our presentation and, if it flies, I'll be the one to get all the credit. But you and I both know that I could never have done it without you. You pulled it all together, kept me on track, greased the wheels, and made it work. We're a team. You know how I think better than my wife does. And she can't type."

I laughed at that, but the feeling in my stomach wasn't very funny. Naturally, I admired and respected him. He always treated me fairly. This had been the first time he had asked me to work late and I felt that he had just rewarded me amply for the extra effort. I would never have thought to define what I felt as love, or anything remotely like it--I guess respect comes closest to what I felt. But at that very minute, as we walked across the parking lot, with his arm around my shoulder and me holding my coat closed against the chilly breeze, something told me that things were about to change between us.

"Monday morning," he said as we stopped beside my car, "I'm going to ask Molly to give you a merit raise. You've earned it. You deserve it. Maybe you can buy yourself a better car. You deserve the best, Abby."

"Thank you, Mr. Charley," was all I could

think of to say. I was starting to shiver, and I don't think it was due to the cold wind.

"And that's another thing," he said, taking me by the shoulders with his arms out straight and looking right into my eyes, "when we're out of the office, my name is Bill,"

"Okay, Bill."

"Good. Now you have yourself a nice Thanksgiving weekend."

And with that he gathered me into his arms and gave me a quick hug, then let me go and walked around to his own car. I watched him start his car as I waied for my old care to warm up--it would stall out on me a dozen times if I tried to put it in gear when it was still cold--and I remember that I kept watching him as he drove away in the distance.

Pretty soon it was Christmastime. The brief time Mr. Charley and I spent together at the office Christmas party was taken up with talk about my car. He had asked me if I had found anything to replace my old car while we were waiting our turn at the punch bowl.

"No. I'm taking my time about that. I want to be sure to get the best possible deal."

"That's wise. As long as you're still looking, I'll keep my eyes open for you as well."

"Thanks," I told him, not believing he would really find time for that sort of thing. After all, I was the one who handled his schedule and I knew how busy he was.

So I was kind of surprised when he called me into the office soon after the holidays and announced that he had found the perfect car for me.

"I've learned that one of our company cars is due for a turnaround," he said. "I think I can get you a very nice deal on it. And you won't have to worry about a trade-in at all."

I knew, of course, that some of our field people drove a car for two or three years and then got a new one. And frequently, the driver was given first option to buy the car he had been driving. I thought that a three- or maybe even a two-year old car would be quite a step up from my old car, which was about eight years old, so I told him I would be happy to take a look at it. Bill had the keys with him and suggested we go down to the parking lot under the building and see it right then.

I was taken aback, and thrilled at the same time, when I discovered the care was not one of the field cars, but one of the executive models--a luxury car. He handed me the keys and told me to get in. I unlocked the doors and got behind the wheel while he got in the other side. It was beautiful. Very plush seats, fully equipped, and it was only a year old.

"Oh, Bill, I can't afford this," I said as I ran

my hands over the steering wheel and tried to make sense out of the many dials and switches on the dashboard.

"Yes, you can," he insisted.

Then he told me how much it would cost me, and told me what kind of terms I could get at the bank. Well, in short, he made it clear that he had already arranged everything and the car was mine. I was speechless.

I threw my arms around his neck to give him a hug, but somehow our lips met and when my brain told me this was wrong, my body did not respond. I just kept on letting him kiss me while his hand pressed against my side and my fingers went through his hair.

Some time later he put some air between us and said, "I take it you like the car."

"Yes," I said, barely able to get the word out. Little firecrackers were going off in my head, popping with thoughts in every direction, and my body was tingling like I'd just stepped off a roller coaster. I was glad I was sitting down.

"Did you bring your purse down with you?" he asked.

I said that I had. I kept it with me any time I left the office as a matter of habit. Then he suggested that I drive to the bank and take care of the loan. He had put all the necessary papers in the glove compartment, and there was a business card clipped to one of them with the name of the loan officer I should talk to. Then he gave me one quick little kiss on the cheek and told me not to worry about the office until I had everything taken care of.

Later, at the bank, I realized it was lucky he had set it up that way. If we had gone back up in the elevator together, the word that we were more than boss and secretary would have shot through the company like wildfire. As it was, I was composed and professional two hours later when I drove my beautiful new car back to the office, parked it in its new stall, and went upstairs.

Bill gave no indication that anything was different between us for the rest of that day, nor for the rest of the week, in fact. On Friday afternoon when I went into his office to say goodnight, he asked me how the car was.

"Wonderful," I told him;

"Well, try not to deplete our petroleum reserves too much, driving it around all weekend," he joked.

"Are you kidding? I'm going to park it somewhere in town where everyone can see me, and just sit behind the wheel and wave at them as they drive by."

We shared a laugh. Then he sobered a bit and said, "By the way, I have a luncheon meeting on Tuesday at the County Inn. I'd like you to be there with me. I think I make a better impression if I don't have to go to the phone to call you every five minutes with another question. And you'd better be prepared to spend most of the day there. We'll go over the things we need Monday morning so we'll be able to present our case as best we can, but I'd best my last dollar that Wilkins and Yaven will rake the idea over the coals, so it may be a rather long session."

"I'll bring my brass knuckles in case the going gets rough," I told him, and then left the office.

Jerry and I had our first big fight that night. I made the mistake of insisting that we take my new car instead of going in his old car, as we usually did. And then I added fuel to the flames by suggesting that he make sure his shoes were clean before he got in. He held himself in check until I was parking my car in the lot at the movies, then he let me have it. Was he angry!

"Damn it, Abby, I'm getting a little sick of having everything we do dictated by that job of yours. It's not bad enough that you're all uppity about your fancy company car, but now we have to walk all the way from out here, just so you won't get a tiny scratch on in. If we'd brought my car like we always do, we would be parking up front and not freezing all the way across the parking lot."

"Jerry, you're acting like a spoiled brat," I told him. "If you're so envious of my success, if you're so afraid of growth, of moving up in the world, why don't you go find yourself someone to match your loser personality. As a mater of fact, you always were sweet on Mary Thompson-- maybe her part-time job would be more your speed."

"You know something? You just said a mouthful. Why don't you just take me back to my old, broken-down car right now? Or would you prefer that I walk?"

"I wouldn't think of letting your poor little body get all cold out there," sneered, jamming the car into gear and wheeling out of the parking lot. "It will be my pleasure to drop you off!"

We didn't say another word to each other as I sped back toward my parents' house. I probably broke a few traffic laws in my hurry to be rid of him. And he had the door open even before I pulled to a stop behind his car, which was parked on the street in front of the house. But he had to add one last little jab. He closed the door very softly, and then pretended to brush his fingerprints off the handle with the sleeve of his coat. Then he got in his car and left a trail of rubber halfway down our street.

Twenty minutes later I was reminded of my little joke with Bill about just sitting in the car and waving to people as they drove by. I took my keys out of the ignition and went into the house, ignoring my parents' questions about why I was home so early, and went straight to my room.

I knew it was really over between us when I discovered I couldn't even shed a tear. I had out-grown Jerry, and now it was time to get down to business. So I was primed and ready for what happened Tuesday.

The meeting, just as Bill had predicted, went on all afternoon. When Mr. Yaven suggested we break for dinner and resume two hours later, everyone except one of the men from the law firm nodded in agreement; and he was, of course, over-ridden. As we left the meeting room, Bill took me by the elbow and headed for the elevators instead of the dining room

"I have a room upstairs, Abby" he told me as we got into the elevator. "We can order something from room service, and eat while we kick out shoes off. It will also give us a chance to consider our strategy without being interrupted or overheard."

I liked the idea of getting out of my shoes and the jacket I had worn that day. In fact, I was thinking that a quick shower--even though I'd have to put the same clothes back on--would be even better.

I guess Bill was doing his mind-reading trick again, because that is exactly what he suggested when we got to the room. He was already on the phone to room service, and told me to take my time.

I suppose you can already guess what happened next. I was drying myself after my shower, my clothes neatly hung over the towel rack, when Bill tapped on the door and opened it just a crack.

"Dinner's here, Abby," he said.

I was standing in front of the sinks and h ad the towel around my back, giving myself a brisk rub to boost the circulation. He'd opened the door just the tiniest bit, but given the way things were arranged, he could see me in the wide mirror over the double sinks. I was about to tell him I'd be right out, not even thinking about what he could or could not see, when I heard him utter two words.

"Oh, wow!" he murmured.

I've wondered a lot about that day. Once in a while I'll decide that Bill planned it all, and that it hadn't really happened by accident. But that idea didn't last in the face of the facts. That day he had taken me down to show me the car, he hadn't made any advances, and I was the one who threw my arms around him. And to be completely objective, there was nothing personal or intimate between us from that time to that moment in the hotel. And there might not have been anything personal or intimate that night if I'd, say, wrapped the towel around myself, or turned away from the mirror, or both. But, of course, I didn't do either of those things.

That first time we made love was all fire and passion, and neither of us did much talking; but every time after that, he always asked me first.

He'd call me into the office and say, "I think we ought to go to lunch when we finish this project. If you'd like, you could reserve a room."

And it was always clear that I could easily say, "Not today, Bill," or "I don't think so."

But I rarely said any of those things. I knew he was married, and at the beginning of our affair there was no talk of him getting a divorce. I knew what I was doing, and I knew that my love was doomed to be a one-way street. But I couldn't help how I felt. I loved him. And I wanted him.

When he suggested, a few months later, that an apartment would be cheaper than continuing to spend so much money on hotel rooms, it seemed like the most natural thing in the world to me. I'm pretty sure I never really believed he'd leave his wife and take up permanent residence with me in that apartment. He promised me that one day he would. He told me that no one understood him the way I did. No one appreciated his desire to do the best possible job at work, to climb the corporate ladder, to feel the satisfaction of being the best. We were a team.

As a matter of fact, I don't think I ever wanted to be Bill's wife. As his secretary I was his partner, in almost every respect, part of a team that was involved in a very exciting life. And of course we shared a love that was just as exciting as our work was. As his wife, I would probably sit at home and be bored to death. Oh, there were nights that Bill would come to the apartment and would just sit and talk business, or we'd just listen to music while I rubbed his feet. But mostly it was beautiful passion and wild fun. I didn't want to be married to him.

I guess things started changing the night Marianne brought the paper by the apartment. She had started coming by during the week, when I was sure Bill wouldn't be there, and we'd share a glass of wine and talk for hours. Fran had moved away months before, and we'd dropped our little Saturday morning meetings. Marianne was the one friend I had who knew everything. And she was the only one I trusted to not lay any big sermons on me about it. She was happy that I was happy, and that was it.

The night she brought the paper, she had it opened to the society page, and she handed it to me.

"I know you've probably already seen this," she said, "but I thought I'd bring it by in case you haven't. Is there wine open?"

"Yes," I answered absently.

It was the announcement of Jerry's engagement. There was a very nice picture of him and his bride-to-be, a girl I didn't recognize. She wasn't from our town, apparently, but the brief article didn't say much more than that she was a student at the local university. What surprised me about the article was that Jerry was also described as a student. It was then I realized t hat it had been almost two years since we had broken up. I still wasn't convinced that either his parents or the reporter wasn't guilty of a little exaggeration.

"Who would have thought he'd go to college?" Marianne commented, rejoining me with a glass of wine in her hand.

Fortunately, we didn't talk much about Jerry that night because Marianne had just received a promotion at the bank, one step away from Operations Supervisor, which was, at that time, her ultimate goal. We spent the evening making plans for how she would spend her new wealth. But later that night, after she'd left, I was straightening up the living room and my eye was caught by the picture again.

I tossed out the paper with the rest of the trash, but I kept being haunted by thoughts of a nice, successful, professional family. I didn't have the kind of life I would have chosen for myself, and I kept thinking about that all week.

Bill didn't come by at all that weekend, and on Monday I found out why. His wife had announced she was pregnant! It would be their third child. I don't know why it hit me so hard--it shouldn't have made any difference one way or the other, but it did.

It took me a while to sort it out, but I finally got a handle on it. Bill and I shared a passionate, loving, romantic relationship. Though I had never given any thought to the idea, I guess I had always felt that Bill was, somehow, faithful to me. I know that must sound silly; after all, I was the *other woman*. But that's how I felt. I was upset.

Nothing changed at the office, but Bill noticed the change a few nights later when he came by the apartment.

"What's wrong?" he asked.

"Nothing, Bill," I lied.

"Come on, Abby. Get it off your chest," he suggested.

I snapped at him with a lot more force than I had intended to use, and he jumped back like I had pointed a gun at him.

"I think I'd better go," he said.

I could tell from his tone that he was expecting me to stop him, but I didn't.

"I'll see you in the morning," he said at the door. "Get some sleep, okay?"

I didn't get much sleep that night, of course. My turning him away like t hat brought even more things about my life up to consciousness, and I went to work with bags under my eyes from lack of sleep and from tears that had flowed most of the night.

He was in his office when I arrived the next morning, so I just went right in.

"Abby, you look terrible," he said, getting up from his desk and closing the door behind me. "What is it?"

"You really don't understand, do you? "

"No, I don't. Is it the pregnancy? Is that what's bothering you? What do you want me to say?"

We argued for quite a long time. In the end, Bill realized there was no way we could continue as we had been. He offered to get me a transfer to a comparable position in the company if I felt I couldn't keep working for him, and I told him I'd think about it.

I'd already thought about it, of course, but I wanted to make my decision myself--for the first time in my life. In the past year a number of men had told me, some of them right in front of Bill, and others in hallways after meetings, that if I ever got tired of making Bill look so good, they would be happy to hire me.

Some of those offers had clearly implied that the men were looking for a mistress. And some of them had just been a kind of backhanded way of complimenting Bill. But I thought that I knew which of them had been serious, and I knew that a few quick phone calls would give me an answer.

I gave my two weeks' notice to Bill at the end of that week, and he politely asked my advice on the choice of a replacement.

It was all very civilized. And I died inside just a little bit more every day I was forced to be with him. After a week on the job his new secretary, Vivian, was as ready as she would ever be, and I asked him if he would let me go a week early.

"Call it a little extra vacation from me," he said.

Marianne came over that night, and surprised me by volunteering to spend the night. I told her everything, until I finally fell asleep as dawn was beginning to lighten the sky.

"Coffee's ready," she said later that morning. "Time to toast the new day and new beginnings."

I don't know what I would have done without Marianne. She kept me going for the next few weeks, listening to my gripes about my new job. She let me cry on her shoulder when something happened to remind me of Bill, and was there for me when I needed her the most.

I started my new job at a slightly lower salary that I had been making with the railroad, but in less than six months I was back up close to that figure. Of course, paying for my apartment myself meant I had a little less at the end of the month than I was used to, but I learned to live with that, too.

In the end I concluded that I had no reason to complain about Bill's behavior, and that I had no reason to beat myself up over what I'd done. I could say I had made a mistake, or maybe it was just the way things happened. Maybe things would have worked out between Jerry and me, maybe they wouldn't have.

But somewhere down the road I'm going to meet someone else--someone single--and I'm going to be a lot wiser about how I handle the relationship.

I know there are no guarantees, but I also know that if I put honesty before convenience, and love before personal gratification, I'll stand a better chance of finding lasting happiness, this time with the right man.

HE CAN'T UNDERSTAND
MY NEED FOR OTHER MEN

Would you believe that I came *so close* to trapping myself in a life of boredom and tedious drudgery that I still get the shakes when I think of it? It's not that I would have minded doing what has to be done to be a good wife, mother, and member of my community--it's just that I wanted to have a little fun at the same time. Is that too much to ask from life?

When I finished high school I joined the Navy. I guess maybe that sounds a little crazy, but I figured it would be the best and cheapest way to have a little adventure, and do a lot of traveling. I also wanted to see if I really wanted to spend the rest of my life in Ohio; or if there was some other part of the country that appealed to me more.

I didn't get very far on my first assignment-- Great Lakes Training Station near Milwaukee--but it was still a change. We received two free days (called liberty) while in Boot Camp, so I spent one in Chicago and the other in Milwaukee. I loved it. Just walking around the streets and riding buses in a strange city was exciting to me, as well as getting the chance to try out new foods in strange restaurants I was easy to please in those carefree days!

After Great Lakes I got sent to San Diego, and boy, was that a change! It took me more than a year to adjust to the idea that swimming outdoors wasn't something that was limited to summer months, and that a heavy overcoat was more of a nuisance than a necessity. But once I got the message, I took to the outdoors like a native. I went boating and learned to sail, took scuba lessons, and even bought a little motor scooter so I could go tooling around from the beaches to the deserts and into the mountains.

I met Dan at a Mexican restaurant. I was having lunch one Saturday after doing some diving in Mission Bay, and I had my face mask and my purse sitting on the seat beside me. He walked in, and just boldly came over to me and asked if he could join me for lunch. I had a mouthful of tortilla chip and salsa at the moment, and I couldn't think of what to do, so I shrugged. I guess he took that as a yes, because he slid right into the booth. I checked him out while he was giving his order to the waitress. He looked okay, had a pleasant voice, so I figured, what the heck?

I think if he had started feeding me some line about how he thought I was the more gorgeous girl in the place, I would have tossed him out of the booth on his ear. Or maybe I would have just left myself. I'm not exactly ugly, but I've never been able to think of myself as anything but plain, Maybe, when I've had a nice hairstyling, and spent a lot of time with my makeup, I might be able to accept "cute" or "good-looking" as a description. But that's about as far as I would be willing to go. Any guy who insisted he thought I was "pretty" or "beautiful" would immediately get classed as a bull-artist who was after just one thing, and he'd never get it from me!

Dan didn't make that mistake. In fact, the first thing he said to me after the waitress left was that he'd noticed my mask and assumed I was a diver. I told him he'd made a correct guess, then waited to see what was next.

"Me, too," he said. "I just got here last week and I've been looking forward to doing some diving, but I don't know anyone to buddy-up with yet. How about it? Would you be my diving buddy?"

As it was, "buddy" was just about the level of relationship I was interested in at the time, and there was something refreshing about an approach like that. I told him I'd like that, and we swapped 'tank talk' and phone numbers. It turned out he was in the Navy, too, but he was stationed at another local naval station. We made a date for the following weekend, and he let me do all the arranging since he was new in town.

Our first dive together turned out to be a lot of fun. He was a photographer and he brought along an underwater camera. I soon learned he had an eye for things I'd missed in my previous dives. And after the dive it was great to have someone to talk to about what we'd seen. We even got into friendly arguments about different species of animals we'd encountered. I got the feeling he wasn't going to be some macho creep who insisted on being the expert in everything.

We went diving a lot together, and we started doing other things, too. When he saw my little Honda, he declared it was the perfect machine, and bought one for himself. We drove all over together: Balboa Park, La Jolla, Tijuana. He even went hiking with me in the desert, bringing along his ever-present camera.

It was in the desert that our relationship moved from being buddies to something more intimate. We had driven out to a spot I knew on the other side of Jamul and we were just hiking, while he looked for interesting cacti to shoot with his camera. I wasn't really paying attention to where I was walking, and I almost stepped on some small creature that was half-buried in the sand. It scuttled away as I pulled myself back. But then I slipped on a rock that was behind me, and when I pulled back, it caught the heel of my boot and threw me off balance. I landed on my rump with a grunt.

Dan was kneeling beside me even before the dust settled or before I could laugh at my own clumsiness. He asked me if I was okay and acting real worried. I told him I was fine, and got to my feet again, with his help. Then he was brushing sand off my bottom and my bare legs, telling me how glad he was that I wasn't hurt.

It wasn't anything he said, or the way he was handling me so carefully, that really got to me, though. While I was standing there, letting him brush me off, I noticed that his camera was lying in the sand a few feet away. Seeing that was what did it, since I knew how much that camera meant to him. When he finished brushing me off and stood beside me, I turned to him and put my arms around his neck. He looked kind of flustered for a minute--then he kissed me.

It was nice--tender and gentle, yet passionate. Not wet and sloppy or anything like that. He just kissed me in a way that I thought it should be done.

We had been buddies for nearly a year at that point, and most of the time we were alone together. Neither of us had many friends outside of the people we were stationed with, so there wasn't really much of a change in our relationship, other than the physical stuff, for a while. He asked me to marry him the night after we'd made love the first time, and I told him I'd think about it. I wanted to see if going from buddies to lovers would change things between us. I didn't tell him that. I just told him I'd have to think about it.

It guess it was about a month after that I finally agreed to an engagement, and I was surprised at how good it felt It looked like I had found a man I could look forward to a very comfortable and exciting life.

The first suspicion I had that anything was wrong about my decision came when he took me home to meet his family. His folks lived in Oregon, and he suggested we spend a long weekend with them and announce our engagement in person, instead of calling them. It sounded like a good idea to me, and besides, I'd never seen anything of the Northwest. In fact, I hadn't seen all that much of California, considering how big it is. I wanted to take a whole week's leave and bike up the coast to Oregon. Dan pointed out that it would take us the better part of a week to make that kind of trip, and it wouldn't leave us much time for visiting. Then he suggested we save our leave for the honeymoon, so I gave in and we flew.

On the flight up he filled me in on his family, telling me stories t hat were, I'm sure, designed to make me more comfortable with them and give me something to talk about. Dan had two brothers, one his senior, and a younger sister. The two younger ones were still living at home, but his older brother had his own farm. I got the impression I wouldn't be meeting the older brother, since Dan didn't tell me much about him. By the time we arrived at the Portland airport, I knew quite a bit about his mother and dad, and his two younger siblings, but the only thing I knew about his older brother was that his name was Terry.

I learned a lot more that weekend, though. It seemed like no matter what the subject of the conversation was, Terry kept coming up. And every time his name was mentioned, Dan kept coming up with some bitter comment. I started wondering about it, since Dan hadn't had much to say before. So when his folks suggested a trip out to Terry's farm on Saturday afternoon, I found myself looking forward to meeting this 'wild man', as they called him.

Terry was sitting in a rocker on his front porch when alal six of us drove in. He waved and whooped and hollered, and just kept rocking away. He certainly looked like a 'wild man', with a long bear, unkempt hair, and bright blue eyes that twinkled all the time. Dan's little sister ran up to the porch ahead of everyone else and sat on Terry's lap, gave him a hug, then dashed into the house with the bread their mom had baked for Terry.

I don't know what got into me--I'm usually pretty reserved with someone new--but Terry seemed so friendly and everything. So after their mom and dad had said hello, and I was being introduced, I gave Terry a hug bear hug and a kiss on the cheek. I guess it was all the crazy stories I had been listening to, or maybe I was just in a holiday mood because of our trip. He lapped it up, grinning from ear to ear, and told Dan that he had found himself a good woman.

Dan's reaction was a little strange, even in light of the weekend's events. He tried to smile at his brother, but all he really managed was a grimace. I joined Dan on the porch steps, taking his hand in mine. Despite all the diving I'd done, I'd never handled fish. But I thought to myself that holding Dan's hand at that moment was probably what holding onto a dead fish was like. The rest of the time we were there, he was down-right sullen and pouty. He answered questions that were put to him with the fewest words possible, and I don't think he put his arm around me once.

I was beginning to think that maybe I had made a mistake in greeting Terry like that, but I immediately told myself that my actions had been completely innocent and only in the spirit that everyone else, except Dan, seemed to be treating this short visit with Terry. Eventually I decided to let Dan pout if he wanted to and I started paying more attention to the conversation around me. I don't know how many times I doubled up with laughter that afternoon as Terry told us stories of life on the farm: troubles with his animals, troubles with his supplies, troubles with his customers. I got the distinct impression he tended to exaggerate a little, but almost all of the stories he told ended up with him being the one who'd goofed, and it was hard not to laugh.

It was real easy to understand why everyone looked forward to a visit with Terry, but when I mentioned my feelings to Dan on the flight back Sunday morning, he shocked me with a very bitter response.

"Sure, everyone loves a clown," he said in a voice loaded with sarcasm. "And it's easy being a clown when you don't give a darn about responsibility."

I started to ask him what he meant, but then I looked at his face and decided against pursuing the subject. He was nearly beet red, and his jaw was set so tight I don't even think a crowbar could have gotten it loose. I changed my mind about asking him what he meant and just said "Yeah," then pretended to be real interested in the magazine I'd taken from the seat pocket. I noticed a while later that he didn't even bother to eat the lunch they served us, and I knew he loved ham and cheese sandwiches.

Once we got back to San Diego the issue seemed to have been put behind him and he was back to his regular self. That is, until the following weekend. We had planned to do some diving together the following Saturday and he was late, so I left a note for him at the front desk of the barracks--as I had done a number of times before--and went down to the docks to get our equipment set up. He arrived about a half hour after I did. I had everything set up and was talking to one of the guys who ran the shop when Dan walked in.

"Couldn't way for me, huh?" Dan said from behind me, startling me just a little.

I turned to tell him I had wanted to get things set up for us, but I was looking at his back. He had spun on his heel and walked over to the equipment--pushing at it with his toe like he expected to see it topple to the ground. I turned back to the guy I had been talking with, and noticed he had a funny look on his face.

"Well, thanks for the advice, Roy."

"Don't mention it, May. You guys have a nice dive."

I was just a little miffed that Dan had seemed so brusque. But Roy hadn't seemed offended, so I decided that no harm had been done.

"We're all ready to go, Hon," I told Dan, joining him.

"Did you check the regulators?" Dan snapped.

"Well, of course!"

"Tanks full?" he spat out.

That did it! I put my hands on my hips and looked him squarely in the eye. I hadn't minded him being in a tiff because I hadn't waited for him, and the bit with Roy didn't matter that much to me, either. But when I said we were ready, I *meant* it. I wasn't going to stand for him cross-examining me like some kind of landlubber who didn't know how to set up her equipment!

"Dan, what is wrong with you?" I demanded, making it clear that I wasn't going to answer another question or budge one inch until I got a satisfactory answer.

I was determined, and I expected him to know that I was; but I was not ready for his reaction. He grew as red as a beet, and began fiddling nervously with the band of his mask. Then he started slapping it against his thigh. It was like I had taken a pin and let the air out of him. He was like a little kid, after a tantrum.

"I'm sorry, May. I guess I'm just in a bad mood. I found out I've got duty tomorrow and I can't get out of it, and..."

Now it was *my* turn to get embarrassed. I realized that I had just taken off, ready to 'do my own thing', without stopping to question what he might be feeling. I felt like I had been pretty insensitive. I gave him a quick hug and told him it was no big deal and suggested we hit the water. I knew we'd both feel better after a dive. He seemed to perk up, and we had a good time. But I couldn't help feeling he was still a little moody.

Later, in the restaurant, Dan made a nasty

comment about some guy giving me the once-over. I finally got him to ease up by flashing my engagement ring and telling him that whoever it was, that guy would just have to eat his heart out. But I couldn't shake the feeling that something about Dan had changed. Where did this jealous streak come from?

About a month after that I had my chance to start asking some questions. It was getting close to Dan's birthday and I wanted to get him something really special. I got the idea to call his mom in Oregon and ask her for some ideas. It also seemed to me that it would be a nice way for me to establish myself with the family. I exchanged pleasantries with his dad, and then his mom got on the phone and I asked her about the present. She gave me a few ideas--one of which corresponded with an idea I'd had--and I thanked her for her help. There didn't seem to be much to say after that, but I didn't want the conversation to end. That's when I got the idea to ask her about Dan's moodiness.

"You know, there is something else I wanted to ask you about," I said. "Ever since our visit with you, Dan has been a little...well, I guess you could say, moody. Is there something I should know?"

There was this long silence on the phone after I'd asked my question, and I was about to say something else, thinking she might have hung up on me. But she finally answered.

"Well, May," she said slowly, as if she wasn't sure about sharing this secret with me. "I guess since you're going to be a member of the family, you might as well know about this. There has been a little bad blood between Terry and Dan. I personally don't feel Dan has the right to feel the way he does, but for some reason he feels he has had to live in Terry's shadow all his life. They have never actually fought about anything, as far as I know; but they haven't got along at all since Terry moved to the farm.

"To tell you the truth," she went on, "we were hoping that Dan's stay in the Navy, and then with you, would make things different. But..."

"I see," I told her, not seeing at all. "Well, thanks for telling me. I'm sure it will work out, and maybe I can work on Dan from my end."

We exchanged a few more bits of chit-chat, and she told me once again how happy they were that I was joining the family. Then she added something, almost like an afterthought, but it set off a little alarm inside. She was saying something about how she and Dan's dad thought I was a "pretty girl", and then she said that Terry thought I was a "fine woman". I thanked her, hung up, and then sat there, staring at the phone, thinking over the exact words she had used.

I considered the idea that if the 'bad blood'

between Dan and Terry she had spoken of had anything to do with a woman, and if Dan had noticed Terry's reaction to me that day at the farm, maybe that would account for Dan's moodiness. Maybe Dan saw his older brother as being in competition with him for--well, for me, or any woman. I decided I needed to talk to Terry, to get the rest of the story. I called information and got his number.

Terry sounded real surprised to hear from me, so I had to explain everything to him--about Dan's pouting, and the phone call to their mom I had just made, and the thoughts I had.

"So, what I really wanted to ask you, Terry, is just what is it between you and Dan?"

He was a lot quicker to answer me than his mom had been, and he had a lot more to say.

"It all really started when Uncle Terrance died," he began. "I was left a little money from his estate, as his namesake, but the rest of the kids didn't get anything. That was bad enough, I guess, but I added to it by taking my legacy to Reno and getting lucky. I managed to turn a few thousand dollars into enough to buy the farm and set myself up in business."

"But that doesn't explain--"

"Hold on! There's more. Dan had always had a resentment toward me--I'm sure it's the same in every family. You know, the older kids get to do things the younger kids can't, and that sort of thing. Anyway, after I bought the farm I guess the folks started bragging about their rich son, and that just added to Dan's resentment. He seemed to start going out of his way to impress the folks, and me, and anyone else who'd listen, with his accomplishments."

I still didn't see what all this could possibly have to do with me, but it was interesting family history, so I let him continue without any more interruptions. I soon found out he was just getting to the point.

"Well, one of Dan's accomplishments, if you can call it that, was that in his senior year he managed to latch onto the prettiest girl in school-- the homecoming queen, no less. I wasn't surprised. After all, he's fairly good-looking, and he's pretty smart, too. Anyway, the weekend of graduation, Dan brought her out to the farm to show her off to me. I knew what he was up to so I played the role of being very impressed and all that.

"The girl took off for parts unknown the following week, without so much as a backward glance. We found out later that she had hot-footed it for Hollywood, convinced that her good looks would land her in the movies. You know the story. But before we learned all that, Dan was convinced that I had somehow stolen her away from him. He never actually accused me directly of any of the nasty things he hinted at around town, but the word got back to me and...well, you can figure it out from there."

Terry repeated pretty much the same things his mom had said, about being glad that I was becoming part of the family, and added his reassurances that Dan would probably come out of his funk soon. He told me Dan and I were welcome at the farm any time. I thanked him for being so honest with me, and hung up, my head spinning with all the new information.

For about a week after those phone calls the tables were kind of turned for Dan and me. Now I was the one who was distracted and moody. More than once Dan had to whistle and wave to attract my attention, even when we were sitting face to face in a restaurant

At first it had all made a lot of sense to me. But as I started thinking about it, I realized there had been a lot of times when Dan had displayed jealousy that had absolutely nothing to do with Terry. To be sure, his reaction to the visit with his older brother made sense now; but my new awareness led me to notice other things that made no sense. Like the way Dan acted when I talked to *any* other man, or when some stranger gave me the eye when we were out together.

My suspicions came to a head one afternoon when we were at the zoo. We had been walking around for a long while, and were taking a break on a bench, sharing a bag of popcorn. An attractive woman in a designer dress stopped nearby and warmly greeted a man. They held each other's hand for a long moment and then sat down on a bench opposite us, talking a smiling at each other the way two friends who didn't see each other that often might.

Dan nudged me and said, "Look at that. Pretty disgusting, eh?"

I couldn't see anything disgusting about it, and told him so.

"No? Look at her left hand," he suggested.

I looked at him first, because his voice had become loaded with sarcasm. He was talking out of the side of his mouth, as though he wanted to be sure no one but me could hear him. Then I did as he suggested and looked at the woman. She was well-dressed, and pretty, and seemed to be enjoying her conversation with her friend.

"What about it?" I asked him.

"Notice her wedding band? *He's* not wearing one."

I took another look and confirmed that Dan was right. She was wearing a band and a nice engagement ring--not as pretty as my own, I thought, but with a larger diamond in it. The man's fingers were free of rings of any kind.

"So?"

"May, don't you see? She's married, but not to him! How dare she talk to any man other than her husband?"

I was getting annoyed at Dan, but I let it slide.

"Disgusting!" he repeated, in that conspirator's voice.

I could feel my heart beating faster and heavier, and I didn't know if it was from anger, or fear, or both. But I knew it would be dangerous for me to say anything at that moment. I suggested we head for the Bird House as we had planned. It took me nearly a half-hour to calm down enough to bring up the subject again. I did my level best to keep my voice calm and disinterested as I questioned him.

"Dan, how do you think married people should act when they're not with each other?"

I didn't get to say another thing for quite a long time. I discovered that Dan had many strict and rigid ideas on the subject, and was quite willing to cite specifics now that he had been asked. I found that it wasn't even necessary for me to agree or disagree with him to keep him going, either. An occasional grunt or nod to let him know I was still listening was sufficient. When he was through sprouting and sputtering, I had to sit down again. My muscles had turned to jelly, and I had a queasy feeling in the pit of my stomach. I hadn't realized how uncompromising Dan was.

Still, I had to press him to say even more--to

satisfy myself that he was telling me how he *really* felt, and not just spouting some academic line.

"Dan, I agree with you that a woman should have sex only with her husband, but do you really believe that it also means a married woman shouldn't have any male friends?"

"Well, that depends on what you mean by 'friend'," he said, side-stepping my question.

"What do *you* mean by it?"

"It's hard to say, in the abstract. But it's not really important. I'm sure the issue won't come up for us, Hon. You wouldn't do anything foolish like that."

I wasn't so sure, but I felt that I had to feel my way through the rest of this conversation carefully.

"Probably not. But let's say, just for the sake of discussion, t hat I met a man while I was diving alone one day, and we shared a little 'tank talk' over a cup of coffee. Would you consider that a violation of the marriage vows?"

"That's a dumb comparison, May. In the first place, you would never be diving alone. And in the second place, why would you want to bother sharing any of your ideas with anyone other than me?"

I'd heard enough by that point, and treated his question like it did not really require an answer. We both watched the monkeys for a while and I decided to let the subject lie where it was. I laughed at the antics of a couple of monkeys, but I didn't feel very happy. My laugh sounded hollow even to my ears.

Throughout the next week I did a lot of soul-searching, and kept away from Dan by claiming that I was having a rough period, complete with cramps. I needed time to think.

It wasn't an easy decision for me to come to. Dan was the first and only man I'd ever felt comfortable with, and my prospects for finding another man like him weren't all that good. Of course his brother had said that I was a 'fine woman'; but there was no way I was even going to consider trading one brother for another. And Terry didn't look all that attractive to me. Besides, I couldn't be sure that Dan's attitudes weren't shared by Terry, after all. I was grateful to Terry for helping me get clear on this important issue, but that wasn't enough to build a relationship on.

I thought about sending Dan's ring back to him with a note, but I felt that I really owed him an explanation in person. I made one last date with him. I tried to soften the blow by telling him that I had discovered changing attitudes in me, instead of letting him know I had seen disturbing things about him. But it didn't help. Dan looked defeated at first, and then he got angry, and (I should have known) he finally accused me of wanting to be free of him so I could "fool around", as he put it, with Terry. In the end, Dan stomped out of the restaurant, leaving me with the check and a feeling of failure. I had wanted to let him down easy, but he had his mind made up.

And I guess the same is true of me. I realized there was no way I wanted to get trapped in a relationship in which I'd have to deny myself. The way I see it, if I can't find a man who will treat me like a person--with individual needs, and desires, and friends (of either sex)--then I'm better off without a man.

Of course, I'm still hopeful. And if I can think of some foolproof way to find out if a man thinks of a woman as a person instead of a cardboard cutout, well...

I LIVED IN A
FOOL'S PARADISE

Sometimes when it's getting close to midnight and quitting time for me, I think about the short drive home and what I'll find there. Most nights I feel like kicking myself for having been so blind and downright stupid, but I'm learning to get over that.

I'm twenty-seven years old now, but I guess my story starts back around the time I was twenty-four or twenty-five. Or maybe even before that.

I went to work right after I got out of high school because I wanted to be on my own. I was a little overweight because I did a lot of late-night munching instead of dating boys. I didn't think much of myself, either.

When I looked at my future, the best I could expect was to find a decent job, pay the rent, and be happy enough that I had my health. I found a job right away, and I took the second shift because it paid a little better. Well, the other reason for working those hours was so I'd have a good excuse for not going out nights. It was boring work. Electronic assembly wasn't exactly a big-time glamour job.

It wasn't that I didn't think I was doing something important. I was smart enough to know that the little pieces I was putting together would wind up in everything from equipment in medical labs all the way to stuff that might go into space. That could make a lot of boredom seem worthwhile.

I had been working on that job for nearly two years when Ed asked me for a date. Well, he didn't really come out and ask me that way--I probably would have fainted or turned him down flat if he had. The way he put it was more like he invited me to be in the same place with him at the same time.

Even that was surprising, though. Ed was, as far as I was concerned, a pretty handsome guy. He stood all of five-eleven, had a nice head of hair, and penetrating eyes. Maybe his nose was shaped a little funny, and when he laughed it looked like he had a few too many teeth in his mouth, but I thought he was good looking.

Ed worked the day shift at the plant, and I had seen him quite a few times, but always in passing. We'd be going in opposite directions in the parking lot, or he'd be coming out of the doors just as I was going in. I didn't pay much more attention to him that I paid to the hundreds of other people that passed through the place. Well, maybe a little more...

When I got to be crew supervisor, I wore a

little gray coat with my name stitched on the pocket--like all the other supervisors wore--and after that he started greeting me by name instead of just smiling and nodding. But I still wasn't prepared for him asking me out.

It was a Friday afternoon in late April, as I remember. I was just going in and he appeared in the doorway, and instead of nodding or smiling or saying "Hi, Connie," and letting me pass, he just stood right there in the doorway, and folded his arms across his chest. I had the choice of jostling people going or coming through the doors on my right or my left, so I just stopped and waited him out.

"Connie, do you like fishing?" he asked.

"Why?" I asked him, not sure how I felt about fishing.

"I'm taking my new boat out to the lake tomorrow, and I thought you might want to come along."

Like I said, I wasn't really prepared for this backhanded request for a date, if that's what it was, and I really didn't know what to say. Then it dawned on me I didn't have a fishing pole, so I told him that, and he just waved it off, said he had plenty enough gear. So I shrugged and said, "Sure."

"Great. I'll pick you up about six?"

Now I was really in a pickle. I didn't get off work until midnight, and I usually didn't get to sleep before one. If I were going to be ready to leave my apartment by six, that meant I'd have to get up at five. Four hours of sleep just didn't seem like enough. On the other hand, a day of fishing didn't seem like that much work, so I decided in favor of it.

"Sure," I said again. "You want my address?"

"You live in the Centerville Apartments, don't you?"

"Yeah," I agreed, a little puzzled about exactly how he'd known that.

"Watch for the green pickup pulling a boat. That'll be me."

And that was how it all started. I was late getting up the next morning, and didn't even have time to brush my hair. I didn't get my morning coffee, either. It turned out none of that mattered. He had a big thermos of coffee in the pickup, and later that day he told me how pleased he was that I hadn't gotten all "prettied up" just to go fishing. I felt a little miffed by the fact he seemed to think of me as 'one of the boys', so when he asked me for a real date the following weekend--dinner and a movie--I knocked his socks off with an elegant hairdo and a new dress that showed my figure to good advantage.

He asked me to marry him about a month after our first fishing date. He didn't have to ask me twice.

We didn't talk a lot, Ed and me. When we were together, it seemed like we both pretty much understood what we were doing, and there wasn't much to say. We worked at the same plant and at pretty much the same kind of job, so there wasn't much point in talking shop. We both felt that eight hours a day was enough time to give to the job without stretching it out by talking about it.a

We had both discovered that first day that I didn't care much for fishing. except for what came after it. I didn't mind cleaning and cooking the catch. I loved really fresh fish, but as far as I was concerned it was just meat on the table. I really didn't care how much time he had to sit, patiently casting into one spot or another to bag that delicious trout. And Ed enjoyed the fishing itself, not bragging about it afterward, so we got along just fine.

We were married in June, and with a whole summer of fishing ahead of us, our pattern of life was pretty much set by the time winter set in. Ed fished in the afternoons and evenings while I worked, and I cleaned fish and kept the house during the days when he worked. It was a good system. When winter rolled around, I had a lot fewer fish to clean, but Ed occupied himself with his remodeling projects, and that gave me a little more housework to fill the gap with.

Weekends, we kept a different kind of schedule, but it was almost as steady as our weekday routine. Saturday nights we'd go out to dinner and a movie, or sometimes a concert. Once in a while we'd just stay home and order a pizza if there was a really good movie on TV, but that was rare.

I got a little closer to one of my sisters because of my marriage. I don't remember what made me so extra talkative that afternoon, but I do remember her reaction when I gave her a rough idea of how Ed and I were living our life together.

"But Connie, don't you find that kind of routine boring, or stifling?"

"Not at all, Carla," I told her. "I guess it depends on where you start out from."

I realized that Carla didn't know anything about the kind of life I had planned for myself when I left high school, so I laid it out for her.

"And then Ed came along," I added. "So now I have this very nice house to call my own, and a good man to share my life with. Far from boring."

"Oh, I get it," she said. "You and Ed have your fun in bed, right?"

I stopped being talkative right there. Our sex life was none of her business, but I didn't tell her that to her face. Ed and I weren't your wild swinger types. Oh, we made love, and Ed was a good lover, I guess. I mean, he was considerate, and he was gentle, and I felt wonderful when I was with him. Since I didn't have any experience outside of our marriage, I chose to believe that what we shared was good.

Maybe it *was* a little routine, like the rest of our life, but that didn't bother me at all. It was, as I thought of telling Carla but didn't, better than the nothing at all I'd had before.

Ed had inherited our house from his grandmother. It still had a mortgage on it because she had borrowed against the equity to cover his grandfather's hospital bills, but the payments were smalls compared to what I knew other people were paying for a house that size.

We had a fairly large lot, so there was plenty of room for Ed to park his boat trailer, and he built a kind of carport for it.

I guess it was knowing that we had so much room that led Samantha to our doorstep. Samantha was my niece, the daughter of Marlene, our older sister. Marlene was the one who had gotten all the looks in our family. Her daughter was just as pretty as she was, but she wasn't as bold. I guessed some of it had to do with the fact that her dad had left when she was very young.

Anyway, they didn't have much of a happy home life, and Samantha had attached herself to me as her 'favorite aunt', even though we didn't see much of them outside of the holidays.

Samantha was eighteen when she showed up, unexpectedly, that Sunday afternoon in July.

Ed and I were doing some yard work in the back, and she came around the garage and said hello.

"Well, Samantha! What a pleasant surprise," I said. Ed just smiled.

"Hello, Aunt Connie," she said, trying to sound cheerful.

It was clear to me right away that something was wrong. She was wearing a pair of cut-off jeans and a baggy tee shirt, and her lovely hair looked rather messy to me--all of which seemed normal enough for a teenager, from what I'd observed. But she was also wearing a little too much makeup, which didn't seem right for her, and there was a little quiver in her chin which her forced smile didn't quite cover up.

"Is something wrong, Samantha?" I asked her.

Well, she started blubbering right there on the spot. Ed got really busy with the weeding at that point, and I put my arm around her shoulder and led her to the picnic table under the maple tree. I told her to tell me all about it. The story she reeled off, between sobs and sniffles, sounded all the more strange for being told under a hot July sun on a beautiful summer's day. It was the kind of story that should have been whispered in a darkened room.

Apparently her stepfather had been abusive since the day he had moved in with them. As she told her story, I could just picture the man expecting a 'party life' with his beautiful new wife, and resenting the kids for making it difficult. When she had finished, I took her into the kitchen and gave her a glass of iced tea and some banana bread I had baked that morning. Then I went back outside to talk to Ed while she sat at the kitchen table.

He'd heard a lot of it, even though he had pretended to be too busy with the weeding to pay much attention, because I never even got around to asking him what I had intended to ask.

"You think she wants to stay here?' he asked.

I just nodded, and he said, "Okay," and that was that. I went back to the kitchen to tell Samantha that she was welcome to stay, and she took me to the front porch where she had left her bags. We put her up in the guest room.

Later that night, while Samantha was unpacking, I called Marlene and told her that Samantha was with us. Marlene tried to make it sound like a 'summer vacation' kind of thing, but I tried to make it clear I thought it was something more permanent than that.

Then she broke down and told me the rest. Her son had already left home--he was only seventeen--a few months before; and the attitude she was now adopting was that it would be best for everyone. She told me that she would send me some money, but I cut her off and told her it wasn't necessary. Even if Ed didn't agree with me, I had enough money of my own to take good care of Samantha, and I didn't feel like letting Marlene get away with easing her conscience that way.

Ed agreed with me one hundred percent. We got her enrolled in school--she was way behind-- and he and I took her shopping for clothes and school supplies. Ed took her fishing, which she seemed to like, and when she wasn't out doing that during the day she helped me out around the house. By the time school had started in the fall, she had pretty much fit into our routine, and I thought things were going to work out just fine.

Ed and I had never talked about children. We hadn't practiced any birth control methods, but I'd never gotten pregnant. I guess we just both assumed that one or the other of us wasn't able to. And it didn't matter which of us it was--we just accepted it.

But after Samantha moved in I got the feeling that--for a few years, at least--I'd have the chance to play 'mother' and satisfy that need. Even thought Samantha was only eight years younger than me, and eleven years younger than Ed, I was still "Aunt Connie" and that was good enough for me. I thought Ed felt the same way, but I was wrong.

The first clue I got that something had gone

drastically wrong was when he moved out of our bedroom.

There wasn't anything all that unusual about him spending a few nights in what we laughingly called The Study. There had been a number of times when one or the other of us had a cold, or Ed had been out late fishing, when he'd slept on the comfortable day bed we'd put in that room. It just made good sense, considering our different schedules, that if one of us was restless, the other one shouldn't have to suffer for it.

So his sleeping in the study wasn't, in and of itself, any big deal. But this time it wasn't for just a few nights. It turned out to be a permanent move. And by the time I realized that, it had been going on for so long I felt a little foolish about talking to him about it. When I finally did get around to mentioning it, he just brushed it off with a comment about him not being able to sleep. I didn't want to make a federal case out of it, so I just let the subject drop.

That wasn't all, though. Samantha's bathing suit was another thing that got me thinking. I hadn't been with her the day she bought it--Ed had gone, and I hadn't thought much about it, then.

The first time I saw the suit was when I went down to the basement one morning to clean the fish they had caught the evening before. Ed had already left for work, and Samantha was still sleeping. When I went down there I got an eyeful.

There were only two fish in the tub, and Ed's clothes were hanging on the hook where he always hung them. Samantha's bathing suit was hanging on the hook next to his things.

It was a one-piece suit, but there wasn't as much material to it as I'd seen in some bikinis. I didn't see how that little bit of a thing could have covered even half of her body.

And then it hit me. Ed usually took off his clothes in this room, and sometimes washed his hands and face in the tub before tossing in the fish. Then he'd usually wrap one of the big towels I kept on a shelf there around himself and head for the shower upstairs.

Had Samantha taken off her bathing suit in the same room? Had she peeled out of that thing while Ed was taking off his clothes? I tried not to think of the pictures that came to my mind, tried telling myself she was just a 'little girl', but it did no good. I soaked all the clothes in the other tub, then put them into the washing machine like I always did. But the pictures kept coming back.

It didn't help matters any when I saw her actually in the suit a short while later. She was lying on a chaise lounge when I came out of that house that day, soaking up some sun. Ed was raking up some grass clippings, and the two of them were talking and laughing about some incident that happened while they'd been out fishing.

The suit just barely covered her: it was cut high on the bottom and low on the top, and most of her back, thighs, and hips were exposed to view. She might as well have been nude. And Ed was acting for all the world like he didn't even notice. Of course, he had already seen her in it a number of times. *And maybe out of it, too,* I thought, even though I tried not to.

I saw even less of Samantha after that, because school started. She was usually gone from the house before I got up, and I was usually gone to work before she got home, so our contact was limited to the weekends. In fact, that was now also true of Ed and me since I no longer had the pleasure of snuggling against him when I crawled into bed at night. I was beginning to feel like an outsider in my own home.

The weekends weren't much better. Saturday mornings she wouldn't usually bother to get dressed. She'd sit around the house in her robe, a pink terry thing I'd bought for her. I started thinking up early-morning projects for her because I couldn't stand the sight.

She'd sit in one of the living room chairs, reading the paper or working on some class assignment, and the robe would part and reveal a shapely leg, and she'd pretend not to notice. I didn't tell her about it because I wasn't going to give her the satisfaction of knowing that she was getting to me.

I couldn't blame Ed for his interest. After all, he was a healthy, good-looking man of twenty-eight. She was a beautiful young girl who was lonely and needed love, and maybe she didn't understand what she was doing to me. But I knew what she was doing to him. I just couldn't do anything about it.

I couldn't do anything about anything, in fact. I thought about a lot of things I might do, but none of them were right. I couldn't very well tell them both to get out of my house, because it wasn't "my" house in the first place. Sure, I'd put two or three years' worth of work into it, but it was Ed's house without question.

And despite what Samantha was doing to Ed, she was still a little girl who already had been battered around, ignored, and tossed out enough in her life. Even if I hadn't practically boasted to my sister that I was taking over where she had 'failed', it just wouldn't be fair to Samantha. Two sets of rejections were too much for anyone to bear, I felt.

Of course, there was one thing I could do, and don't think it didn't cross my mind a time or two. I could have moved out myself. But the simple fact was I loved Ed--no matter what he had done. He was my husband, and I was determined to stick it out. If he wanted to leave me, he would have to ask me himself, or file for divorce. I wasn't about to just walk out. I'd said "for better or worse" and I'd meant it.

I just kept on living my life, hoping that he'd soon tire of his little fling, and that we'd get back on an even keel. I prided myself on how understanding I would be when he finally ended it, letting him know that I accepted him no matter what.

I also did my best to encourage Samantha to find someone her own age. Every time I got the chance, I'd ask her if she was seeing any boys, what the boys in her school were like--things like that. She didn't say much, but once in a while she'd tell me about a friend or two.

Mostly, she kept to herself, though, and really applied herself to her studies. In her first year with us she managed to make up one of the two school years she'd been set back, and I felt very proud of that fact. It was a clear indication I was doing something right.

Samantha's second summer with us was a long one, though. Even though she was taking two classes in the summer session to get even further ahead, she still had a lot of time on her hands, and I had a lot of worries in my head. She bought a new bathing suit that summer, and I was pleasantly surprised to see that it was of a more modest cut than the one she'd worn the summer before.

Our vacation that year was the only period I could think of where I got close to being happy--

the way I'd been before Samantha moved in. We usually rented a cabin at the lake, but since Samantha was with us, Ed suggested we get rooms at the lodge. Ed and I slept in the same bed together for more than a week. It was heavenly.

Of course, we did a lot of fishing, so Samantha was with us for a big part of the time. I was surprised at how good she was. Either she had a natural knack for it, or Ed had been a good teacher. They fished, and I got in a lot of reading in the shade of my straw hat between handing out bait and sandwiches, and we all got nice tans.

The lodge had a policy of giving guests credit for the fish they caught. We'd pick out the fish from our catch that we wanted for dinner that night, and they'd serve the others to guests who hadn't been so lucky. I'd bet we paid less for our rooms that summer than any of the other guests.

It turned out to be the calm before the storm, though. When we got back home, we went right back to the same old routine: Ed sleeping in the study, which I had taken to calling "his" room by then, and he and Samantha spending more time together.

Then, in late October, Samantha got sick and went to see our family doctor. After her second visit she dropped the news in my lap like a bomb. She was pregnant.

I couldn't keep my tongue still. The first thing I asked, was "Who's the father?"

I held my breath, waiting to hear the worst, but she concocted a lie instead. "Some boy I met at the lodge," she said.

I knew it was a lie because I hadn't seen her with any boy. She also didn't bother to make up a name for this fictitious boy, expecting me to believe that she had been so carefree she hadn't even learned his name, or didn't care to remember it.

Ed confirmed my suspicions with his reaction. He just grunted when I told him. He didn't even pretend to be interested in knowing who the father was. I cried myself to sleep for a lot of nights after that.

Oddly enough, this momentous news didn't change things all that much. Samantha insisted on having the baby. She told me that she expected to finish high school before the baby was born, and that she'd find some way to care for it herself.

Ed and I didn't talk about it, but I got the clear impression he was all for her staying with us until she was darn good and ready to leave--or until he was ready to acknowledge their relationship and throw me out.

I became even more stubborn than I had been before. I'd play out the game, and, when the time came, I was prepared to make him pay dearly for what he had done to me. My biggest worry was how I could possibly explain things to Marlene.

It was a cold, crisp, clear day in mid-November when reality came crashing down around my ears. I heard a knock at the front door just as I was preparing to leave for work. I grabbed my lunch pail and my jacket, and headed for the door, prepared to tell the salesman I expected to find there to get lost.

The young boy standing on our doorstep was no salesman. Salesmen didn't wear jeans and sneakers.

"Yes?" I asked.

"Uh...are you...does Samantha live here?" he finally managed.

I told him she did, wondering why a boy of his age wasn't in school. He was having trouble explaining himself, and I didn't feel like helping him out.

"You must be her Aunt Connie," he finally said. "I'm Larry."

He looked like he thought that announcement was supposed to mean something to me, but I decided he had already wasted enough of my time. Instead of being polite and telling him that I was pleased to meet him, I just said, "So?"

"Uh, ma'am, could I see Samantha? I mean, do you think she'd want to see me? I..."

Suddenly, the nervous, almost pathetic look on his face got to me. I decided it wouldn't matter all that much if I were a few minutes late. I invited him in.

"Samantha isn't home from school, yet," I told him after he'd perched himself on the edge of the couch. "Don't you go to the same school?"

"Uh, no," he told me. "I graduated last year, from Kearny," he added, naming the next town. "I met her at the lake this summer."

You could have knocked me over with the proverbial feather! I wanted to ask a few questions, but he was hurrying on with what he'd come to say before he lost his nerve. I listened, and I learned.

"We--I--I fell in love with Samantha up there at the lake. I couldn't tell her that then, but I want to tell her now and ask her if she's interested in, uh, having a relationship with me," he blurted out.

I was smiling in spite of myself. I tried to not let him know, because I was sure that if I laughed, he would have bolted out the door, or broken down and cried all over the coffee table.

I wasn't sure what to say, and then it dawned on me there was no way I was moving from that house until I had some answers. I excused myself and went to the kitchen to call in sick. I told them not to bother Ed with the news--there was nothing to worry about, but I just wasn't up to coming in to work. I hung up and went back to the nervous boy in the living room.

I offered him something to drink, but he

politely declined, so I decided to get some answers.

"Why did you wait so long to get in touch with Samantha, Larry?"

"I'm in love with her," he said again, making me wonder why kids today seemed to be able to toss around words like 'love' and 'relationship' so easily. He was quite sincere.

"I...I guess I got scared when I realized how I felt about her. I didn't know that she was...that I was..."

There was a pounding in my ears that made it difficult for me to hear him. I had a feeling I knew what he was trying to say, and I couldn't stop my racing heart, nor prevent my mind from leaping to a premature conclusion.

As it was, I didn't get a chance to hear a whole lot more just then. The front door burst open, and a wild bundle of beauty came rushing into the room like a whirlwind. I heard her call his name, and then the two of them were wrapped up in each other's arms.

While they 'said hello' I had time to reflect on the fact that she must have recognized his car at the curb, and that she had clearly undergone an amazing memory recall--remembering such details as the name of the boy she had been so uncon-cerned about only weeks before.

They finally realized that I was still in the room with them, watching them with a motherly fondness, and they separated.

"Aunt Connie, this is Larry," Samantha announced proudly--and unnecessarily.

"Yes, we've met," I told her. "He was just telling me about this summer at the lodge."

"Oh." She sat down on the couch, pulling him down with her. "Then you know all about it."

She was talking to Larry, not to me, and he gave her a puzzled look. She looked at me then, and I shook my head to let her know I hadn't told him about her condition.

"I think I need some cocoa," I announced, heading for the kitchen.

I heard Larry repeat his desire to "have a relationship" with her as I left. I didn't hear much of the conversation that followed because I made as much noise as I could with the pot, the milk, and the cocoa mix.

She must have informed him of her pregnancy, because he whooped in pleasure--then stifled it rather quickly as he remembered my presence.

Ed walked through the door as they were concluding their conversation. It took us quite a while to sort out his confusion over what I was doing home, and what was going on.

Larry stayed for dinner, and between courses Ed and I learned of their plans. Samantha was going to remain in school as planned, and

Larry already had a nice job with his father's lumber business. I vetoed the idea of him moving in with us or her moving in with his folks, and insisted they wait until after their wedding to take up housekeeping. I knew it must have sounded a little like closing the barn door after the horse was out, but my feeling was it wouldn't hurt them to try to do things in the right order.

The other thing that had occurred to me was that even though Larry had told his folks about Samantha, they didn't know about the baby. I didn't want either of them getting carried away until they were sure of how his folks would respond. I needn't have worried.

The Carltons loved Samantha, and they were happy as larks about the youngsters getting married right away. Larry's mother called me on Sunday, and we had a nice long talk, making preliminary wedding plans even before we got to know each other. She told me how Samantha had impressed her husband with her knowledge of fishing, and even insisted she remembered seeing all of us at the lake that summer.

I had to admit, when we met them later, that I didn't remember them, but I went along with everyone else and pretended that I had and that, had we known the kids were attracted to each other, we would have become good friends on the spot.

One thing I didn't have trouble remembering

was that Ed had moved out of our bedroom shortly after Samantha's arrival. It was easy to remember because he was still sleeping in the study. One evening the following week I came home determined to get an answer out of him, even if it meant that neither of us would get any sleep that night. He was grumpy when I first woke him up, but he rubbed the sleep out of his eyes and sat up.

"What is it, Hon?" he asked, looking at the clock.

"Ed, I want to know why you moved out of our bedroom," I demanded.

"Shhh, she'll hear us," he whispered, nodding in the direction of the closed door.

I lowered my voice a little, but my tone stayed just as persistent, and my resolve was just as firm.

"I really don't care if she does, Ed. I want an answer, and I don't care what Samantha might hear."

"Well, that's just the point," he whispered back, his voice cracking with the effort to be quiet and forceful at the same time.

"Huh?" I was dumbfounded.

"She might hear us," he repeated, like some kind of broken record. "She might...you know, *hear* us..."

Suddenly, as I looked into his eyes, everything became clear to me.

"You mean, she might hear us making

love?"

"Yes," he croaked.

We'd never talked about sex. We did it, but we didn't talk about it. We were from a very different generation. Sex was something a couple did in complete privacy. Ed would have been immensely uncomfortable around Samantha if he had thought she had ever heard us making love.

I remembered those rare weekend afternoons when she had been out of the house, and that week at the lodge, and suddenly I felt both foolish and proud. I threw my arms around him and pushed him back to the pillow.

We didn't make love that night. We didn't need to. I slept in his study with him, and the next night he moved back into our bedroom. We didn't have long to wait after that because Larry's folks had agreed to an early wedding, and they gave the couple a six-month's deposit on an apartment as a wedding present.

Ed looked more handsome than I'd ever seen him when he walked Samantha down the aisle. I don't know which one of us--my sister or me--cried the most as the young couple exchanged their vows. The second best present I got that day was when Marlene told me that as far as she was concerned, Samantha had two moms she could count on.

The best present I got that day came when Ed and I got home after the reception. Suffice it to say we made up for lost time.

These days, when it's getting close to quitting time, I think about going home and slipping into bed to snuggle up against my husband. I know I could have avoided a lot of agony for myself by confronting Ed earlier. I kick myself for being so stupid. But I can't change who I am, and I'm just grateful everything worked out in the end.

I WAS A MAIL-ORDER BRIDE

I've been dreaming about home quite a lot lately. Not the house I lived in here in Florida--I was never able to think of that place as home even thought I once looked forward to being there and thought of it as becoming my 'new home'. That house--Teddy's house--now belongs only to my nightmares.

The home I dreamt of was from a happier time, the place where I grew up, in Thailand. It was a small village on the river. My hometown wasn't much to look at or talk about, and my parents' home wasn't a luxurious house with lots of fancy gadgets in it. Still, I dream of it. And in my dreams it is a place of peace and comfort where everyone is loving and kind.

My new friends in Florida, where I'm now trying to recover from my nightmares, tell me that my dreams are quite natural. They say I need a "dream place" like Thailand to help me become "centered" so I can face my nightmares and learn to cope with them.

I didn't understand at first, but as some of

the other women told me about their dream places, I began to feel less alone. Their hometowns had names that sounded American to me--Omaha, Detroit, Bakersfield--but when I heard my friends talk about these places, they seemed as far away as Thailand. Perhaps, as one of the women--who came from just across the street--said, "Where you come from in not as important as the experiences you have had along the way."

My experiences started innocently enough, with an exchange of letters between me and a girl I grew up with in Thailand. My friend, Jirapon, is a few years older than I. We weren't all that close, but after she met an American sailor, married him, and then moved to the United States with him, we started writing letters to each other. She would frequently ask me to pass along personal messages to her relatives--a cousin's birthday or her parents' anniversary. I could tell she missed the people she had left behind, but she didn't seem to miss Thailand as much. I guess she liked having that connection to home, but the picture she painted of her life in Key West told me she was very happy in her new home.

Jirapon and her husband had opened a small bakery in Key West after he got out of the Navy, and her letters were filled with the joys of working together, of meeting new people, and of being part of their new community. I grew quite envious of her life and frequently expressed this in my letters to her. She'd answer that I shouldn't envy the long hours of work she put in every day at the bakery, but even as I read her words I could feel the satisfaction her work gave her, the sense of joy she experienced.

I suppose my life would have been like the other girls with whom I grew up. I would have finished school and worked until I'd married some local boy. After marriage I would have settled down to raise a family. All this might have happened if it hadn't been for Jirapon's letters. For one thing, my correspondence with Jirapon led me to study English with a greater intensity, one none of my classmates could match. I read everything printed in English that I could get my hands on-- books, magazines, pamphlets, cereal boxes--everything. I kept trying out new phrases on Jirapon in my letters to her, and composed many more letters I never mailed.

I promised myself that one day, after I learned English very well, I would get a job at one of the American companies based in Thailand, like Jirapon had done. There I would meet a handsome American who would take me to the United States. But fate dealt me another hand.

One day I was reading an American magazine I'd read many times., when I noticed an advertisement in the back. I must have read it before, I told myself, because the magazine was rather worn, but I hadn't thought about the meaning of the words on those earlier occasions, evidently. That day I not only understood the meaning, but immediately decided to answer the ad. It was for a pen-pal club which promised "American men for correspondence and friendship."

I wrote a letter to them and received an immediate reply. They wanted a photograph, which they said they would publish, along with my name and address, in their catalog. There was a small fee involved.

I could hardly eat for weeks after I sent in my picture and my money order. I expected a flood of letters from American men. I had bought such a supply of paper and pens that my mother asked me if I were going to open a stationery store.

Teddy was the first man who wrote to me. I think I wasted a whole box of stationery trying to get my first letter to him to sound just right. I received letters from other men, too, and answered some of them. But Teddy had started it all, and he remained my favorite pen pal right from the start. After we had exchanged a few letters, he sent me a picture of himself, and I put it in a frame on my little writing desk. He looked so handsome in his suit, and the car he was standing in front of seemed like a beautiful bronze chariot to me. It was love at first sight.

Teddy told me a little about himself, but many of his early letters were filled with questions about me. He wanted to know everything about me, it seemed, and of course I found that flattering. In almost every letter he asked me for another picture. I had pictures taken in front of my parents' house, at the docks with my father's boat in the background, and so forth. With each picture I'd tell him more about myself and my life. It was a very uplifting experience because in writing to Teddy, I began to see my life differently. Things I'd taken for granted became subjects for long discussions on paper, and my heart went out to him for the way he caused me to examine my life.

One of Teddy's requests presented me with a small problem. He asked me to send him a picture of myself in a bathing suit. I forget his exact words now, but he had written that he wanted to imagine me 'frolicking on the beach' or something like that. The idea seemed very foreign to me since the ocean represented a livelihood for our family and not a place for frolicking.

When I went to the water, it was to work at repairing nets or cleaning the guts out of fish. I didn't realize at that time that Teddy had seen too many movies with all those bare-breasted tropical beauties giggling and bouncing over clean white sand. Of course, I was living in a dream world of my own at the time, which made it more difficult to understand the true intention of his request.

My problem was that I didn't even own a

bathing suit. I thought of borrowing one, but most of my friends didn't own one, either. I did the next best thing. I put on a pair of shorts and knotted a blouse around my midriff, and I tried to strike a 'frolicking' pose. My girlfriends ruined most of the photographs they took because they jiggled the camera while they laughed at my antics. But Teddy liked the pictures, so I didn't mind what I'd had to go through to get them for him.

I suppose if I'd been more honest with myself I might have realized what Teddy was really interested in. But honesty had to take a back seat to pride in those days. I couldn't even be honest with my friend Jirapon. When one of her letters took on a negative tone, accusing me of not keeping up my end of our correspondence, I explained about Teddy. But even then I couldn't bring myself to tell her the truth--about how I'd actually paid to find a pen pal--and I told Jirapon that we'd started writing through a mutual friend. I ignored her requests for details and filled my letters to her with news of home, the way I had in the past, but my main focus was always on Teddy.

When Teddy started dropping hints about how much he'd like to meet me in person, I forgot about justifying my actions. I also forgot about the many unanswered questions I'd asked him-- details about his life in Orlando he'd never given me--and about my own motivations that had led to our correspondence in the first place. I wrote back to him that I would love to meet him and hoped he would some day come to Thailand.

It wasn't long after that when Teddy suggested the very thing I had been hoping for. He explained how difficult it was for him to "get away from his business" and how it might be better for both of us if I came to visit him. I replied that his idea sounded heavenly, but admitted I hadn't enough money to make the trip. Money, he told me in his next letter, was no object, and he offered to send me the plane fare. I thought he must be very rich indeed if he could do that, and I started to imagine the mansion he must live in and the life style he had never told me about. I even convinced myself that he had kept this information from me so that our friendship could develop in a pure state of innocence.

That all sounds so foolish and naive now, but between my ignorance and the beautiful pictures of American life I had created out of Jirapon's letters from Key West, it was an easy mistake for me to make.

It took many long months for this new dream to become a reality. In addition to the many details of the trip itself--passport, inoculations, things like that--there were the objections of my parents to overcome. It seemed to me they worried about everything, and they raised objections more than once. I thought my plans would never become a reality. Between us, though, Teddy and I handled all of it.

For example, when my mother asked where I would stay, I reminded her that Jirapon lived in the same state as Teddy, and I suggested that I would probably stay with her. Of course, when I said that, I had no idea of how far apart Key West and Orlando were. I had not mentioned this arrangement to Teddy, and I had not even discussed it with Jirapon. I sent letters to both of them immediately, however, and soon received replies which I read, in part, to my parents to calm their fears.

Of course, I didn't tell my parents that I had simply mentioned that I was "thinking about a visit" in my letter to Jirapon, nor that her reply had been written with the mistaken idea I was planning to visit her alone. I also didn't read them the part of Teddy's letter where he said he'd thought I would stay with him. I only read the part where he mentioned his cousin who lived nearby.

His next letter managed to put an end to all the objections about his true intentions. He wrote that he'd given the matter careful consideration and wanted me to accept the ring he was enclosing as a token of "our new understanding". Wrapped in tissue paper and taped to the bottom of his letter was lovely little ring with a small stone. I put it on, then showed my parents the "engagement ring" he'd sent. For my parents this meant that Teddy's intentions were honorable, and their objections ended.

I truly believed that we'd be married soon. I'd be a mail-order bride!

Later I would remember all this and tell myself that I had no one to blame but myself for what happened to me. My new friends here in Florida keep pointing out to me that my guilty feelings are misplaced. Wanting to believe in someone who tells lies, they remind me, is not the same as being the one who tells the lies.

The truth was, though, I had told a few lies of my own. Even if they weren't in the same league with the whoppers Teddy had told, I couldn't hold myself blameless. I wanted to believe that Teddy had somehow fallen in love with me through our letters, and I kept acting on that belief long after I had learned the truth about him.

The last few weeks before my departure for Orlando were so frenzied, I didn't have time to think about what I was doing. I must have packed and repacked my small suitcase a dozen times the day before I left for the airport. I was so excited I almost left my suitcase in my cousin's truck when he dropped me off at the terminal.

The long flight seemed endless to me, and I'm sure I didn't sleep a wink. I kept pulling Teddy's picture out of my purse and staring at it, as though I hadn't already memorized every feature.

I wanted so much to be sure I'd recognize him when I arrived that I didn't trust my own memory.

I shouldn't have worried. He was wearing the same suit he had worn for the picture, and the first words he spoke to me erased all the nagging doubt I had carried with me.

"Nitty, honey, you're even prettier than your pictures. I'm so glad you came."

All the phrases I had practiced went out of my head in that instant, like the air being let out of a balloon. I was speechless and suddenly very weak in the knees. I just hugged him and felt his laughter bubbling in his chest as I pressed my face against it. I finally found my voice, but I just kept saying his name over and over.

He took charge of things right from the start, hurrying me though the airport and baggage claim, whisking me and my suitcase out to the parking lot where he had left his car. It wasn't the same beautiful bronze chariot I had seen in the picture he'd sent me, but at that point I didn't care. I was in the United States with my fiancé and nothing else mattered.

He took me to dinner first. We went to a restaurant which seemed quite fancy to me at the time. While I picked at my food, he told me of the plans he'd made for our first few days. He said he'd managed to get a few days off work--a fact which sounded strange in itself because I had the distinct impression he owned his own business--

and he told me about the places we'd visit. None
of he places he told me about, except Disney
World, made any sense to me, but I told him his
plans sounded wonderful, and they did.

When he finally took me to his home that
evening I got my first major shock. His 'beautiful
mansion' turned out to be a small one-bedroom
apartment. I didn't understand at first and made a
comment about the odd design of his house,
thinking the entire building belonged to him. He
laughed so hard I thought I would die of embar-
rasment right there on the spot, and we hadn't even
crossed the threshold yet. But then he calmed
down and started explaining things about the
economy and the housing shortage. Things I only
half understood.

I understood his tenderness, though, and his
gentlemanly behavior. A short time later my
yawns began to signal what the rest of my body
had known for hours. I was very tired.

"Darling," he said, "I want you to take the
bed tonight. I know you must be very tired, so I'll
sleep out here on the couch."

I wanted to protest that I couldn't ask him to
give up his bed, but he took my suitcase into the
bedroom and turned down the sheets of the bed.
He told me that he'd emptied a drawer in the
dresser for me to use, showed me where the extra
towels were, and so forth. Then he kissed me
lightly on the cheek and left me alone with my

thoughts.

I barely managed to get undressed before my eyes started closing. The very next thought I had was that the coffee smelled very good. And that thought came just before I opened my eyes and discovered it was morning. Then next thing I realized was that Teddy was sitting on the edge of the bed, pouring coffee from a shiny silver coffee pot. There was toast and jam on the tray he had prepared, and a cheery smile on his face. I forgot about the smallness of the apartment in the face of this royal treatment.

"Ready to take in the sights of Orlando, Darling?" he asked as he handed me a cup of coffee.

The only thing I was ready for at that moment was the bathroom, but I was naked under the bedcovers and Teddy was sitting right beside me, sipping coffee. I put on a brave smile, took the mug from him, and tried to ignore the pressure.

Teddy munched on a piece of toast, then he seemed to notice my discarded clothes. He put his cup back on the tray and stood up, saying something about how I'd have to learn to be more tidy--but I wasn't listening. My full attention was on the open bathroom door and the robe which hung there. The moment he turned his back, I made a dash for it.

I felt better as I came out of the bathroom, dressed in his robe, and my behavior didn't seem to have disturbed Teddy. He said something about there being no need for me to be so shy among friends. He was anxious to tell me about his plans for the day, so he incident was soon forgotten.

I'll never forget my first day in Orlando with Teddy. He kept telling me things like how big the city was and what a rich history it had--most of which didn't impress me because Chiengrai was twice as big and had a much longer history. But I did see things which impressed me. I couldn't explain it to Teddy at the time since I didn't really understand it myself, but I figured it out later. Compared to Chiengrai, most of the people I saw in Orlando seemed to be on holiday. The whole city seemed like one giant amusement park to me. But the real difference took me longer to figure out because it dealt with something I that I wasn't seeing. Not once during that whole day, as we went from Disney World to Sea World, hurried through wax museums and went to an alligator show, did I see people physically working hard.

I held on tightly to Teddy's arm and let him show off his city to me, feeling very alive and protected--and loved. The only sour note in the whole day came when we were having lunch. My thoughts turned to Jirapon for some reason, and I mentioned to Teddy how much I was looking forward to visiting with her. He asked me where she lived and I told him.

"Key West? You've got to be kidding,

darling," he said, giving me a look that made me feel very stupid. "Key West's a long way from here, maybe four hundred miles. It would take whole day just to drive there. Forget it!"

I was stunned and ashamed. I realized I had made a grave error in estimating the true size of the United States, and I later learned, with some careful reading, that all of Thailand would fit into one average-sized state in the United States. I suddenly felt very alone and exposed.

My sense of vulnerability was greatly increased that night when we returned to Teddy's apartment. I was exhausted from the day, and Teddy said he was "pooped" also. He suggested I make some coffee while he took a shower, and he went off to the bedroom. More than anything I just wanted to sink into the cushions of his sofa and rest my tired feet, but I found the coffee and the pot and did my best to honor his request.

Not a minute after I'd finished and slipped out of my shoes, Teddy emerged wearing the robe I'd put on that morning.

"Your turn, sugar pie," he said. "I put a little present on the bed for you. Something for you to wear when you finish your shower."

The prospect of a nice hot shower brightened my spirits a little, and I went to the bedroom to undress.

Then I saw his present, and suddenly I was face to face with another harsh reality. The insubstantial thing he had laid out could hardly be called a garment, let alone a robe, as I had been expecting. What material there was could only be described as flimsy. I'd seen spider webs that had more substance to them.

I took a long time with my shower, my thoughts about the short gown and its implications far into both the past and the future.

Teddy seemed upset that I was taking so long. I heard him call out to me a number of times before I managed to dry myself and drape the little piece of nothing over my shoulders. I seriously thought of putting the plain cotton shirt I had packed as a nightgown over the see-through thing, but I didn't want to insult Teddy. I compromised by wearing panties and a bra and decided to brave it out, at least for a little while.

As I look back on it now, I realize that the moment I stepped out of the bedroom wearing that piece of nothing was the point of no return. By accepting his gift and doing as he asked, I had put my life in his hands and surrendered myself to his will.

Teddy was gentle with me that first night, but that doesn't excuse my part in it. I gave myself to him as surely as if it had been my own idea, and I paid the price for my foolishness and my pride.

We didn't leave his apartment the next day. As with the night before, we stayed in the bedroom most of the time. Teddy was quick to assure me of his 'good intentions' and just as quick to make promises about 'taking care of me' in the future.

I cried the first time he made love to me, and he kissed the tears from my cheeks and murmured love sounds in my ear. He told me I'd learn to like it, told me he'd "teach me"; but I had the sense he was more interested in his own feelings than in mine. I got the distinct impression he felt like he had just accomplished some glorious conquest and was immensely proud of himself.

The truth was that I did have feelings within myself that suggested I might, as he put it, learn to like it, but it was all happening too quickly for me to absorb. I told myself that if he'd just given me a little time, taken things slowly, it might have been different. But Teddy was too intent on feeding his own appetite, satisfying his own desires.

Among the distressing thoughts I had in those first few days was how I could possibly manage to hide my shame when I returned home to Thailand and faced my family. I was sure that my giving in to Teddy's lust would be as obvious as he color of my dress, and I couldn't imagine justifying my actions to anyone.

Teddy noticed my mood and asked me about it, though his question made it clear he had only one thing on his mind.

"What's the matter, sweetheart?" he asked. "Don't you like it yet?"

"It's not that," I told him, even though he was right. "I was just thinking that you said you wanted to marry me."

It wasn't exactly what I had wanted to say, but I didn't know how I could explain to him that I had pictured us getting to know each other, falling in love gradually, having a period of courtship--if they still call it that--before all the rest occurred. His response, however, turned everything around. At least for a while.

He laughed and hugged me, ran his rough hands over my body, then assured me that he did intend to marry me.

"As a matter of fact," he said, "I've been thinking we could cash in your return ticket to pay for the wedding. It won't be anything fancy, but..."

I was so relieved. I hugged him back--for the first time--and promised him I'd do my best to adjust. He laughed again, then told me we had plenty of time to 'work out the details' and that I should leave it all to him.

Leaving it all to him became a way of life, I was soon to discover. The next day he left me alone in the apartment to do a little shopping. While he was gone I began composing a letter to Jirapon, telling her of our coming wedding and inviting her to participate if she could get away. Teddy came home with packages in his arms while

I was writing and wanted to know what I was doing. When I told him about the letter he put the packages down on his kitchen table and told me to put the things away.

As I turned from the refrigerator where I had put the beer and the other things, I saw he was reading my letter. He sighed heavily, then told me I was "jumping the gun". I didn't understand his phrase, and I guess he saw my puzzled look, because he sighed again and explained. He said he had things to plan and didn't known exactly when we were going to be married. Then he made a suggestion t hat it would be better if *he* wrote to Jirapon, since he could more clearly explain where we lived, and where the wedding was going to be, and so forth.

He finished by tossing my letter into the trash, then told me to put a pizza into the oven and pour him a beer. I was so stunned I couldn't even react, couldn't think of any reasonable arguments to counter his action. I did as I was told.

That night he introduced me to a new "training aid", as he called it. He had a VCR in his living room and had purchased some videos which he told me would help me make the transition to married life. I couldn't believe my own eyes as I watched the first of these movies. But that was nothing to the shock and disgust I felt when Teddy explained that he wanted me to do the very things we were watching.

The first time I protested, he tried to convince me with words. He pointed out that the women in the movie were obviously enjoying what they were doing. He also said things like if I wanted to be a "real woman" and stop being "a baby" I'd learn to do those things.

I tried, but it was too sudden, too revolting. After a while he stopped trying to convince me with words and began threatening me with his fists.

I know it must seem hard to understand why I didn't just run away from him. I realize now that I could have left him, found a policeman, begged to be sent home, or found a way to contact Jirapon. But at the time I couldn't imagine any of those things. I felt I was completely at Teddy's mercy, and I tried to convince myself that he would become loving and gentle toward me if only I learned how to please him.

The very next time he left me alone in his apartment I found out just how vulnerable and unprotected I was. My return ticket was gone from my purse. He had left the few coins from Thailand I possessed, but I had no idea how much they were worth in America, and I wasn't even sure if there were busses or taxicabs. I knew it would do me no good to ask him about the plane ticket--he had already told me he planned to use it to finance our 'wedding'.

I did think about going to the police. But when I pictured myself trying to tell them why I was so afraid of the very man I'd voluntarily come halfway around the world to see, I imagined them laughing at me in the same way Teddy did, and telling me to go home and be a good girl.

I just sat down on the floor and cried. Later, when I was drained of tears, I got up and put some ice on the bruises I'd received when Teddy knocked me against a chair. After that I cleaned the apartment. I had finally convinced myself that I had brought all my troubles on myself, and I was determined to make the best of it.

My efforts led me nowhere. Teddy seemed to take my submission as a sign of complete surrender, and his only reaction was to become even more demanding. He began to complain, with his voice and his fists, about everything from my behavior in bed to the way I washed dishes. Nothing I did was good enough for him, and he demonstrated his displeasure with angry shouts and blows..

What saved me from sinking into the bottomless pit Teddy was digging for me was the television. After our first week Teddy had to go back to work at the radiator shop (another of his lies--he had never owned his own business), and I got into the habit of turning on the television for company when he was gone. I cleaned the apartment each day, and tried to plan meals that would please him, using the strange foods he brought home some evenings. The friendly voices from the television helped to keep me from the depressing thoughts that held me in their grip day and night.

I was eating a little soup for lunch one day when I heard a woman on the television ask a question that immediately caught my attention.

"Are you a victim of abuse?" she asked.

I found myself nodding sorrowfully in response to her question. She went on to say some things about women having choices in their lives-- I don't remember much of the rest of it. But there was a phone number flashing on he bottom of the screen under the word "Shelter". I grabbed for the pad I had been using to write down a recipe and wrote down the phone number.

I stared at the television, not really seeing or even hearing it any longer, and thought about that word--shelter. I'd never used Teddy's phone before, but I decided right then and there that the time had come for me to make that choice.

I didn't know what to say when a woman's voice answered my call. She seemed friendly and helpful, and willing to let me stammer out my story. When I started to cry she made soothing sounds and told me that she knew what I was going through and that she'd try to help.

I finally calmed down enough to tell her I

didn't know how to get to the shelter she spoke of, and she patiently explained that she wasn't allowed to come to get me. But then she told me that if I wanted to call a taxi to take me to the shelter, they would pay for it. I started blubbering all over again--I had convinced myself that I'd never hear such a compassionate voice again in my life.

After I'd done as she instructed, I was amazed at how easy it was. Once I got to the shelter, I had to answer a lot of questions for a woman who wrote some things on a clipboard. My bruises were examined by a nurse. All the women were so helpful and didn't seem to mind at all when I broke into tears instead of answering them. They were all so patient with me. I thought my heart would burst with all the joy and relief I felt.

Some time later the nurse gave me a pill, which she explained would help me to sleep, and they assured me that someone would be there to assist me when I woke up. They also told me that even if Teddy tried to find me, he wouldn't succeed.

I slept through the rest of that day and into the late morning of the next day, though my sleep was not an untroubled one. I remember a nightmare where Teddy had dressed me in something which made me look more than if I'd worn nothing at all, and was parading me up and down the street. Men with big, rough hands were sneering and grabbing at me; and my family stood nearby, hanging their heads as the sight of my shame.

When I awoke, a woman I'd never seen before was sitting by the side of my bed, reading a book. She put her book down when I stirred and asked me if I felt rested.

Talking was an important part of what they did there at the shelter, I learned. Some women were so frightened, it took them a long time to be able to just talk, but the fact that everyone in the shelter--even the nurse--had been through similar experiences helped.

I also discovered, in a broader context, that I'd been fortunate in that I'd suffered no broken bones or any permanent physical damage.

My friends in the shelter helped me to find Jirapon's phone number in Key West, and put in a collect call to her. Jirapon was shocked at first-- she hadn't even known for sure I'd made the trip to Orlando. When I told her that I was too ashamed to think about going back home, she promised to send me a bus ticket to Key West, and said we'd talk about my future plans when I arrived there. I let her talk to one of the directors of the shelter to work out the details. Then I had myself another good cry--this time from relief instead of from pain.

Jirapon called me the next day to let me know that she'd put my ticket in the mail. She also told me she'd talked with her husband and that they agreed I could stay with them as long as I wanted. Between their generosity and the unexpected kindness of my new friends in the shelter, I'm beginning to think that America is not as bad a place as my nightmarish time with Teddy made it appear to be.

It will probably take many years and a lot more healing before I learn to trust another man, but I've decided I can use the time to learn how to be a good citizen of my adopted country. And maybe, in my own small way, I can find a way to pass along the kindness and understanding I've been shown.

MY BABY WAS BORN
BEHIND BARS

I have nothing but time. I sit here on my tiny bed in my tiny room with lots of time on my hands.

My "room" is actually a cell, and my address is the Women's Prison. Some of the corrections officers tell me I won't be here long, as prison sentences go--just long enough, one of them said to me the other day, to learn my lesson.

I think I've already learned my lesson, but I'm still trying to figure out how it happened, how I let myself get into this fix in the first place.

I don't think of myself as a bad person, and most people I know have always told me I have a pretty good attitude. I sure can't blame my background, because I had a pretty normal home when I was a kid. My dad worked most of the time, and Mom was usually home, though she sometimes worked at a part-time waitress job when things were tight.

My little sister and I always had enough to eat, a warm place to sleep, and nice clothes.

Mom was more strict than Daddy, but if we did things like help her clean house or wash dishes, she always gave us a treat or let us watch a little extra television. I certainly couldn't blame my folks for the mess I made of my life.

I used to try to blame my teachers, blame school for my problems. Most of the time I made barely passing grades in my classes, and I thought it was because the teachers didn't like me. They were always telling me I talked too much and didn't pay attention to my lessons. But I studied hard sometimes, spent longs hours reading the books and trying to figure out the questions, and I still didn't get good grades. Mom tried to help me out once, but she didn't even understand the books they gave us to study, and she lost interest after a few nights.

I never did figure out school. My best friend in high school, Nicole, did, and I still think she might have been right.

"School is all baby-sitting, Nicole said. "Think about it. What's the real reason we come to this place every day? So our parents can go to work or do the shopping or whatever. This," she went on with a wave of her arm that took in the whole school, "is just nothing more than advanced day care."

I was about to tell her she was full of it, but Nicole didn't give me or anyone else a chance to get a word in edgewise.

Nicole had a lot more to say, but I wasn't listening any more. I was having a particularly hard time with geometry then, and I remembered thinking in class while our teacher was talking about angles, that the only angle I was interested in was the one I needed to be able to shift gears in my boyfriend's car.

I was going with Eric by that time, and I remembered the first time he'd taken me for a ride in his car. He was a senior in high school, and I was a junior. He'd offered to take me home one day, and that was how we'd started going together.

I didn't think we were going to last after that first day. I mean, I liked him and everything, but I thought he was turned off by me after what I did. The thing is, he wanted me to shift gears for him while he was driving. He said it was more comfortable for him to drive with his arm around me, and that meant I'd have to do the shifting. So he told me to watch him go through the gears a couple of times, and then take over.

I watched, but I found out seeing it wasn't the same thing as doing it. The first time I tried it I stalled the car. He just kind of sneered at me and told me I'd put it in fourth instead of in second, then said something else about "lugging" which I didn't understand at the time. It just meant I'd shifted too soon. I felt really foolish, and I felt sure he was just going to drop me off at my house and that would be that.

He didn't let me shift any more until he got me home, but then he turned off the engine and said I could practice some more if I wanted to. He put the clutch in and held it down so I wouldn't wreck any gears, then showed me how to go from first through fourth and then into reverse.

Anyway, I sort of got better at it after a while, because Eric let me practice until I got the feel of it. I still wasn't sure how he felt about me, though, because when he said I was making progress and doing well, he also told me it was time for him to go! The only thing he said when he left was that he'd see me around.

I didn't even tell Nicole about that first date, because I figured if he didn't ask me out again, no one would have to know, and I wouldn't be embarrassed.

Eric wasn't in school the next day, which was Friday, and I didn't see him again until the following Monday, but I thought about him all that weekend. Every time I could sneak away to my room, I'd grab the old baton that had been in my closet for years. I'd clench it between my knees and practice shifting with my left hand. By the time Monday rolled around, I felt pretty sure I could handle shifting--if Eric asked me to.

I tried being cool about it, but when I bumped into Eric coming out of his history class on Monday afternoon, and he told me he'd take me home that night, I almost fainted right there in the hall.

That night after school I got a few lessons in

'practical geometry' that no teacher ever bothered to tell us. For one thing, my practice all that weekend paid off. I figured out that if I sat real close to Eric, and tucked my left leg under me, the gear shift was in just about the same position as the baton had been.

The other thing I learned was that Eric was interested in geometry, too. He spent a lot of time studying curves and angles during the drive--*my* curves and angles, that is. He was a gentleman about it, though. He just said he thought I was beautiful. He didn't try anything, either--which I liked. He treated me with respect, and when he kissed me good night, it was like nothing I'd ever felt before.

After that, Eric and I were an item. Nobody made a big deal about it, though one of the girls in my crowd tried to make something out of the fact that Eric drove the ugliest car around. We all just thought she was jealous, since she didn't have a boyfriend.

Anyway, the more time I spent with Eric, the more school seemed like a big waste. I was worried, too, that after Eric finally got out of high school and went to college--he was planning to go to the local community college--we would grow apart. But we were together all that summer after he graduated, and I was pretty sure we were going to stay together. The prospect of not seeing him art all while I was a senior in high school was kind of scary. I figured there'd be a lot of other college girls around him, and maybe he wouldn't want to have anything to do with a high-school girl any more, even after what we'd started to mean to each other.

We hadn't gone all the way yes, but we'd come pretty close a couple of times. Eric was the first guy I wanted to make love with, but I was still a little scared. And because Eric was so mellow about everything, he agreed to wait until I was ready.

One day that summer Eric told me he was buying a new car. I told him I didn't care what kind of car he got, except it had to have regular seats in it because I was tired of sitting on the emergency brake all the time. That's when I found out for sure he really cared for me, because he said right away he'd remember when it came time to decide . And he did.

The two-year-old car he ended up buying may not have been the prettiest car in the parking lot, but it looked pretty enough to me. And best of all, it was an automatic. I could snuggle right up next to Eric on the front seat and not have to worry about shifting at all.

Nicole and all the rest of my friends were jealous. She asked me where Eric had gotten the money, and I told her he had some kind of part-time job. Then she asked me where he worked, and I had to admit I didn't know--I just knew Eric always had money.

I'd never told anyone, but that summer Eric and I almost broke up, and it was all because I wasn't into smoking pot. I'd tried cigarettes once, years before, but I'd never tried again.

Anyway, the night we argued we'd been at a drive-in movie. Eric and I had been kissing for a while, not even bothering to watch the movie, when he told me to get his change box out of the glove compartment. It was an old box that Eric kept to put his change in. He was very neat that way, didn't like to have coins rolling around in the glove compartment. I thought he was going to get us some sodas or something, but when I opened the box I saw there wasn't much change in it. What he wanted was the hand-rolled cigarette he'd stashed in there.

I knew right away it was a joint. Everyone talked about smoking pot all the time, the same way they talked about making love with their boyfriends. Eric lit up the joint while I was putting the change box away, took a big drag on it and then passed it to me.

I told myself it was no big deal. I'd take a couple of hits on it, let the stuff do whatever it was going to do, and then go back to kissing Eric. Well, that's what I told myself, anyway. My throat, lungs, and nose had a different idea. I took a drag the way I'd done when I tried smoking, but before

I even got it all down I started coughing and choking and gasping for air.

I vaguely heard Eric mutter something as he tried to find the joint--I'd dropped it on the floor of the car, apparently--but I was too involved with my coughing and gagging to pay attention to what he said.

What was worse than anything, though, was Eric's reaction. You'd think I had thrown up on his upholstery or something the way he was carrying on. First he chewed me out for dropping the joint and almost putting a hole in the carpeting, then he got real mad because I wouldn't stop coughing. After that he started calling me a baby and a lot of other things. I was starting to get a little angry at his attitude, and if I'd been able to stand up without bending over in a coughing fit, I might have walked out on him and tried to hitch a ride home.

It wasn't long afterward that Eric and I made love for the first time. I'm not saying there was any connection between my not wanting to smoke pot and us making love, but I guess I did feel I needed to show him I really did care for him and that we didn't really need drugs to have a good time. We'd been close to it, anyway, and I guess I wanted to as much as he did, so it just sort of happened.

Something else happened that summer that

got me kind of worried about Eric, even though it didn't really have anything to do with us, exactly. We usually hung out all weekend together, but one Saturday he said he had some business to take care of and would pick me up that night instead of early in the morning like he usually did. I told him that was fine, because I figured my mom would be happy to have me stick around for a day and help her with housework. I did help her around the house that morning, but as it turned out she and Dad had planned something for that afternoon and left before lunch.

Nicole and one of the other girls came over in the afternoon, and we just sat in the back yard and talked. They were going to stay until Eric came to get me, but it was getting later and later, and he never showed up. Nicole wanted to wait with me, but her friend wanted to do something else. They were in her car, so they left.

I tried calling Eric, but there wasn't anybody home. I called a few other people and kind of casually got around to asking if they'd seen Eric, but I got nowhere. Nobody knew where he was.

I didn't find out until Sunday afternoon what had happened to him. He'd been in jail.

"In jail!" I screamed into the phone.

For a minute I thought he'd hung up on me, but he said he was just holding the phone away from his ear so I wouldn't destroy his hearing. So I calmed down, and asked him to tell me about it.

He said he'd been arrested for reckless driving and that they'd kept him overnight in the city jail to teach him a lesson. I thought it sounded pretty strange that they'd throw someone in jail just for speeding, which is what he'd made it sound like, and I told him so. He kept insisting that's all there was to it, then said something about his parents bothering him about being on the phone so long, and that he had to go.

He came over Monday morning after our parents had gone to work, and by that time I'd heard some things from some friends of his. I told him what I'd heard and demanded he tell me the truth. He asked me to get him a soda, then drank some before he said anything.

"Okay," he finally said, "the truth is, I was doing a deal with these guys."

"What kind of a deal?" I asked, sitting next to him on the couch.

He let out this big sigh, then told me the whole story. He said he knew these guys who wanted to buy some marijuana, but they didn't have a car, and they didn't have any connections. He also knew these other guys who had some marijuana to sell, but they didn't know the other guys and didn't want to get mixed up with strangers. So Eric had agreed to act as the go-between. He was on his way to the buyers with the marijuana in his glove compartment when he noticed a cop car behind him. He panicked, started driving faster and faster, and naturally the policemen started chasing him. He said he got lucky and managed to throw the drugs out of his car in a way the police didn't see him do it, but they finally caught him and booked him into jail.

Eric told me the whole story then--all about the police telling him they knew he was dealing but didn't have any evidence, so they'd just decided to book him for reckless driving. That's why they kept him over night until his dad bailed him out on Sunday.

I guess if I'd had any sense I'd have handed him his walking papers right then and there. But he looked so pathetic and so helpless, I didn't have the heart to do it. What I tried to tell him then was that I didn't want him to ever do something stupid like that again.

And that was the point where everything started going downhill. A short time after that, Eric moved out of his parents' house and got a place of his own. He told me he'd had a big fight with his dad, but when I tried to get more details from him, he didn't say much.

Anyway, he told me he'd carried some clothes to his car, planning to spend a few days with one of his buddies, and his dad started throwing things out of his bedroom window onto the lawn. When he came by to pick me up that night, his backseat and truck were stuffed with things all in a jumble, so I figured he'd been telling me the truth.

He stayed with a friend of his for a while, but the weekend after school started, he got a place of his own. I helped him move into his apartment and even donated an old blender my mom had stashed in a kitchen cupboard. It was fun setting up house and shopping together for food. I stayed with him all weekend and got a ride to school with Nicole on Monday morning.

Eric said there wasn't any point in him going to college, so he said he'd have to get serious about making some money to pay the rent. I thought he meant he'd have to get a job. He did get a job, but it was only part-time, pumping gas, and it didn't take a lot of brains to figure out he wasn't making enough money to pay for the apartment, and food and gas for his car on what they paid him. I guess I just decided to look the other way instead of being a pest about it.

My parents didn't mind my spending a lot of time with Eric as long as I stayed in school, and at first I did go to all my classes. But keeping house was a lot of work, I found out, and I started cutting classes, then skipping whole days. I guess I could have gotten into trouble about that, eventually, if I hadn't gotten into some other kind of trouble first.

It was just after my eighteenth birthday that I found out I was pregnant. I guess it was bound to happen. Eric and I were practically living together by then, and sooner or later, I guess, one thing led to another. We were both very upset about it, and we had to decide what to do. We talked over a lot of options, and finally decided I'd have the baby and put it up for adoption.

In the end it didn't really matter what we'd decided. Eric's new life-style put an end to any plans we may have made.

One afternoon Eric drove home in a brand-new car. I couldn't believe my eyes when I saw it. I just kept looking from Eric to the car and back again, and Eric practically popped all his buttons, strutting around like he owned the world.

"It's beautiful," I finally said, "but how can we afford the payments?"

"No payments," he boasted. "I paid cash for this beauty."

The minute the words were out of his mouth I could see he regretted saying them. I don't know how much longer he could have kept up the fiction we were living on his gas station salary, but at that point the cat was, was they say, out of the bag. He didn't even wait for me to say anything.

"Look, babe," he said, stuffing a hand into the pocket of his jeans, "we're making it, and we're making it big. As long as we keep on making smart decisions from here on out, the sky's the limit. Tomorrow we're leaving this dump," he said, jerking his thumb at the apartment house behind us, "and the only question is--are we leaving together or do I go alone?"

I took a long time thinking about what I would say. I tried to imagine what people would think if I just walked out, how I would explain what had happened without sounding like a fool.

I didn't think much of his boast about the sky being the limit--flashy cars and a nice address weren't all that important to me. But I guess I wasn't very clear about what *was* important to me. In the end, I simply decided to hold onto what I had--even if it did turn out to be the tail of a tiger.

"I'll start packing our things," I told him.

He didn't say anything to me when he followed me into the apartment a little later. He stood there in the bedroom doorway and watched me putting things into a pile, saw that I wasn't separating his stuff from mine, then left me alone. I heard him whistling in the bathroom a little later, and I went out and told him I'd need some boxes. He just shrugged and left. I had all our clothes on the bed by the time he came back, and I just put everything in the boxes, and he carried them out to the car.

Eric didn't turn mean or anything like that. It just seemed he didn't care about anything but making more money. Even when we made love it just seemed like something we had to do to get through the day -- like having lunch. I started dying inside, I guess, but I was too numb to notice.

I'd made my choice to ignore what was right

from what was wrong, and it seemed to me that nothing much mattered after that. I stopped seeing my friends--even Nicole. After a while, even having Eric didn't seem to be that important. I just kept going through the paces, and the pace seemed pretty frantic most of the time.

Eric bought me a new car of my own. He put it in my name, just like he'd put our new condo in my name. It didn't matter They were just things--empty, meaningless things.

I didn't scrub floors any more, but I was kept busy pouring drinks and toting ashtrays for our flashy new visitors most of the time. I didn't cook because we ate out all the time or had something delivered. The old blender I'd so proudly donated to our first apartment had re-mained behind--part of the "junk" that Eric had insisted we not bother to take with us.

They caught him, of course. His boastful pride made him too easy a target for them to miss him. They followed him home one night after he made a deal selling cocaine at some fancy restau-rant downtown and stopped him right outside the apartment. I was so numb I even asked the under-cover cops what they wanted to drink before I realized what was going on.

They charged me with being an accessory, since they couldn't prove I'd had anything to do with the actual selling of the drugs, which they called Distributing a Controlled Substance. When the judge asked me if I had anything to say before she pronounced sentence, I just stared at her. I wanted to say it wasn't fair, that I hadn't really done anything but just stay with my man, but I knew that wasn't the point. I didn't say anything.

They don't have big iron bars that slam in your face in a modern prison. They don't have a bunch of horrible men standing around, just waiting for an excuse to beat you, either. But it's still hell. It didn't even take one day for me to know I didn't ever want to do anything that would put me back inside these walls again. I went through all the thinking about who or what was to blame for my misfortune. Eric came first, of course, then the drugs, then the money. Finally I worked my way down to myself. It was hard to face that.

The hardest thing to face was that my baby girl was born in prison. The anguish I felt about giving her to the authorities when she was born so they could put her up for adoption was and still is more than I can bear. I only hope God can forgive me, because I can't forgive myself.

My folks came to visit me, but sitting there across that table from them, seeing the looks on their faces--the guilt and the accusations all mixed together-- was too much for me. I told them they didn't have to come visit me again, and they seemed relieved.

I called Nicole a couple of times. She

always accepted my collect calls, but she steadfastly refused to come to the prison to visit me.
She said I could call her any time to talk, and she
promised me that when I got out, she'd be happy to
see me, but she didn't want to see me "behind
bars". Remembering the look on my folks' faces, I
didn't want to press her about it--I didn't want to
see that same look in Nicole's eyes I'd seen in my
mom's.

Nicole had finished high school and was the
assistant director of a daycare center. We laughed
about that a lot, and I teased her about the way she
used to hate school and called it "advanced baby
sitting". Her answer kind of hit me just the right
way. She said something about there being a
difference between attitude and behavior.

"Not many people really care about your
attitude," she said, "It's only your behavior that
counts."

Once that sunk in, I stopped trying to blame
others for my troubles, and like I said, I started
focusing on me. In particular, I started looking at
my own behavior. I saw a lot of things I could
have done differently, but more importantly I saw
the kinds of things I had to do to make it right
once I got out of prison.

If the corrections officers are right about me
not being here for very long, I probably wont have
time to take advantage of their GED program, but
that won't matter. The first thing I'm going to do

when I get out is sign up for night school and get my high school diploma.

In other words, I'm going to stop being a taker and start being a contributor.

One of the other inmates told me yesterday that she heard that Eric--who is at the men's prison across the street--got put in solitary confinement for a few days. I asked her if she knew why, and she said she'd heard he just had a bad attitude. She gave me a strange look when I laughed at that, but I didn't bother to try to explain it to her. I did think about trying to find a way to talk to Eric, to explain to him what I'd learned, but I decided against it. For one thing, he's probably not interested enough to hear what I'd have to say. And for another, I really would rather not see him again, or even talk to him.

I don't know if I'll be lucky enough to find another man I can care about as much as I once cared about Eric. I do know that I have to start with me, that I have to learn to care about the quality of my own life. Maybe once I get that nailed down, I'll be able to attract a man who cares about the quality of his life. I guess that's a pretty big order, but at least it gives me something positive to work for.

And maybe some day, if the fates ever decide to smile on me, I can see my baby's face again. I know I don't deserve more. I pray that the couple who adopted her love her and give her a good life. I know I couldn't have. But that doesn't mean I don't love her, don't worry about her being hungry or cold or crying. Not a day will go by when I don't think about my innocent baby. That is the worst punishment of all.

Also from

Anthony French

Past Perfect Terror

A romantic thriller set in 1983

Dee Johansen is running from her past when she, literally by accident, meets Jeff Westman, who appears to have no past at all.

They form a somewhat rocky partnership, and with each new revelation their lives become increasingly entangled -- with terrifying results.

Filled with tension, suspicion, doubts, and misleading information, the couple flee from the foothills of the Oregon Cascades above Silverton, to Seattle, Denver, Dallas, the forests of Western Michigan, and finally Chicago's Daley Plaza in their efforts to resolve the issues of their pasts while staying one step ahead of their antagonists.

Available at:
www.amazon.com/author/anthonyfrench

Making Lemonade

The author's memoirs--31 anecdotal tales spanning more than 60 years, from 1956 through 2017. Bouncing from pillar to post, across North America and the Pacific Ocean in his unique, hop-scotch way, it covers eight years in Naval Aviation, a decidedly non-conformist academic career, and a tour of Oregon state government.

His encounters prove to be adventurous, mysterious, audacious, mystical, often upside-down or backward, occasionally whimsical, sometimes heart-warming, and always thought-provoking as well as entertaining.

And woven through it all runs the suggestion that when life hands you lemons, just make lemonade.

Available now at:

www.amazon.com/author/anthonyfrench

Coming Soon

Wrongful Targets
The sequel to Past Perfect Terror

Dee Johansen and Jeff Westman return to the rustic cabin in Oregon's Silverton Hills to enjoy a little recuperation, and plan their future. Their idyll is interrupted by Sammy, who asks them, in their guise as private investigators, to join in the search for a missing teenager, Maria Spense. Maria left her parents' ranch in Prineville weeks before and hasn't been seen since.

They, not very reluctantly, agree, and soon discover there's more to the job than finding a missing runaway. Maria's father has the ear of the Oregon State Police and has posted a reward of $100,000 . Their investigative skills are needed, but they first have to do some fence-mending among various agencies. Their initial successes only serve to throw them into an increasingly complex web of sleazy criminal activity.

Watch for it at:
www.amazon.com/author/antonyfrench

Made in the USA
Columbia, SC
06 June 2018